Capitalism in the 21st Century

'A tour-de-force of Marxist analysis; both a significant addition to the literature on Marx's theory of value and an accessible introduction to why it is essential to understanding the multiple crises of 21st-century capitalism.'
—Murray E.G. Smith, Professor of Sociology, Brock University

'Carchedi and Roberts make killer arguments that Marx's labour theory of value is indispensable for understanding capitalism's environmental destructiveness, economic crises, impact on knowledge production, and aspects of its financial processes.'
—Rick Kuhn, author of the Deutscher Prize-winning
Henryk Grossman and the Recovery of Marxism

'Fundamental: it explains the characteristics of the current world through its most objective dimension—the theory of value—which, in an anti-dialectical way, has been forgotten by the left in recent decades. In this book economics is politics and politics is economics.'
—Raquel Varela, author of *A People's History of the Portuguese Revolution*

'This book offers a rigorous Marxist interpretation of some of the major issues in contemporary capitalism. Its analysis is firmly based on the Marxist labour theory of value and is coupled with meticulous empirical support.'
—Stavros Mavroudeas, Professor of Political Economy,
Panteion University, Greece

'Capitalism will always be capitalism, but in the 21st century new forms, controversies and challenges have appeared […] This book masterfully descends to the concrete to show the strength of Marx's law of value and the alternative socialist planning.'
—Juan Pablo, Professor of Applied Economics,
Complutense University of Madrid

'[Carchedi and Roberts are] two of the most accomplished and prominent Marxist authors.'
—Lefteris Tsoulfidis, Professor of Economic Thought,
University of Macedonia, Greece

'Brilliant Marxian theoretical and empirical analysis […] as if updating Ernest Mandel's *Late Capitalism* for the 21st century.'
—Seongjin Jeong, Professor of Economics, Gyeongsang National University

Published in association with the International Initiative for Promoting Political Economy (IIPPE)

Edited by
Ben Fine (SOAS, University of London)
Dimitris Milonakis (University of Crete)

Political economy and the theory of economic and social development have long been fellow travellers, sharing an interdisciplinary and multidimensional character. Over the last 50 years, mainstream economics has become totally formalistic, attaching itself to increasingly narrow methods and techniques at the expense of other approaches. Despite this narrowness, neoclassical economics has expanded its domain of application to other social sciences, but has shown itself incapable of addressing social phenomena and coming to terms with current developments in the world economy.

With world financial crises no longer a distant memory, and neoliberal scholarship and postmodernism in retreat, prospects for political economy have strengthened. It allows constructive liaison between the dismal and other social sciences and rich potential in charting and explaining combined and uneven development.

The objective of this series is to support the revival and renewal of political economy, both in itself and in dialogue with other social sciences. Drawing on rich traditions, we invite contributions that constructively engage with heterodox economics, critically assess mainstream economics, address contemporary developments, and offer alternative policy prescriptions.

Also available

Beyond the Developmental State:
Industrial Policy into the Twenty-First
Century
Edited by Ben Fine, Jyoti Saraswati
and Daniela Tavasci

Microeconomics:
A Critical Companion
Ben Fine

Macroeconomics:
A Critical Companion
Ben Fine and Ourania Dimakou

Money and Society:
A Critical Companion
Axel T. Paul

Dot.compradors:
Crisis and Corruption in the Indian
Software Industry
Jyoti Saraswati

Capitalism in the 21st Century

Through the Prism of Value

Guglielmo Carchedi and Michael Roberts

First published 2023 by Pluto Press
New Wing, Somerset House, Strand, London WC2R 1LA
and Pluto Press Inc.
1930 Village Center Circle, Ste. 3-384, Las Vegas, NV 89134

www.plutobooks.com

British Library Cataloguing in Publication Data
A catalogue record for this book is available from the British Library

ISBN 978 0 7453 4088 3 Paperback
ISBN 978 1 786806 96 3 PDF
ISBN 978 1 786806 97 0 EPUB

This book is printed on paper suitable for recycling and made from fully managed and sustained forest sources. Logging, pulping and manufacturing processes are expected to conform to the environmental standards of the country of origin.

Typeset by Stanford DTP Services, Northampton, England
Simultaneously printed in the United Kingdom and United States of America

Contents

Figures

Tables

Introduction

The purpose of this book is to bring to the reader a Marxist interpretation of some of the major issues in contemporary capitalism in the 21st century. We rely on the tool of Marx's value theory to deliver scientific explanations of the laws of motion in 21st century capitalism. Marx's theory of value in capitalism is the red thread running through the book.

What is value? Marx starts from the view that value is the result of the exertion of human labour. Without any exertion by humans nothing is produced that keeps human beings alive and well. So that means value is not some metaphysical abstraction, but actually physical – it exists in objective reality. Think of it this way: electricity is real; it is the movement of electrons through atoms of usually copper. We cannot always see it (although we can experience its results: light, heat and shocks). And it can be measured in volts, watts and amps. Similarly, the exertion of human labour (both objective and mental) is material and so can be measured in labour time (hours, minutes etc.).

Nature also has value (to us) in that, without air, the planet, trees, forests, water etc., there would be no human life. So it has (use) value to humanity. But it requires the exertion of human labour to turn this intrinsic use value of nature into other use values for humanity: from forests to timber to houses involves the exertion of human energy (and thus labour).

Marx calls this aspect of human labour, its use value. But it is only under capitalism that the use values required and generated by human labour turn into commodities for sale on a vmarket for private profit. The results of human labour are converted into commodities which then have value with dual aspects: use value for the purchasers of those commodities and value, also called exchange value because it becomes manifest as money through exchange. These two aspects of value within the commodity reveal the basic contradiction of capitalist production ie between production for social need (use value) and for profit and the accumulation of capital (exchange value). That's why Marx starts with the commodity in *Capital*.

Under capitalism the only objective way of valuing a product of human labour (a commodity) is by measuring the labour time involved, not by each consumer's subjective opinion of its value. Commodities have two aspects, a use value and a value because they are the products of both a specific (concrete) type of labour (which produces its use value) and of abstract labour, which produces its value. Abstract labour is the expenditure of human energy irrespective of the specific type of activity.

1

The alternative theory to Marx's labour theory of value is utility theory, which argues that each individual's personal estimate of use value or utility should be somehow aggregated to get the total utility of the products of human labour. This is impossible. How can the use value of a product that is estimated by one person be measured against another's?

It is the transformation of abstract human labour into the value of the commodities which is the focus of the law of value. Marx holds that there is a law-like relation between the labour expended under the capitalist production and value: the quantity of labour (measured in time) determines both the quantity of value produced, since value is labour, and the quantity realised through redistribution. *This is the kernel of the law.*

But value does not emerge from abstract labour immediately, only after some intermediate processes. The generation of value goes through different stages.[1] If the capitalist production process has been started but is not yet finished, the labourers are performing abstract labour and are *in the process of creating* the commodity's value. At this stage, the value is *potential*, that is, not yet realised because the commodity itself, not being finished, is still being created and thus it exists only potentially. When the production process is completed and the commodity is finished (but not yet sold), the abstract labour which has gone into it becomes the value produced, or *contained* or embodied in the commodity. The material substance of this value is abstract labour.[2] Since a commodity must be sold in order to realise its value, the value contained in the commodity is also its *potentially realised* value. When the commodity is sold, the value contained in it becomes *realised* value. This realised value is represented by money, the universally accepted form of value.

In a capitalist economy, due to competition among the many producers of the same commodity, a commodity sold on the market may not realise the value contained in it and so not all the labour which has been needed for its production. Competition on the market decides the *socially necessary labour time* required to produce and realise the value of a commodity. Profitability varies for different producers, but through competition there is a tendency towards an average profitability. So the price of a commodity will tend to be set by the cost of production plus the average rate of profit across the economy. The value contained in a commodity is thus modified into a price of production.

The major factor influencing profitability is technology. New technologies replace workers with means of production. They produce less value and surplus value but realise more value at the cost of the technological laggards. The latter, in their turn, will shift to more efficient technologies. It is this continual process of modification driven by changes in technology and competition that tells you that Marx's law of value is not a static equilibrium theory, instead, that the process of commodity production is in continual motion. When a production process (P1) terminates, another one (P2) begins, that is, the outputs of P1 become the inputs of P2. The value of the inputs of P2 is then their value contained as output of P1. This is the basis of the *temporalist* theory of the transformation of (1) labour into value and of (2) value contained into value realised, which is usually referred to as the transformation of value into price.

There are three other aspects that are essential to the law of value and crucial to explaining developments in 21st century capitalism. Marx's great discovery in his law of value is *surplus value*. In capitalist production, there are owners of the means of production (factories, land, finance etc.) and there are the rest of us who own only their own labour power. The owners of the means of production employ human labour power to produce value contained in the commodities which are owned and sold by the owners/controllers of the means of production. But the owners do not pay the full value contained in the commodities to those selling their labour power to produce them. The owners of the means of production pay for the use of the machines and raw materials and the wages of the workers employed. But they receive in the value contained in the commodities and realised on the market a greater value than their costs. So there is a surplus value that is appropriated by the owners. This can be broken down into profits to the producer capitalists, interest to the finance capitalists and rent to the landlords.

As mentioned above, individual capitalists are continually striving to increase their surplus value in competition with other capitalists. They can do so by increasing the workforce and/or by increasing the intensity and hours of work by labour. But there are physical and social limits in doing this. Moreover, other capitalists may introduce new technologies that speed up the productivity of their workforce and so reduce the hours of work (or cost in value) necessary to make a commodity below the average. Such capitalists can then undercut those with less advanced technology. This forces all capitalists to invest more and more in technology/machinery to raise the productivity of labour and reduce relatively the use and cost of labour power. So the ratio of investment in constant capital (machinery and raw materials) will tend to rise relative to investment in labour power (variable capital). This ratio is called the organic composition of capital and in this book, we continually show its importance in our prism of value.

The law of value says that only human labour can create value. Machines can produce more units of commodities per worker, but without the exertion of human labour, machines cannot make commodities. (We have not yet reached a world of total automation where all use value is produced by robots and if we ever do that will not be capitalism.) As the rise in the organic composition of capital can only come about by capitalists investing more surplus value in machines relative to investing in human labour power, there is a tendency in capitalist production for the subsequent increase in new value to be less than the increase in investment employed. In other words, the rate of profit in a capitalist economy tends to fall over time. There are many counter-tendencies to this tendency, in particular, increased exploitation of the human labour force, that is, a higher rate of surplus value; and in the case of national economies, increased trade and investment by technologically advanced capitalists in foreign markets with less efficient means of production in order to appropriate surplus value. Again, this counteracting factor is a key feature of our analysis of modern imperialism in this book.

Thus, the law of value leads to surplus value, the organic composition of capital and the rate of profit on capital. With these categories, we have the basis of a Marxist theory of 21st century capitalism.

However, our analysis is not only on theory but also based on empirical evidence. This is not a book full of quotes from Marx and Engels, although they are there. And it is not filled with lengthy theoretical arguments. More, it is a narrative backed by the best data we have to expound our explanations.

We start in Chapter 1, not with a discussion of the nature of value in modern capitalism, but with the value of nature. This is literally a burning issue. The planet and all its living species are increasingly being degraded by the capitalist mode of production, where the accumulation of capital for the few overrides the interests of the many, and not just humanity. Environmental degradation has always been a feature of capitalist production for profit, but in the 21st century this has reached an existential point with global warming and climate change which threaten to sacrifice nature and humanity on the altar of profit: the ultimate insanity of an irrational system. In this chapter, we attempt to show that market forces cannot reverse the disaster ahead and only ending the domination of the law of value can do so.

In Chapter 2, we consider the basic relationship between value and money in modern capitalism. Money is the universal expression of value in motion. And with the rise of finance, the sector of capitalism where money supposedly makes more money without the intervention of human labour, we analyse the allegedly new theories of the role of money in the 21st century, modern monetary theory (MMT) and the new digital and cryptocurrencies and their role. And we offer an original Marxist theory of inflation in modern economies against the flawed mainstream alternatives.

In Chapter 3, we turn to the major fault-lines of capitalism since its emergence as the dominant mode of production some 200 years ago. We cover the various theories offered in the past to explain regular and recurring crises of production and investment under capitalism over the last 150 years. But we base our approach on Marx's laws of value and profitability to explain the causes

4

of crises and why the macroeconomic policies of government and monetary authorities won't work in ending regular and recurring slumps.

In Chapter 4, we move onto the international arena to analyse the economic foundations of imperialism in the 21st century with new empirical evidence. We show that modern imperialism, which emerged towards the end of the 19th century, is still with us (with the same usual suspects). The appropriation of value by the imperialist countries continues on an even grander scale than 100 years ago. There is no prospect of any so-called 'emerging economy' catching up to join the imperialist elite.

Modern capitalism is increasingly no longer dominated by the production of things for profit. Capital now needs to appropriate knowledge or mental labour and commodify the product of that labour. Mental labour is just as material as objective labour; and as available for exploitation by capital in the 21st century as the production of tangible things was in the 19th and 20th centuries. In Chapter 5 we present an analysis that shows the conditions under which knowledge has value for capital and human mental labour is exploited and commodified. And we consider the impact of the rise of the robots and artificial intelligence in the 21st century, and even quantum computers, designed to replace human labour. We argue that machines do not think like humans and so can never fully replace human activity.

In our final chapter, we pose the alternative to capitalism in the 21st century: socialism. In particular, we apply value theory to understanding the features of the transition from capitalism to socialism and from a system of value creation to one of meeting social need. To do that, we look at the 'case studies' in the 20th century of such transitions as in Soviet Russia and China, to draw lessons for the 21st century. We review the old debate on the feasibility of democratic planning over value in the light of new studies in the age of quantum computers and algorithms.

Time is running out for capitalism and for the planet. To paraphrase Gramsci, 'the old is dying, but the new is not yet born'. The 21st century will decide whether the new will replace the old before it is too late.

1

Value and Nature

1.1 MARX AND ENGELS ON NATURE

Marx and Engels are often accused of what has been called a Promethean vision of human social organisation, namely, that human beings, using their superior brains, knowledge and technical prowess, can and should impose their will on the rest of the planet or what is called 'nature' – for better or worse. The charge is that other living species are merely playthings for the use of human beings. There are humans and there is nature – in contradiction. This charge is particularly aimed at Friedrich Engels who, it is claimed, took a bourgeois 'positivist' view of science: scientific knowledge was always progressive and neutral in ideology; and so was the relationship between man and nature. Indeed, the 'green' critique of Marx and Engels is that they supposedly were unaware that Homo sapiens were destroying the planet and thus themselves. Instead, Marx and Engels had a touching Promethean faith in science and capitalism's ability to develop the productive forces and technology to overcome any risks to the planet and nature. This critique runs contrary to the writings of Marx and Engels. Marx wrote:

> Nature is man's inorganic body, that is to say, nature in so far as it is not the human body. Man lives from nature ... and he must maintain a continuing dialogue with it if he is not to die. To say that man's physical and mental life is linked to nature simply means that nature is linked to itself, for man is a part of nature.[1]

This conception of humans and nature as parts of a single totality can be found throughout Marx and Engels' work. That Marx and Engels paid no attention to the impact on nature of human social activity has been debunked recently in particular by the groundbreaking work of Marxist authors like John Bellamy Foster and Paul Burkett.[2] They have reminded us that throughout Marx's *Capital*, Marx was very aware of capitalism's degrading impact on nature and the resources of the planet. Marx wrote that

> the capitalist mode of production collects the population together in great centres and causes the urban population to achieve an ever-growing preponderance ... [It] disturbs the metabolic interaction between man and the earth,

i.e., it prevents the return to the soil of its constituent elements consumed by man in the form of food and clothing; hence it hinders the operation of the eternal natural condition for the lasting fertility of the soil. Thus, it destroys at the same time the physical health of the urban worker, and the intellectual life of the rural worker.

As Paul Burkett says: 'it is difficult to argue that there is something fundamentally anti-ecological about Marx's analysis of capitalism and his projections of communism'.

Far from promoting an instrumentalist approach to animals, what Marx emphasised is the material relation that governs the existence of humans and all species. Marx's classical historical-materialist analysis argues that human beings share a close kinship with other animals biologically and psychologically. Marx was a strong critic of Cartesian metaphysics, for its removal of the mind/soul from the realm of the animal and the reduction of the latter to mere mechanical motions. In Marx's words, 'Descartes in defining animals as mere machines, saw with the eyes of the period of manufacture. The medieval view, on the other hand, was that animals were assistants to man.' Marx's analysis of the historical development of capitalism highlighted this transition in animal relations. For him, Descartes' depiction of animals as machines represented the status that animals were accorded in capitalist commodity production. Marx took note of the ongoing changes, such as the reduction of non-human animals to a source of power and the altering of their very existence in order to further the accumulation of capital. He specifically focused on how the historical development of capitalism, including the division of town and country that accompanied it, shaped these conditions, reducing animals simply to instruments and raw materials, as reflected in the general logic of the system.

But he suggests that the human species is distinctive in its capacity to produce more 'universally' and self-consciously, and thus is less one-sidedly limited by specific drives than other animals. Humanity is therefore able to transform nature in a seemingly endless number of ways, constantly creating new human needs, capacities and powers.

Engels too must be saved from the same Promethean charge. Actually, Engels was well ahead of Marx (yet again) in connecting the destruction and damage to the environment that industrialisation was causing. In his first major work, *Outlines of a Critique of Political Economy*, again well before Marx looked at political economy, Engels notes how the private ownership of the land, the drive for profit and the degradation of nature go hand in hand.[3]

To make earth an object of huckstering – the earth which is our one and all, the first condition of our existence – was the last step towards making oneself an object of huckstering. It was and is to this very day an immorality surpassed only by the immorality of self-alienation. And the original appropriation – the monopolization of the earth by a few, the exclusion of the rest from that which is the condition of their life – yields nothing in immorality to the subsequent huckstering of the earth.

Once the earth becomes commodified by capital, it is subject to just as much exploitation as labour.

Engels' major work (written with Marx's help), *The Dialectics of Nature*, written in the years up to 1883, is often subject to attack as extending Marx's materialist conception of history as applied to humans into nature in a non-Marxist way.[4] And yet, in his book, Engels could not be clearer on the dialectical relation between humans and nature. In a famous chapter 'The Role of Work in Transforming Ape into Man', he writes:

> Let us not, however, flatter ourselves overmuch on account of our human conquest over nature. For each such conquest takes its revenge on us. Each of them, it is true, has in the first place the consequences on which we counted, but in the second and third places it has quite different, unforeseen effects which only too often cancel out the first. The people who, in Mesopotamia, Greece, Asia Minor, and elsewhere, destroyed the forests to obtain cultivable land, never dreamed that they were laying the basis for the present devastated condition of these countries, by removing along with the forests the collecting centres and reservoirs of moisture. When, on the southern slopes of the mountains, the Italians of the Alps used up the pine forests so carefully cherished on the northern slopes, they had no inkling that by doing so they were … thereby depriving their mountain springs of water for the greater part of the year, with the effect that these would be able to pour still more furious flood torrents on the plains during the rainy seasons. Those who spread the potato in Europe were not aware that they were at the same time spreading the disease of scrofula. Thus at every step we are reminded that we by no means rule over nature like a conqueror over a foreign people, like someone standing outside nature – but that we, with flesh, blood, and brain, belong to nature, and exist in its midst, and that all our mastery of it consists in the fact that we have the advantage over all other beings of being able to know and correctly apply its laws.

Engels goes on:

> in fact, with every day that passes we are learning to understand these laws more correctly and getting to know both the more immediate and the more

8

remote consequences of our interference with the traditional course of nature. … But the more this happens, the more will men not only feel, but also know, their unity with nature, and thus the more impossible will become the senseless and antinatural idea of a contradiction between mind and matter, man and nature, soul and body.

Engels explains the social consequences of the drive to expand the productive forces.

But if it has already required the labour of thousands of years for us to learn to some extent to calculate the more remote natural consequences of our actions aiming at production, it has been still more difficult in regard to the more remote social consequences of these actions. … When afterwards Columbus discovered America, he did not know that by doing so he was giving new life to slavery, which in Europe had long ago been done away with and laying the basis for the Negro slave traffic.

The people of the Americas were driven into slavery, but also nature was enslaved. As Engels put it:

What cared the Spanish planters in Cuba, who burned down forests on the slopes of the mountains and obtained from the ashes sufficient fertilizer for one generation of very highly profitable coffee trees – what cared they that the heavy tropical rainfall afterwards washed away the unprotected upper stratum of the soil, leaving behind only bare rock!

Now we know that it was not just slavery that the Europeans brought to the Americas, but also disease, which in its many forms exterminated 90 per cent of Native Americans and was the main reason for their subjugation by colonialism.[5]

Humans can work in harmony with and as part of nature. It requires greater knowledge of the consequences of human action. Engels said in his *Dialectics*:

But even in this sphere, by long and often cruel experience and by collecting and analyzing the historical material, we are gradually learning to get a clear view of the indirect, more remote, social effects of our productive activity, and so the possibility is afforded us of mastering and controlling these effects as well.

But better knowledge and scientific progress is not enough. For Marx and Engels, the possibility of ending the dialectical contradiction between man and nature and bringing about some level of harmony and ecological balance would only be possible with the abolition of the capitalist mode of production. As Engels said: 'To carry out this control requires something more than mere knowledge ... it requires a complete revolution in our hitherto existing mode of production, and with it of our whole contemporary social order.'

1.2 LABOUR AND NATURE: THE SOURCE OF WEALTH

'Labour is not the source of all wealth. Nature is just as much a source of use values (and it is surely of such that material wealth consists!) as labour, which is itself only the manifestation of a force of nature, human labour power,'[6] so says Marx. 'The use values ... of commodities, are combinations of two elements – matter and labour. If we take away the useful labour expended upon them, a material substratum is always left, which is furnished by Nature without the help of man ... We see, then, that labour is not the only source of material wealth, of use values produced by labour.'

Marx writes in *Capital* of labour as a process 'by which man, through his own actions, mediates, regulates, and controls the metabolism between himself and nature. He confronts the materials of nature as a force of nature.'[7] There has been much academic discussion among Marxists and 'green ecologists' recently on the relation of humans to nature. The argument is around whether capitalism has caused a 'metabolic rift' between Homo sapiens and the planet, that is, disrupting the precious balance among species and the planet, and thus generating dangerous viruses and, of course, potentially uncontrollable global warming and climate change that could destroy the planet.

The debate is around whether using the term 'metabolic rift' is useful because it suggests that at some time in the past before capitalism there was some metabolic balance or harmony between humans, on the one hand, and 'nature', on the other. According to Saito, with *The German Ideology*, written in 1845, there was a turning point in Marx's travel towards an 'ecological dimension' in his critique of capitalism. Saito reckons this is when he begins to use the term 'metabolism' and refines his understanding of the concept as the general metabolic tendency of capital. Saito argues that Marx progressively realises that Capital's continuous expansion exploits not just labour, but also nature in the search for profit, leading to the destruction of the soil, deforestation and other such forms of the degradation of natural resources. Capital wants more and more value and, in particular, surplus value. That becomes the purpose of production and the metabolic harmony that existed between humans and nature before capitalism is broken. There is now a metabolic rift caused by capitalism.

However, any emphasis on rifts or ruptures has the risk of assuming that nature is in harmony or in balance until capitalism disturbs it. But nature is never in balance, even without humans. It is always changing, evolving, but with 'punctuated equilibriums', such as the Cambrian explosion, with many species evolving as others go extinct.[8] The rule of the dinosaurs and their eventual extinction had nothing to do with humans (despite what the movies may depict). And humans have never been in a position to dictate conditions on the planet or with other species without repercussions. 'Nature' lays down the environment for humans and humans act on nature. To quote Marx: 'Men make their own history, but they do not make it just as they please; they do not make it under circumstances chosen by themselves, but under circumstances directly encountered and inherited from the past.'[9]

It's true that Marx refers to the robbing of the soil by capitalist production. In *Capital*, Volume I, Chapter 15 on machinery Marx says:

> Moreover, all progress in capitalist agriculture is a progress in the art, not only of robbing the worker, but of robbing the soil; all progress in increasingly the fertility of the soil for a given time is a progress towards ruining the more long-lasting sources of that fertility. The more a country proceeds from large-scale industry as the background of its development ... the more rapid is this process of destruction. Capitalist production, therefore, only develops the techniques and the degree of combination of the social process of production by simultaneously undermining the original sources of all wealth – the soil and the worker. (Marx, 1995 [1887])

But does Marx reckon, as Saito claims, that he saw the main contradiction of capitalist production in the 'metabolic rift' between humans and nature? Contrary to Saito's conclusion, Marx rejected Liebig's soil exhaustion theory of the limits of capitalism and rejected its implied Malthusianism that population would outrun the availability of food and the necessities for human life.

For Marx, capitalism was a system of 'brutal exploitation' of labour power in production for profit, not one of robbery or dispossession. Capitalism is not only subject to regular and recurring crises in production and employment. It fails to use effectively the scientific and technological discoveries that could end toil and disease globally. It is indeed degrading nature, exterminating species, and threatening to destroy the atmosphere of the planet, but these outcomes are the result of the contradictions to be found in the capitalist mode of production itself, not in some existential threat from outside the system.

1.3 MEASURING THE DAMAGE

Can we quantify the damage to nature imposed by capitalism? We cannot, if damage is defined as destruction of value. Nature, inasmuch as it is unaffected by human action, that is, inasmuch as it does not incorporate human labour carried out by labour for capital, has no value (for capital). Therefore, no value is destroyed and no quantification of damage is necessary for capital. A tropical forest, inasmuch as it is not privatised and left uncultivated, has no value for capital. However, if it is privatised, it is attributed a price (not value) on the basis of the price of other similar pieces of land. It enters the market without having a value, only a price. This is one of the examples to be found in Marx of a commodity having a price without a value. If an element of nature enters a market where no equivalent element exists that can serve as an indication of its price, then that element's price is determined simply by the relative strength of demand and supply.

Yet neoclassical economics insists in attributing value (in its distorted view is its money price) to nature. Given that nature, if isolated from human action, is a use value, the question is: how does neoclassical economics attribute a price to use values and therefore how does it calculate the loss (in terms of prices) when nature is destroyed?

If I buy a piece of virgin land whose price is determined either by a similar piece or, lacking this, by the interchange of supply and demand, that price is a title to participating in the redistribution of value produced elsewhere. If I sell that land, I give up my right to that redistribution, which is acquired by the purchaser. But if by accident a fire destroys that land before I commodify it, there is no loss of value; only a loss for me personally due to the impossibility to participate in the redistribution of societal value. But from the perspective of the economy, there is a destruction of use values, of wealth. The value has not changed (it is only differently redistributed), but wealth has decreased. It follows that the damage inflicted on the Amazon rainforest can only by computed in terms of how many square kilometres have been destroyed by capital in a given period and thus in terms of use values, but it is wealth that has been destroyed. Logging transforms one type of use value (trees) into a different use value (logs). If performed by labour for capital, it is productive labour. The capital invested in logging is circulating capital. The problem is that logging transforms a renewable form of wealth into a non-renewable one. Neoclassical economics attempts to measure a country's wealth – obtained through a methodology called 'wealth accounting' – that includes all assets that contribute to our economic wellbeing, from buildings and factory machines, to infrastructure, human and social 'capital' and 'natural capital'. This method is deeply flawed so that computations are meaningless. More specifically, natural capital accounts (NCA) are sets of data for material natural resources, such as forests, energy and water. While national accounts are limited to the production boundary of the economy, natural capital accounts go beyond that, to account for natural goods and services that aren't subject to market transactions and don't necessarily have well-established market prices. In this methodology, nature is turned into 'natural capital'. Recently, the World Bank has made attempts to calculate wealth including fixed assets (produced capital), wages (human capital) and natural resources (natural capital).[10] Produced capital includes the value of machinery, buildings, equipment, and residential and non-residential urban land. Human capital is computed as the present value of future earnings for the working population over their lifetimes. Natural capital includes the valuation of fossil fuel energy (oil, gas, hard and soft coal) and minerals (bauxite, copper, gold, iron ore, lead, nickel, phosphate, silver, tin and zinc), agricultural land (cropland and pastureland), forests (timber and some non-timber forest products) and protected areas.[11] But if the method is faulty, the estimates are meaningless in measuring value or wealth.

The basic approach is the one recommended by the System of National Accounts, namely: 'to value the quantity of ecosystem services at market prices that would have occurred if the services had been freely traded and exchanged'. This ensures that the value of such services to their consumers is equal to the value provided by the owner of the assets that supplied such services, since it represents the point at which the supply and demand curves cross. When such services are traded in a market, the exchange value can be directly observed as the market price.

But many ecosystem services have no such market, in which case the exchange value must be attributed or 'imputed'. This is not just a problem for natural capital accounts but one which has been faced in national accounting for many years. Most of the goods and services considered in the national accounts are valued based on market prices. But for a sizeable proportion, nearly a third by value, their values must be imputed. These include the value of owner-occupied housing and the value of public services such as hospitals, schools, and public order and safety.

Given this means of valuation, the relevance of the paradox of diamonds and water should be noted. Adam Smith posed the question, but failed to answer to his own satisfaction, of why diamonds should apparently be valued so much more highly than water, given that the intrinsic value of the latter would apparently seem much greater. Marx addressed this issue. In a land where water is abundant and diamonds very rare or non-existent, the former is cheaper and the latter very expensive. But if the quantity of the endowment is reversed, their prices are reversed too. This reversal is due not to changes in demand, but to the different quantities of labour needed for their production.

So this neoclassical approach cannot measure value in nature.

1.4 NATURE AND RENT

The World Bank's calculation of depletion depends on measuring 'rents' on resources. The estimates of natural resources rents are calculated as the difference between the price of a commodity and the average cost of producing it. And here Marx's discussion of rent is relevant. As mentioned above, because no exploited labour goes into the production of, say, a naturally occurring forest, when a capitalist monopolises that forest and charges rent for its use, there is no increase in capital to the system as a whole. That is, no labour has gone into producing the forest, so no surplus value can be extracted from it. Nor has it taken up any investment of capital. What's more, all the conditions that make labour possible – land, air, water – are, at the outset at least, 'free gifts of nature'.

To Adam Smith, rent was a 'monopoly price'. 'The rent of the land ... is naturally a monopoly price. It is not at all proportioned to what the landlord may have laid out upon the improvement of the land, or to what he can afford to take; but to what the farmer can afford to give' (Smith, 1970 [1776], p. 249). That rent arose at a particular historical juncture when land became private property was not lost to Smith: '[a]s soon as the land of any country has all become private property, the landlords, like all other men, love to reap where they never sowed, and demand a rent even for its natural produce' (p. 152). For Ricardo '[r]ent is that portion of the produce of the earth, which is paid to the landlord for the use of the original and indestructible powers of the soil'.

Marx demurred. For him, land has no 'original' powers either, since the land is in no way 'original', but rather the product of an 'historical and natural process'. Landed property does not create the portion of value that is transformed into surplus profit. Landed property is not the cause of this surplus profit's creation, but simply of its transformation into the form of *ground-rent*. Any difference in soil fertility creates surplus profit in superior plots. But by itself it does not create rent. This was Ricardo's folly. To explain rent, one needs the existence of *landed property* in addition to 'power of the soil'. Generally, the additional surplus earned by capital in a sector gets distributed across sectors through competition between capitals. Capital would flow into the sector with a higher rate of profit to lap up the extra profit, as a result output would rise. Price, which could have been close to value, would fall. How far would it fall? The fall will be to the extent that the rate of profit gets equalised across sectors. This uniform rate of profit is the average rate of profit. However, the spontaneous flow of capital described above gets stalled due to the presence of landed property. Landed property restricts capital inflow, thereby crop output is kept low and market price remains high. The gap between the value of output and price of production remains. This difference gets extracted by landlords in the form of rent.[12] In other words, rent is really a transformed form of surplus profit, which arises in agriculture because the organic composition of capital in agricultural production is lower than the economy-wide average rate of profit, but is transformed into rent because of landed property, that is, ownership of land by a class of landowners (who are different from the class of capitalist-farmers).

While Marx had analysed the emergence of ground-rent with reference to agricultural production in the presence of landed property, the analysis can be equally well applied to understand rent income to mining, real estate, oil and natural gas production. What is important is the structure of the relationship that is established in the production process between, on the one hand, the capitalist commodity producer, and on the other, the owner of some non-produced resource that is used for that production. As long as capitalist commodity production uses some privately owned non-produced resource that is limited in quantity, as is the case, for instance, in mining, in oil and natural gas production, or in real estate development, the owner of that resource can bargain away a part of the surplus value in the form of rent.[13]

1.5 RAW MATERIALS AND PROFITABILITY

Marx's law of the tendency of the rate of profit to fall is the basis for predicting the transient future of the capitalist mode of production. The law forecasts a secular decline in the profitability of capital that increasingly puts the capitalist production into crises that become more difficult to extricate from. The law has counter-tendencies that can slow the pace of falling profitability and even reverse the decline for periods. But in the long run, these counter-tendencies cannot overcome the tendency.

One of the counter-tendencies is capital's drive to reduce the costs of production and raise profitability by intensive use of natural resources to lower the cost of raw materials (or circulating capital) in capitalist production. The rate of profit is thus 'inversely proportional to the value of the raw materials' (Marx, 1967, III, p. 111). The cheaper the raw materials and energy, the higher the rate of profit. And yet, the dynamism of capitalist production leads the 'portion of constant capital that consists of fixed capital ... [to] run significantly ahead of the portion consisting of organic raw materials, so that the demand for these raw materials grows more rapidly than their supply' (pp. 118–19). Raw materials become 'scarce' relative to the rise in fixed asset investment.

> The more capitalist production is developed, bringing with it greater means for a sudden and uninterrupted increase in the portion of constant capital that consists of machinery, etc., the greater is the relative overproduction of machinery and other fixed capital, the more frequent the *underproduction* of plant and animal raw materials, and the more marked the previously described rise in their price and the corresponding reaction. (Marx, 1981, p. 214)

Jason Moore has taken up this aspect of Marx's law.[14] A priority of capitalism has been to drive down the share of circulating relative to fixed capital, so driving down the value composition of inputs and energy while simultaneously expanding the material volume of commodity production. The great energy transitions of the modern world, from peat and charcoal (1450s–1830s), to coal (1750s–1950s), to oil and natural gas (1870s–present) were appropriations of nature's 'free gifts' that were sufficiently massive to induce a rising productivity of labour while reducing the capital intensity of production in general. Such revolutions cheapened raw materials (circulating capital) and, indirectly, reduced the value composition of fixed capital itself. Cheaper steel, for example, rendered the mass production of fixed capital cheaper as well. In so doing, these revolutions created the necessary conditions for new long waves of accumulation. Marx once observed that the 'natural fertility of the soil can act like an increase of fixed capital' (1973, p. 748), and is this not equally true for the wealth of forests, of peat bogs, of coal seams and oil fields?

If a sufficient mass of cheap energy and raw materials can be mobilised, the rising organic composition of capital can be attenuated – especially if 'capital saving' innovations run strongly alongside labour saving movements – and the tendency towards a falling rate of profit, is not only checked, but (for a time) reversed. The same logic applies to variable capital. If a sufficient volume of cheap food can be supplied, the rate of surplus value may be augmented.

José Tapia has argued that the transitions from peat and charcoal to coal, and from coal to oil, were major technological revolutions that initiated periods of accelerated accumulation in the history of global capitalism, since cheap energy 'powerfully checks the falling rate of profit'.[15] Conversely, expensive oil reduces profitability and pushes towards crisis, as clearly illustrated by what happened in the early 1970s, late 1980s, late 1990s, and in the years immediately before the Great Recession. The global slump of the mid-1970s has often been called the Oil Crisis, and indeed a peak in the world price of oil occurred in 1974. But there were also peaks of oil prices in 1980, 1990, 2000 and 2008, which means that oil prices were rising in the period immediately previous to each of the five crises.

The econometrician James Hamilton reported a statistically significant correlation between oil price shocks and economic recessions in post-war US data.[16] Hamilton's conclusion was that the evidence 'makes it difficult to reject the historical correlation as entirely spurious', meaning that oil price increases might be the shocks that push the economy into recession. The evidence indicating a correlation between oil price shocks and the last five crises of the world economy is solid.

Indeed, we can find a high inverse correlation between the change in the price of crude oil and the change in the average rate of profit (Figure 1.1). The average

16

rate of profit is defined here as the internal rate of return (IRR) in the G20 economies since 1950.[17] We find an inverse correlation of −0.76 between the price of crude oil and the G20 IRR between 1950 and 2019. However, between 1950 and 1966, when the IRR rises by about 8 per cent, the oil price also rises by 14 per cent and thus there is no negative correlation. This was the golden age of high profitability and low oil prices. However, in the profitability 'crisis' period between 1966 and 1982 when the IRR falls 34 per cent, the oil price rises ten times. Between 1982 and 1997, the oil price falls 39 per cent and the IRR rises 17 per cent. From 1997 to 2019, the IRR drops 12 per cent coinciding with a tripling of the oil price. In all these periods, there is a significant inverse correlation.

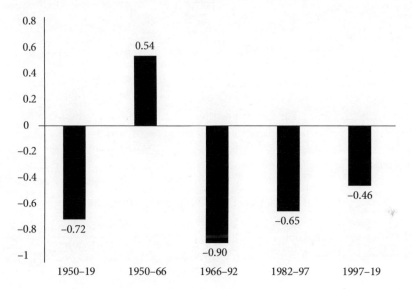

Figure 1.1   Crude oil price and IRR correlations

Similarly, we find a high inverse correlation between the changes in US IRR and the official price index of raw materials in US industrial production (Producer Price Index, PPI) (Figure 1.2). Again, in the periods when the US rate of profit fell (1966–82) and (1997–2019), there was a large rise in the production price of raw materials in US industrial production. In the periods of rising profitability (IRR) of 1950–66 and 1982–97, there was also a rise in the rate of PPI. This suggests that rising profitability could absorb inflation in raw materials prices, but not indefinitely.

Capitalism thus turns the 'free gifts of nature' into profit. And in the incessant drive to raise profitability, it depletes and degrades natural resources. And as nature is privatised and turned into private property, the owners of 'nature'

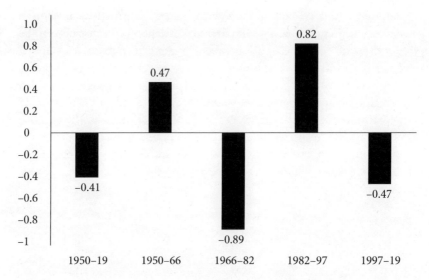

Figure 1.2   Correlations between annual changes in US PPI and US IRR

can also extract rent from the exploitation of labour. However, there is a continual battle by capital to control and lower rising raw material prices as natural resources are depleted and not renewed, adding another factor to the tendency of the rate of profit to fall.

1.6 GLOBAL WARMING AND CLIMATE CHANGE

The drive for profit has led to an uncontrolled expansion of industrialisation, energy and commodity production in agriculture that emits carbon emissions and provokes natural resource depletion that is heating up the planet to levels that threaten its very existence.

The United Nations (UN) has said that: 'Currently, the world is on course for a temperature increase of 3.2 degrees Celsius or more, unless industrialized nations can deliver reductions in greenhouse gas emissions of at least 7.2% annually over the next 10 years in order to keep to the limit of 1.5°C degree target agreed in Paris.' Although the Paris Agreement aimed to hold global warming as close to 1.5°C as possible, that doesn't mean it is a 'safe' level. Communities and ecosystems around the world have already suffered significant impacts from the 1°C of warming so far, and the effects at 1.5°C will be harsher still. Poverty and disadvantages will increase as temperatures rise to 1.5°C. Small island states, deltas and low-lying coasts are particularly vulnerable, with increased risk of flooding, and threats to freshwater supplies, infrastructure and livelihoods. Warming to 1.5°C also poses a risk to global economic growth, with the tropics and southern subtropics potentially being hit hardest. Extreme weather events such as floods, heatwaves and droughts will become more frequent, severe and widespread, with attendant costs in terms of health care, infrastructure and disaster response.

The sixth report from the Intergovernmental Panel on Climate Change (IPCC) states clearly that climate change and global warming is 'unequivocally caused by human activities'. But can climate change be laid at the door of the whole of humanity or instead on that part of humanity that owns, controls and decides what happens to our future? Sure, any society without the scientific knowledge would have exploited fossil fuels in order to generate energy for production, warmth and transport. But would any society have gone on expanding fossil fuel exploration and production without controls to protect the environment and failed to look for alternative sources of energy that did not damage the planet, once it became clear that carbon emissions were doing just that?

Scientists warned of the dangers decades ago. Nuclear physicist Edward Teller warned the oil industry all the way back in 1959 that its product will end up having a catastrophic impact on human civilisation.[18] The main fossil fuel companies like Exxon or BP knew what the consequences were, but chose to hide the evidence and do nothing – just like the tobacco companies over smoking.[19] The scientific evidence on carbon emissions damaging the planet, as presented in the IPCC report, is about as uncontroversial as smoking in damaging health. And yet little or nothing has been done because the environment must not stand in the way of profitability.

The culprit is not 'humanity' but industrial capitalism and its addiction to fossil fuels. At a personal level, in the last 25 years, it is the richest 1 per cent of the world's population, mainly based in the imperialist centre, who are responsible for more than twice as much carbon pollution as the 3.1 billion people who make up the poorest half of humanity.[20] The richest 10 per cent of households use almost half (45 per cent) of all the energy linked to land transport and three-quarters of all energy linked to aviation. Transportation accounts for around a quarter of global emissions today, while SUVs (sport utility vehicles) were the second biggest driver of global carbon emissions growth between 2010 and 2018. But even more to the point, just 100 companies have been the source of more than 70 per cent of the world's greenhouse gas emissions since 1988.[21] It's big capital that is the polluter even more than the very rich.

The IPCC provides various scenarios on when global temperatures will reach the so-called Paris target of 1.5°C above average pre-industrial levels. Its main scenario is called the Shared Socioeconomic Pathway (SSP1-1.9) scenario, in which it is argued that if net carbon emissions are reduced, then the 1.5°C target will be reached by 2040 at the latest, then breach the target up to 2060 before falling back to 1.4°C by the end of the century.

But this is the most optimistic of five scenarios on the pace and intensity of global warming in the 21st century and it's bad enough! The other scenarios are way bleaker, culminating in SSP5-8.5 which would see global temperatures rise 4.4°C by 2100 and continuing upward thereafter. There isn't a scenario better than SSP1-1.9 and these are ignored by the IPCC.

No probabilities are offered for any of these scenarios – just the hope and expectation that SSP1-1.9 will happen. But the pace of emissions growth and temperature is already on a much faster trajectory. The planet has already warmed 1.0–1.2°C depending on how you want to measure it (current or ten-year average). The trend is well established and is tending to surprise on the upside, not the downside. Furthermore, the rate of change in atmospheric chemistry is unprecedented and continues to accelerate.

Even if we assume the SSP1-1.9 objectives can be met by 2050, cumulative global carbon dioxide (CO_2) emissions would still be a third higher than the current 1.2 trillion tons of CO_2 emitted since 1960. That would push atmospheric CO_2 beyond 500ppm, or 66 per cent higher than where things stood in the pre-industrial period (Figure 1.3). That pathway implies 1.8°C of warming by 2050, not 1.5°C.

The reality is that the IPCC's very low emissions scenario is improbable, and the global temperature is likely to hit 1.5°C much earlier than 2040 and reach a much higher level, even with the conditions of SSP1 in place, namely, a 50 per cent reduction in CO_2 emissions by 2050. More likely, global warming will reach around 1.8°C by 2050 and 2.5°C by the end of the century. A plausible worst case of 3.5°C is possible (10 per cent chance). These projections assume Paris Agreement signatories meet their nationally determined contributions

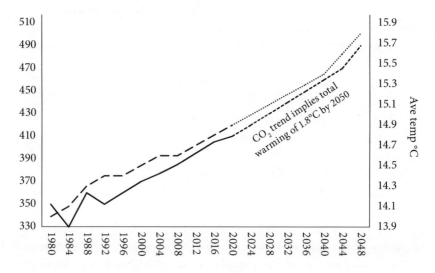

Figure 1.3 Atmospheric CO_2 (ppm) and average global temperature (°C) since 1980

(NDCs). If they fail to do so, the probability of extreme temperature increases is non-negligible. Indeed, unless countries start achieving 'negative' emissions, and not just a reduction, then current target limits will not be met.

That means even more drought and flood events than currently forecast and so even more suffering and mounting economic losses from the mix – a loss in world GDP of 10–15 per cent on current trajectories and double that in the poor dominated countries, the so-called 'Global South' (Figure 1.4).

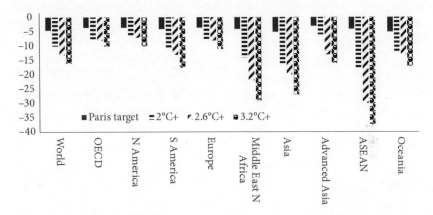

Figure 1.4 Mid-century GDP losses by region generated by global warming (%)

If emissions do not come down drastically before 2030, then by 2040 some 3.9 billion people are likely to experience major heatwaves, twelve times more than the historic average. By the 2030s, 400 million people globally each year are likely to be exposed to temperatures exceeding the workability threshold. Also, by the 2030s, the number of people on the planet exposed to heat stress exceeding the survivability threshold is likely to surpass ten million a year.[22]

The UN forecasts that unless global warming is stopped the planet will turn into 'uninhabitable hell' for millions.[23] Even at 1.5°C, we will see sea level rises of between two and three metres. Instances of extreme heat will be around four times more likely. Heavy rainfall will be around 10 per cent wetter and 1.5 times more likely to occur. Much of these changes are already irreversible, like the sea level rises, the melting of Arctic ice, and the warming and acidification of the oceans. Drastic reductions in emissions can stave off worse climate change, according to IPCC scientists, but will not return the world to the more moderate weather patterns of the past.

Much of the difference is explained by a rise in climate-related disasters including extreme weather events: from 3,656 climate-related events (1980–99) to 6,681 climate-related disasters in the period 2000–19. The last 20 years has seen the number of major floods more than double, from 1,389 to 3,254, while the incidence of storms grew from 1,457 to 2,034. Floods and storms were the most prevalent events with major increases in other categories including drought, wildfires and extreme temperature events. There has also been a rise in geo-physical events including earthquakes and tsunamis which have killed more people than any of the other natural hazards. The International Monetary Fund (IMF) says: 'Climate change affects economic outcomes through multiple channels. Rising temperatures, sea-level rises, ocean acidification, shifting rainfall patterns, and extreme events (floods, droughts, heat waves, wildfires) affect the economy along multiple dimensions, including through wealth destruction, reduction and volatility of income and growth.'[24] The IMF goes on: 'The broad consensus in the literature is that expected damages caused by unmitigated climate change will be high and the probability of catastrophic tail-risk events is nonnegligible.' And: 'There is growing agreement between economists and scientists that the tail risks are material and the risk of cata-strophic and irreversible disaster is rising, implying potentially infinite costs of unmitigated climate change, including, in the extreme, human extinction.'

Rising heat and humidity is threatening to plunge much of the world's pop-ulation into potentially lethal conditions, the study finds. The climate crisis is pushing the planet's tropical regions towards the limits of human liveability, with rising heat and humidity threatening to plunge much of the world's population into potentially lethal conditions, new research has found. Should governments fail to curb global heating to 1.5°C above the pre-industrial era, areas in the tropical band that stretches either side of the equator risk changing into a new environment that will hit 'the limit of human adaptation', the study warns.

Human ability to regulate body heat is dependent upon the temperature and humidity of the surrounding air. We have a core body temperature that stays relatively stable at 37°C (98.6F), while our skin is cooler to allow heat to flow away from the inner body. But should the wet-bulb temperature – a measure of air temperature and humidity – pass 35°C, high skin temperature means the body is unable to cool itself, with potentially deadly consequences. The global number of potentially fatal humidity and heat events has doubled between 1979 and 2017, with the coming decades set to see as many as three billion people pushed beyond the historical range of temperature that humans have survived and prospered in over the past 6,000 years.

1.7 MAINSTREAM ECONOMICS AND CLIMATE CHANGE

However, mainstream economics remains steeped in complacency. Integrated assessment models (IAMs) are used to calculate the social cost of carbon (SCC). They attempt to model the incremental change in, or damage to, global economic output resulting from 1 tonne of anthropogenic CO_2 emissions or equivalent. These SCC estimates are used by policymakers in cost–benefit analyses of climate change mitigation policies. Using IAMs, Nobel Prize winner William Nordhaus claimed he could make precise the trade-offs of lower economic growth against lower climate change, as well as making clear the critical importance of the social discount rate and the micro-estimates of the cost of adjustment to climate change. His results showed that things would not be that bad even if global warming accelerated well beyond current forecasts.

The IAM neoclassical growth accounting approach is fraught with flaws, however. The IPCC mitigation assessment concluded from its review of IAM outputs that the reduction in emissions needed to provide a 66 per cent chance of achieving the 2°C goal would cut overall global consumption by between 2.9 per cent and 11.4 per cent in 2100. This was measured relative to a 'business-as-usual' scenario. But growth itself can be derailed by climate change from business-as-usual emissions. So the 'business-as-usual' baseline, against which costs of action are measured, conveys a misleading message to policymakers that fossil fuels can be consumed in ever greater quantities without any negative consequences to growth itself. Steve Keen points out that

> If the predictions of Nordhaus's Damage Function were true, then everyone – including Climate Change Believers (CCBs) – should just relax. An 8.5 percent fall in GDP is twice as bad as the 'Great Recession', as Americans call the 2008 crisis, which reduced real GDP by 4.2% peak to trough. But that happened in just under two years, so the annual decline in GDP was a very noticeable 2%. The 8.5% decline that Nordhaus predicts from a 6 degree increase in average global temperature (here CCDs [climate change deniers] will have to pretend that AGW [anthropogenic global warming] is real) would take 130 years if nothing were done to attenuate Climate Change, according to Nordhaus's model. Spread over more than a century, that 8.5% fall would mean a decline in GDP growth of less than 0.1% per year.

IAM values often depend crucially on the 'discounting' used to translate future costs to current dollars. The high discount rates that predominate essentially assume that benefits to people in the future are much less important than benefits today. Most current models of climate change impacts make two flawed assumptions: that people will be much wealthier in the future and that lives in the future are less important than lives now. The former assumption ignores the great risks of severe damage and disruption to livelihoods from climate change. The latter assumption is 'discrimination by date of birth'. It is a value judgement that is rarely scrutinised, difficult to defend and in conflict with most moral codes.

The discount rate used to calculate the likely monetary damage to econo-mies is arbitrary. If we use a 3 per cent discount rate, that means the current rise in global warming would lead to $5 trillion of economic damage (loss of GDP), but the cost in current money of global warming would be no more than $400 billion, about what China spends on hi-speed rail. So, on this discount rate, global warming causes little economic damage and thus the social cost of carbon (SCC) is only about $10/ton, so mitigation action can be limited. This is what Nordhaus uses in his model. But why 3 per cent? Nicholas Stern, of the famous *Stern Review on the Economics of Climate Change*, took Nordhaus' data and applied a 1.4 per cent discount rate. The SCC then rises to $85/ton – meaning that it costs economies $85 for every ton of CO_2, or closer to $3 trillion now! If you take a median range discount rate on likely damage, the SCC is probably about $50/ton. But the carbon price before COVID was about $25/ton. So the social cost is not being 'internalised' in any market prices.

The argument about the discount rate exposes the argument about the future. The IAMs assume that the world economy will have a much larger GDP in 50 years so that even if carbon emissions rise as the IPCC predicts, governments can defer the cost of mitigation to the future. And if you apply stringent carbon abatement measures, for example, ending all coal production, you might lower growth rates and incomes and so make it more difficult to mitigate in the future. That is what Nordhaus' IAMs can lead us to conclude.

Also, because the IAMs omit so many of the big risks, SCC estimates are often way too low. As the IPCC acknowledged, published SCC estimates 'lie between a few dollars and several hundreds of dollars'. For example, a new analysis draws upon several public health studies to conclude that for every 4,434 metric tons of CO_2 pumped into the atmosphere beyond the 2020 rate of emissions, one person globally will die prematurely from the increased temperature.[25] This additional CO_2 is equivalent to the current lifetime emissions of 3.5 Americans. Under Nordhaus' DICE model the 2020 social cost of carbon is $37 a metric ton but the addition of the mortality cost brings this figure up to $258 a ton.

Finally, as with all these neoclassical growth accounting models of which the IAM of Nordhaus is one, there is no allowance for recurring crises of produc-tion in capitalism or rising inequality of income and wealth. Growth accounting is the mainstream version of explaining long-term economic growth. Neoclas-sical theory assumes perfect competition and free markets and it assumes what it should prove: that capitalist economic expansion will be harmonious and without crises as long as markets are free and competition is operating.

Applying these microeconomic assumptions to long-term growth was the province of factor productivity models, originating with Solow and Swan in 1956.[26] Based on marginal utility theory, each factor of production (capital and labour) contributed to growth according to its marginal productivity.

The problem with this factor accounting model is two-fold. First, the nature of 'capital' could not be defined or measured – what was it: numbers of different machines or the present value of the interest rate for borrowing 'capital'? This led to the so-called Cambridge controversy, where the neoclassical school was confounded by those who showed that you needed a common measure of value (labour?), otherwise the definition of capital was circular (namely, its marginal productivity was the rate of interest on borrowing, but the amount of capital was the present value of the rate of interest!).[27] The second problem was that adding up the marginal contributions of capital and labour factors to GDP growth would lead to a 'residual', which was designated as 'technical innovation', the productivity growth of all the factors. This appeared to be 'exogenous', that is, from outside the market system of marginal productivity. Mainstream economics has no explanation for technological innovation.

And IAMs also exclude the feedback – namely, that global warming leads to more natural disasters, droughts and floods and thus to massive disruption and migration of affected populations and thus a sharp reduction in GDP growth rates. The world will not be much 'richer' in the next generation if global warming goes unchecked.

1.8 MEASURING GLOBAL WARMING AND GROWTH

It is undoubtedly true that when economies accelerate in growth and industrial output, based on fossil fuel energy, then carbon emissions also rise inexorably. José Tapia, has produced firm empirical evidence of the correlation between economic growth and carbon emissions. Indeed, whenever there is a recession as in 2008–09, carbon emission growth falls. Tapia and Carpintero have shown that there is a pro-cyclical correlation between the rate of increase of atmospheric CO_2 and the rate of growth of the global economy, providing strong evidence that the world economy is linked with the build-up of the greenhouse effect and, therefore, with the process of global warming.[28]

Tapia uses multivariate analysis of the influence of the world economy on CO_2 levels to show that the annual increase in atmospheric CO_2 is significantly linked to the growth of the global economy. Years of above-trend GDP growth are years of greater rise in CO_2 concentrations, and similarly, years of below-trend growth are years of smaller rise in CO_2 concentrations. So global emissions of CO_2 have increased at rates strongly correlated with the absolute growth of the global economy. When capitalist production stops, so does global warming, as in 2009 and 2020.

Tapia goes on to say:

However, even in 2009 when the global economy contracted 2.25%, global emissions did not decrease, they just ceased growing to start growing again next year when the world economy somewhat recovered. This shows how dependent on fossil fuels the world economy has become in recent years. In earlier recessions of the global economy – in the mid-1970s, early-1980s, early-1990s and late-1990s – emissions not only decreased in many countries, as we have shown, but also worldwide. The notion that economic growth will reduce the carbon intensity of the world economy (the ratio of global emissions to world GDP) is inconsistent with the fact that the carbon intensity of the global economy has increased in recent years. In 2010, after the Great Recession, world GDP grew 5.0%, but emissions grew faster, 5.9%. Furthermore, the average growth of global CO_2 emissions was 3.1% per year in 2000–2011, while it had been 1.0% per year in 1990–2000, and 2.0% per year in 1980–1990.

Most of the rise in emissions comes from emerging economies where economic growth has been fastest. China was responsible for 24 per cent of the global total emissions in 2009, against 17 per cent for the US and 8 per cent for the eurozone. But each Chinese person emits only a third as much as an American and less than four-fifths of a resident of the eurozone. China is a relatively wasteful emerging economy, in terms of its emissions per unit of output. But it still emits less per head than the high-income countries because its people remain relatively poor. As emerging countries develop, emissions per person

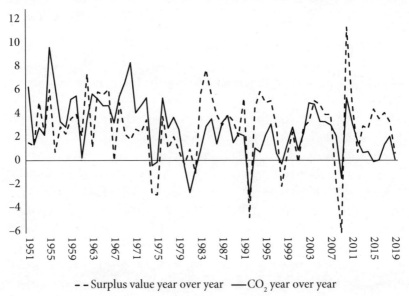

- - Surplus value year over year   ——CO_2 year over year

Figure 1.5   Yearly change in global CO_2 and total profits (%)

will tend to rise towards levels in high-income countries, raising the global average. This is why global emissions per person rose by 16 per cent between 2000 and 2009, which was a period of fast growth in emerging economies.

We find a high correlation between carbon emissions growth and total profits (Figure 1.5). There is a positive correlation (0.48) between the annual change in global carbon emission and the annual change in total profits of the G20 top economies and the annual change in profitability (0.41). The faster the rise in profits, the faster the rise in CO_2 emissions.

1.9 THE MARKET SOLUTION

European Climate Commissioner Connie Hedegaard said: 'If your doctor was 95 percent sure you had a serious disease, you would immediately start looking for the cure.' But what are the solutions? The chairman of the IPCC reckoned that the only way to reduce large-scale fossil fuel use is to 'price' carbon emissions: 'Unless a price could be put on carbon emissions that was high enough to force power companies and manufacturers to reduce their fossil fuel use, there seemed to be little chance of avoiding hugely damaging temperature increases.'

For some time, the IMF has been pushing for carbon pricing as 'a necessary if not sufficient' part of a climate policy package that also includes investment in 'green technology' and redistribution of income to help the worst-off cope with the financial burden. The IMF is now proposing a global minimum carbon price. Nordhaus calls for a 'climate club' of countries willing to commit to a carbon price. 'A key ingredient in reducing emissions is high carbon prices', he said, adding that a 'climate club' would have to impose a penalty tariff on countries that did not have carbon pricing in place. Nordhaus said that such an approach would help solve the problem of 'free riding', which has plagued existing global climate agreements, all of which are voluntary.

Market solutions to climate change are based on trying to correct 'market failure' by incorporating the nefarious effects of carbon emissions via a tax or quota system. The argument goes that as mainstream economic theory does not incorporate the social costs of carbon into prices, the price mechanism must be 'corrected' through a tax or a new market. The first problem with this is that climate change is not one market failure (like tobacco) but several: in capitalist transport, energy, technology, finance and employment.[29] Economists who have attempted to calculate what the 'social price' of carbon should be have found that there are so many factors involved and the pricing must be projected over such a long time horizon that it is really impossible to place a monetary value on the 'social damage' – estimates for the carbon price range from \$14 per ton of CO_2 to \$386! 'It is impossible to approximate the uncertainties in low-probability but high-damage, catastrophic or irreversible outcomes.'[30] Indeed, where carbon pricing has been applied, it has been a miserable failure in reducing emissions, or in the case of Australia, dropped by the government under the pressure of energy and mining companies.

And while there is much talk about raising carbon emission prices, little or nothing is said about the huge subsidies that governments continue to make to fossil fuel industries. EU Commissioner Gentiloni admitted as such: 'Paradoxically, [the current energy taxation directive] is incentivising fossil fuels and not environmentally friendly fuels. We have to change this.'

The G20 countries have provided more than $3.3 trillion (£2.4 trillion) in subsidies for fossil fuels since the Paris Climate Agreement was sealed in 2015 (Figure 1.6), despite many committing to tackle the crisis. G20 member states continue to provide substantial financial support for fossil fuel production and consumption.[31] China provided nearly a quarter of the 2019 count. But with a per capita total of $104, it was well below the G20 average of $313. In contrast, Saudi Arabia ($1,962), Argentina ($734) and Russia ($523) came top. The G20 as a whole has cut this funding by 10 per cent in 2015–19. But this masks significant variation across countries, with eight members boosting support – notably Australia, Canada and the US.

Australia increased its fossil fuel subsidies by 48 per cent over the period, Canada's support rose by 40 per cent and that from the US by 37 per cent. The UK's subsidies fell by 18 per cent over that time but still stood at $17 billion in 2019. The biggest subsidies came from China, Saudi Arabia, Russia and India, which together accounted for about half of all the subsidies; 60 per cent of the

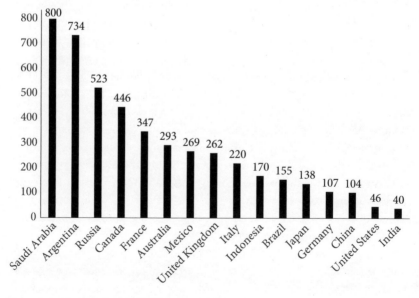

Figure 1.6   Fossil fuel subsidies per capita ($)

fossil fuel subsidies went to the companies producing fossil fuels and 40 per cent to cutting prices for energy consumers. And yet, reforming fossil fuel subsidies aimed at consumers in 32 countries could reduce CO_2 emissions by 5.5 billion tonnes by 2030, equivalent to the annual emissions of about 1,000 coal-fired power plants and also save governments nearly $3 trillion by 2030.[32] The International Energy Agency's (IEA) road map for net-zero emissions by 2050 calls for a 6 per cent decline in coal-fired generation annually. Yet coal production continues to rise.[33]

More than 80 per cent of emissions are covered by carbon price schemes in France, Germany and South Africa. In the UK, only 31 per cent of emissions are covered but the UK has one of the highest carbon prices at $58 per tonne of CO_2. Just 8 per cent of US emissions are covered and at the low price of $6 per tonne (Table 1.1). Russia, Brazil and India do not have any carbon prices. Indeed, the current average global carbon price is under $2 and 80 per cent of global emissions have no carbon emissions pricing market at all![34]

So the carbon pricing and taxation solution, even if it worked to lower emissions, is a pipedream as it can never be implemented globally before global warming reaches dangerous 'tipping points'.[35] Market solutions are not working because for capitalist companies it is just not profitable to invest in climate change mitigation:

Private investment in productive capital and infrastructure faces high upfront costs and significant uncertainties that cannot always be priced. Investments for the transition to a low-carbon economy are additionally exposed to important political risks, illiquidity and uncertain returns, depending

Table 1.1 The carbon price landscape

	% of region covered	Carbon price ($/tCO$_2$)	Effective price ($)	% of global emissions
Sweden	40	127	50.8	<1
Norway	60	59	35.4	<1
Switzerland	33	96	31.7	<1
British Columbia	70	26	18.2	<1
France	33	50	16.5	1
California	85	16	13.6	2
European Union	43	25	10.8	8
Japan	70	3	2.1	5
Argentina	20	6	1.2	<1
China	40	3	1.2	1
North East US	18	5	0.9	1
Mexico	45	1	0.5	1.5
The rest	100	0	0	80
Global average			1.7	

on policy approaches to mitigation as well as unpredictable technological advances. (Krogstrup and Oman, 2019)

Indeed:

The large gap between the private and social returns on low-carbon investments is likely to persist into the future, as future paths for carbon taxation and carbon pricing are highly uncertain, not least for political economy reasons. This means that there is not only a missing market for current climate mitigation as carbon emissions are currently not priced, but also missing markets for future mitigation, which is relevant for the returns to private investment in future climate mitigation technology, infrastructure and capital.

Another solution offered is regulation of the carbon emitters. Former Bank of England governor, Mark Carney calls for 'clear, credible and predictable regulation from government' with 'Air quality rules, building codes, that type of strong regulation. If you can have strong regulation for the future, then the financial market will start investing today, for that future. Because that's what markets do, they always look forward'.[36] Although the IEA recently said that if the world was to stay within 1.5°C Paris target increase in global heating, there could be no more exploration or development of fossil fuel resources, Carney argues that countries and companies could still carry on exploiting fossil fuels if they use technology such as carbon capture and storage, or other ways of reducing emissions. 'With the right regulation, with a rising carbon price, with a financial sector that is oriented this way, with public accountability of government, of financial institutions, of companies, yes, then we can, we certainly have the conditions in which to achieve [holding global heating to 1.5°C].'

Apart from carbon pricing and taxes, the IMF proposes a green investment stimulus – investments in clean public transportation, smart electricity grids to incorporate renewables into power generation, and retrofitting buildings to make them more energy efficient. Supposedly, this green infrastructure push will achieve two goals. First, it will boost global GDP and employment in the initial years of the recovery from the COVID-19 crisis. Second, the green infrastructure will increase productivity in low-carbon sectors, thereby incentivising the private sector to invest in them and making it easier to adapt to higher carbon prices.

The IMF claims this could actually boost global GDP in the first 15 years of the recovery by about 0.7 per cent of global GDP on average, and employment for about half of that period, leading to about twelve million extra persons being employed globally. As the recovery takes hold, preannounced and gradually rising carbon prices will become a powerful tool to deliver the needed reduction in carbon emissions. 'If implemented, such a policy program would put the global economy on a sustainable path by reducing emissions and limiting climate change. The net effect would approximately halve the expected output loss from climate change and provide long-term real GDP gains well above the current course from 2050 onward.'

However, the IMF does admit that, despite the long-run benefits and an initial boost to economic activity, its policies do impose costs along the transition. Between 2037 and 2050, the mitigation strategy would hold global GDP down by about 0.7 per cent on average each year and by 1.1 per cent in 2050 relative to unchanged policies. Also, the IMF recognises that 'low-income households are more likely to be hurt by carbon pricing, as they spend a relatively large share of their income on energy and are more likely to be employed in carbon-intensive manufacturing and transportation.' But governments can use various policies to limit the adverse effects of higher carbon prices on households, for example, cash transfers and public spending. Talking in terms of 'human capital', about workers, the IMF reckons that jobs can be saved by 'retooling workers which will also help to smooth job transitions to low-carbon sectors.'

However, the IMF model assumes no financial and investment crises in capitalist production for the next 30 years! It projects average annual global growth of 3.3 per cent up to 2050. And yet it also reckons its 'mitigation' strategy would knock 1 per cent a year off that rate. On that basis, per capita real GDP growth would be barely above population growth in many countries of the Global South. The model does not really avoid the conflict between lives and livelihoods (see below).

It would be so much easier to avert crisis if we could just capture carbon and re-bury or store it in some energy-efficient, cost-efficient way. But to this point, hopes of carbon capture and storage (CCS) being a sort of silver bullet have been little more than 'magical thinking'. It simply doesn't work as we imagine it should in our minds.

While CCS can work, at least in theory, it is prohibitively expensive and may even become part of the problem. For example, a consortium including Amazon and Microsoft invested in CarbonCure Technologies, a Canadian firm seeking to slash the CO_2 emissions of concrete. But producing cement, the key ingredient in concrete, creates so much CO_2 that if the industry were a country, only China and the US would emit more over the course of a year. Moreover, carbon capture is still in its infancy – there are only about 20 projects in commercial use worldwide, according to the IEA.[37]

The world's most authoritative body of energy analysts, the International Energy Agency, found in its latest annual flagship report that the world is headed towards global warming higher than the Paris Agreement's most aggressive limit of 1.5°C. The agency reckons that getting fossil fuels substantially out of the energy system would cost 25 per cent more than the $54 trillion the world is already expected to invest by 2040.

The IEA reckons that 'The era of global oil demand growth will come to an end in the next decade, but without a large shift in government policies, there is no sign of a rapid decline. Based on today's policy settings, a global economic rebound would soon push oil demand back to pre-crisis levels.'[38] Bringing about a 40 per cent reduction in emissions by 2030 requires, for example, that low-emissions sources provide nearly 75 per cent of global electricity generation in 2030, up from less than 40 per cent in 2019 – and that more than 50 per cent of passenger cars sold worldwide in 2030 are electric, up from 2.5 per cent in 2019.

JP Morgan economists tried to work out what could be the minimum reduction in fossil fuel use to avoid losses for the energy companies and financial markets. The lower the target limit on greenhouse gas emissions, the greater the risk of 'stranded assets' (unused) on the books of the companies. The size of stranded assets would depend on the temperature target, which in turn would depend on government policy decisions and on technology innovations to reduce energy use and carbon emissions over the next generation. The IEA has a 'Sustainable Development Scenario' which it claims to limit the global warming increase to 1.8°C relative to pre-industrial times, with a 66 per cent likelihood. In this scenario, energy-related CO_2 emissions are assumed to peak immediately and then fall to reach zero in 2070. If that actually happened, then, according to JPM, 87 per cent of the current proved coal reserves, 42 per cent of current proved oil reserves and 26 per cent of current proved natural gas reserves would need to be left in the ground if the temperature gain were to be limited to 1.8°C.

The IEA also has a 'Stated Policies Scenario' which is intended to reflect the effects of policies that governments have already implemented with an assessment of the likely consequences of policies that governments have announced but not yet implemented. Finally, there is the 'Current Policies Scenario' which is where governments ignore or do not implement all stated current climate policies. What the IEA finds is that the Stated Policies Scenario shows some relative improvement in reducing carbon emissions compared to the Current Policies Scenario, but it is a long way short of the Paris 2°C objective. Indeed, the Stated Policies Scenario would be consistent with an increase in the global temperature of around 3°C ! That would have devastating effects on the climate.

Even in the IEA Stated Policies Scenario, the stranded assets for coal are still large, at 67 per cent of the proved reserves. But there are no stranded assets for either oil or natural gas. Indeed, the cumulative extraction of oil from 2019 to 2070 exceeds the level of proved reserves in 2018 by 215.7 billion barrels (12 per cent of proved reserves in 2018), while the cumulative extraction of natural gas from 2019 to 2070 exceeds the level of proved reserves in 2018 by 68,525 billion cubic metres (35 per cent of proved reserves in 2018). JPM comments: 'These calculations help to explain why companies are still exploring for new oil and gas deposits, despite some dire warnings about stranded assets.' In other words, existing government agreements to reduce fossil fuel use and carbon emissions will not damage the profits of the oil and gas multinationals at all, but also will fail to stop the inexorable rise in global warming to increasingly destructive levels.

Then there is the Nightmare Scenario. Some recent scientific projections suggest that a 'business-as-usual climate policy scenario' is expected to deliver a temperature increase of around 3.5°C ; dangerous enough. But the impact of climate change is likely to come just as much from an increase in the variance as from an increase in the mean. Up to now scientists concur that the Earth could warm 3°C if CO_2 doubles. But the latest models suggest even faster warming – recent model projections on global warming from various sources are suggesting a rise in global temperature in excess of 5°C. Indeed, a Pareto probability distribution function of the current projections have 'fat tails' that suggest there is a 1 per cent likelihood of a 12°C increase in temperature. Weitzman finds that 'the most striking feature of the economics of climate change is that its extreme downside is non-negligible. Deep structural uncertainty about the unknown unknowns of what might go very wrong is coupled with essentially unlimited downside liability on possible planetary damages.'[39] With that kind of temperature increase, human life would probably not survive. But even worse, says JPM economists, 'in such a catastrophic outcome, all financial and real assets would likely be worthless'!

And yet governments continue to allow energy companies to search for and develop more fossil fuel resources. And this is not just in so-called emerging economies which need growth. Canada's Liberal government claims to be a leader in fighting global warming. But the government has still agreed to allow the development of the biggest tar sands mine yet: 113 square miles of petroleum mining. A federal panel approved the mine despite conceding that it would likely be harmful to the environment and to the land culture of indigenous people. These giant tar sands mines (easily visible on Google Earth) are already among the biggest scars humans have ever carved on the planet's surface. But Canadian authorities ruled that the mine was nonetheless in the 'public interest'. Canada, which is 0.5 per cent of the planet's population, plans to use up nearly a third of the planet's remaining carbon budget.[40]

And yet the technology for introducing renewable energy to replace fossil fuels and other environmentally damaging energy production is available now – and the cost per unit is falling fast.

Nuclear power remains problematic as an alternative source of energy. It is dangerous, wastes water, it takes a long time to construct nuclear plants at huge cost, and construction materials have considerable greenhouse gas emissions. A 2017 report by WISE International estimated nuclear life cycle emissions at 88–146 grams of CO_2 per kilowatt hour. By contrast, estimates of life cycle emissions for wind power sit at about 5–12 grams. Carbon emissions from uranium mining will also rise over time as the most easily recoverable ores are mined out. Mining uranium is dangerous in itself and nuclear 'waste' will be with us forever.

1.10 THE 'DEGROWTH' SOLUTION

Degrowth was originally termed by André Gorz in 1972. Gorz argued that the global environmental balance, which is predicated upon non-growth (or 'degrowth'), is not compatible with the capitalist system, which requires 'accumulation for the sake of accumulation'. Degrowth, according to Gorz, is thus a challenge to capitalism itself.

Degrowth has become increasingly popular among many environmentalists and leftists. There are some who even call themselves 'degrowth communists'. Jason Hickel, a prominent proponent of degrowth, defines it like this: 'The objective of degrowth is to scale down the material and energy throughput of the global economy, focusing on high-income nations with high levels of per-capita consumption.'[41] The degrowth perspective asks why society is so obsessed with 'growth' (as measured by GDP) and seeks to deconstruct the entire 'ideology of growth'. The 'ideology of growth' is used by the capitalist class to argue that more and more growth is needed to overcome poverty and to create jobs.

Giorgos Kallis, another major proponent of the movement, says that 'degrowth envisages radically reducing the surplus' and advocates so-called 'self-limitations' where there are 'collective decisions to refrain from pursuing all that could be pursued'. Rather than the typical Malthusian 'natural' external limits, degrowth calls for a collective enforcement of limits and constraints.[42]

The target of degrowth, Kallis declares, is 'not just capitalism, but also productivism'. Proponents of degrowth argue that any type of 'economic growth is ecologically unsustainable – whether it is capitalist growth or socialist does not make a difference'. Kallis justifies this claim by arguing that if we did not change consumption levels in a post-carbon energy regime, then nothing would really change in terms of environmental destruction because 'the manufacturing of renewable energies requires lots of earth materials. And the fact that they cost more than fossil fuels might have something to do with their lower energy returns and higher land requirements.' Thus, degrowth does not really have an ecological theory of capitalist accumulation. For degrowth, any type of accumulation is bad.

But accumulation simply means reinvesting the surplus back into production to expand the means of production. The difference is that accumulation under socialism is guided by the workers themselves who collectively determine what and how much surplus to produce and how to use it. Under capitalism, accumulation happens for accumulation's sake, to invest more and thus to make more profits without a plan and purely in the interests of private profit.

When workers are in control of the surplus, will we not develop and grow the productive forces to make life better and easier for ourselves and more sustainable for the earth and its inhabitants? Wouldn't we especially grow green productive forces to build more (and better) schools, public transportation etc.? Shouldn't socialists strive to repair the underdevelopment of imperialism by assisting in the development of productive forces in the formerly colonised world?

'Yet for all its stinginess, capitalist production is thoroughly wasteful with human material, just as its way of distributing its products through trade, and its manner of competition, make it very wasteful of material resources, so that it loses for society what it gains for the individual capitalist' (Marx).[43] The wasteful and environmentally unsustainable consumption patterns of the working class are not produced by 'personal' choice but are system-induced. Every day, millions of workers in the US commute to work in single occupant vehicles not because we 'choose' to drive. It's because public transportation is so unreliable (if it exists at all), jobs in the labour market are so unstable and temporary that few workers are actually able to live close to work, and the rents around major industries tend to be unaffordable for our class. Then there is planned obsolescence, such as when commodities like cell phones are produced to break every two years. When capitalism is overthrown and replaced with socialism, we can produce things that are 'built to last' because our aim is to satisfy society's needs and not private profit.

Proponents of degrowth argue that there are absolute 'planetary limits' and a fixed 'carrying capacity' that cannot be surpassed by humans if we want to avoid ecological collapse. There's no distinction between socially produced limits and natural limits. Kallis argues that 'only social systems of limited size and complexity can be governed directly rather than by technocratic elites acting on behalf of the populace ... Many degrowth advocates, therefore, oppose even 'green' megastructures like high-speed trains or industrial-scale wind farms.'

The same can be said about degrowth solutions to the problems the capitalist agricultural system creates. Proponents of degrowth propose small-scale (both urban and rural) methods of agriculture production to replace industrial-scale agriculture. They, in fact, glorify and romanticise 'peasant economies'. Despite the problems of capitalist industrial agriculture, there are two main benefits of industrial-scale agriculture. First, it has drastically increased yields. There is enough food produced to feed eleven billion people. Second, industrial farming has thoroughly decreased the backbreaking labour needed for agricultural and food production. In 1790, 90 per cent of the US workforce laboured on farms. In 1900, it was 35 per cent. Now only 1 per cent of the US workforce works on farms. Certainly, in any just society we would want to spread out food production more evenly amongst the population. But getting rid of industrial-scale agriculture and reverting to small-scale peasant and small landowner agriculture would require massive numbers of workers to go back to the land and perform backbreaking agricultural work. Such a transformation would inevitably reduce agricultural yield substantially, increasing the possibility of food insecurity and hunger among vast swathes of the population.

Matt Huber, a Marxist environmental geographer, argues that a 'truly humane society must commit to relieving the masses from agricultural labour' and that we cannot act as if 'small-scale agricultural systems are much of a "material basis" for a society beyond industrial capitalism'.[44] Ernest Mandel writes: 'it is simply not true that modern industrial technology is inevitably geared towards destroying the environmental balance. The progress of the exact sciences opens up a very wide range of technical possibilities'.[45] Increased rates of pollution and environmental degradation occur because capitalists pursue profits at the expense of the environment, not because of the technologies themselves. Socialists have to distinguish between instruments of production and their use under capitalism.

Jason Hickel argues that degrowth is not about reducing GDP.[46] Rather, it is about reducing excess resource and energy throughput, while at the same time improving human well-being and social outcomes. Excess resource and energy use is being driven by rich nations, not poor nations. So rich nations need to reduce their resource and energy use. Hickel reckons that we could end global poverty and ensure flourishing lives for everyone on the planet (for ten billion people by the middle of the century), including universal health care and education, with 60 per cent less energy than we presently use (150 EJ, well within what is considered compatible with 1.5°C).

Capitalism is highly inefficient when it comes to meeting human needs; it produces so much, and yet leaves 60 per cent of the human population without access to even the most basic goods. Why? Because a huge portion of commodity production (and all the energy and materials it requires) is irrelevant to human well-being. In an actual degrowth scenario, the goal would be to scale down ecologically destructive and socially less necessary production (what some might call the exchange value part of the economy), while protecting and indeed even enhancing parts of the economy that are organised around human well-being and ecological regeneration (the use value part of the economy).

Who are the biggest emitters or consumers of carbon apart from the fossil fuel industry? It is the richest wealth and income earners in the 'Global North' who have excessive consumption and fly everywhere. It is the military (the biggest sector of carbon consumption). The waste of capitalist production and consumption in autos, aircraft and airlines, shipping, chemicals, bottled water, processed foods, unnecessary pharmaceuticals etc. is directly linked to carbon emissions. Harmful industrial processes like industrial agriculture, industrial fishing, logging, mining etc. are also major global heaters, while the banking industry operates to underwrite and promote all this carbon emission.

The solution to these multifaceted and compounding environmental crises is not 'degrowth', but rather, as Mandel formulates it, 'controlled and planned growth': 'Such growth would need to be in the service of clearly defined priorities that have nothing to do with the demands of private profit ... rationally controlled by human beings ... The choice for "zero growth" is clearly an inhuman choice.' Two-thirds of humanity still lives below the subsistence minimum. If growth is halted, it means that the underdeveloped countries are condemned to remain stuck in the swamp of poverty, constantly on the brink of famine. 'Planned growth means controlled growth, rationally controlled by human beings. This presupposes socialism: such growth cannot be achieved unless the "associated producers" take control of production and use it for their own interests, instead of being slaves to "blind economic laws" or "technological compulsion".'

1.11 THE PLANNING SOLUTION

A global plan could steer investments into things society does need, like renewable energy, organic farming, public transportation, public water systems, ecological remediation, public health, quality schools and other currently unmet needs. And it could equalise development the world over by shifting resources out of useless and harmful production in the North and into developing the South, building basic infrastructure, sanitation systems, public schools, health care. At the same time, a global plan could aim to provide equivalent jobs for workers displaced by the retrenchment or closure of unnecessary or harmful industries. And a global plan could start to utilise new technology in food production. Damaging and cruel livestock farming could be phased out with plant-based 'meat' production and organic farming.

1.12 PANDEMICS: NATURE STRIKES BACK

COVID-19 appeared to be an 'unknown unknown', like the 'black swan'-type global financial crash that triggered the Great Recession over ten years ago. But COVID-19, just like that financial crash, is not really a bolt out of the blue –

a so-called 'shock' to an otherwise harmoniously growing capitalist economy. In early 2018, during a meeting at the World Health Organization in Geneva, a group of experts (the R&D Blueprint) coined the term 'Disease X': they predicted that the next pandemic would be caused by an unknown, novel pathogen that hadn't yet entered the human population.[47] Disease X would likely result from a virus originating in animals and would emerge somewhere on the planet where economic development drives people and wildlife together. Disease X would probably be confused with other diseases early in the outbreak and would spread quickly and silently; exploiting networks of human travel and trade, it would reach multiple countries and thwart containment. Disease X would have a mortality rate higher than a seasonal flu but would spread as easily as the flu. It would shake financial markets even before it achieved pandemic status. In a nutshell, COVID-19 was Disease X.

As socialist biologist, Rob Wallace, has argued, plagues are not only part of our culture; they are caused by it.[48] The Black Death spread into Europe in the mid-14th century with the growth of trade along the Silk Road. New strains of influenza have emerged from livestock farming. Ebola, SARS, MERS and now COVID-19 have been linked to wildlife. Pandemics usually begin as viruses in animals that jump to people when we make contact with them. These spillovers are increasing exponentially as our ecological footprint brings us closer to wildlife in remote areas and the wildlife trade brings these animals into urban centres. Unprecedented road-building, deforestation, land clearing and agricultural development, as well as globalised travel and trade, make us supremely susceptible to pathogens like corona viruses.

There is now firm evidence of a strong link between environmental destruction and the increased emergence of deadly new diseases such as COVID-19. Indeed, increasing numbers of deadly new pathogens will afflict the planet if levels of deforestation and biodiversity loss continue at their current catastrophic rates. Almost a third of all emerging diseases have originated through the process of land use change. As a result, five or six new epidemics a year could soon affect Earth's population. 'There are now a whole raft of activities – illegal logging, clearing and mining – with associated international trades in bushmeat and exotic pets that have created this crisis', says Stuart Pimm, professor of conservation at Duke University. 'In the case of Covid-19, it has cost the world trillions of dollars and already killed almost a million people, so clearly urgent action is needed.'[49]

It is estimated that tens of millions of hectares of rainforest and other wild environments are being bulldozed every year to cultivate palm trees, farm cattle, extract oil and provide access to mines and mineral deposits. This leads to the widespread destruction of vegetation and wildlife that are hosts to countless species of viruses and bacteria, most unknown to science. Those microbes can then accidentally infect new hosts, such as humans and domestic livestock. Such events are known as spillovers. Crucially, if viruses thrive in their new human hosts, they can infect other individuals. This is known as transmission and the result can be a new, emerging disease. Zoologist David Redding, of University College London explains what happens in places where trees are being cleared, mosaics of fields, created around farms, appear in the landscape interspersed with parcels of old forest.[50] 'This increases the interface between the wild and the cultivated. Bats, rodents and other pests carrying strange new viruses come from surviving clumps of forests and infect farm animals – who then pass on these infections to humans.'

In the past, many outbreaks of new diseases remained in contained areas. However, the development of cheap air travel has changed that picture and diseases can appear across the globe before scientists have fully realised what is happening. 'The onward transmission of a new disease is also another really important element in the pandemic story', said Professor James Wood, head of veterinary medicine at Cambridge University. 'Consider the swine flu pandemic. We flew that around the world several times before we realised what was going on. Global connectivity has allowed – and is still allowing – Covid-19 to be transmitted to just about every country on Earth.'

The blame for the 2019-nCoV outbreak is supposedly open markets for exotic animals in Wuhan, but it could also be due to the industrial farming of hogs across China. Or even a leak from a lab. But whatever the specific source of COVID-19, there appears to be an underlying structural cause: the pressure of the law of value through industrial farming and the commodification of natural resources. Commoditising the forest may have lowered the ecosystemic threshold to such a point that no emergency intervention can drive any outbreak low enough to burn out. For example, in relation to the Ebola outbreak in the Congo (which is also happening again).

Deforestation and intensive agriculture may strip out traditional agroforestry's stochastic friction, which typically keeps the virus from lining up enough transmission. And anyway, 'even the wildest subsistence species are being roped into ag value chains: among them ostriches, porcupine, crocodiles, fruit bats, and the palm civet, whose partially digested berries now supply the world's most expensive coffee bean. Some wild species are making it onto forks before they are even scientifically identified, including one new short-nosed dogfish found in a Taiwanese market.' All are increasingly treated as food commodities. As nature is stripped place-by-place, species-by-species, what's left over becomes that much more valuable. Spreading factory farms meanwhile may force increasingly corporatised wild foods companies to trawl deeper into the forest, increasing the likelihood of picking up a new pathogen, while reducing the kind of environmental complexity with which the forest disrupts transmission chains.

That theory has now been supported by a new study suggesting that high pork prices in China after the recent swine flu epidemic there led to increased consumption of wild animals from markets. These animals were the conductors of the new pathogens. So industrial farming was the likely cause of COVID-19.

> If more wildlife enters the human food chain, either through [individuals] hunting ... or going to market and getting different meat sources. If that increases, it could just increase the contact opportunity, said the author of the study, David Robertson, professor of viral genomics and bioinformatics at Glasgow University. 'You're just increasing the opportunity for the [SARS-CoV-2] virus to get into humans.[51]

It is very likely that there will be more and possibly even deadlier pathogens ahead.

As for COVID, we can reasonably identify the following factors. First, the uncontrolled growth of (otherwise necessary) industrial agriculture has led to the use of problematic hygienic methods that, however, enhance capitalist profitability and has already caused significant problems (e.g. salmonella). Second, due to the internationalisation of capital (the so-called globalisation), increasing competition internationally imposes the dominance of these production methods as they involve lower costs. Third, the uncontrolled growth of the capitalist agro-industrial complex dramatically limits virgin areas and brings humanity into contact with diseases and viruses that were previously restricted there and concerned small indigenous communities. The latter had either acquired relative immunity to them or the epidemics were limited to these communities and did not spread significantly. Fourth, the internationalisation of capital with the proliferation of transport and communication routes between remote areas of the world facilitates the rapid transmission of epidemics throughout the world, while in the past was more limited and therefore more controllable. Fifth, the commodification of the use and consumption of exotic species enhances zoonotic disease.[52]

Some health expert studies that point out that every day, hospital doctors must make decisions on what is the most 'cost effective' from the point of view of health outcomes. Should they save a very old person with COVID-19 if it means that some younger person's cancer treatment is delayed because beds and staff have been transferred to the pandemic? 'If funds are not limitless – then we should focus on doing things whereby we can do the most good (save the most lives) for the least possible amount of money. Or use the money we have, to save the most lives.' Health economics measures the cost per QALY. A QALY is a

Quality Adjusted Life Year. One added year of the highest quality life would be one QALY. 'How much are we willing to pay for one QALY? The current answer, in the UK, is that the NHS will recommend funding medical interventions if they cost less than £30,000/QALY. Anything more than this is considered too expensive and yet the UK's virus package is £350 billion, almost three times the current yearly budget for the entire NHS. Is this a price worth paying?' This expert reckoned that 'the cost of saving a COVID victim was more than eleven times the maximum cost that the NHS will approve.' At the same time cancer patients are not being treated, hip replacements are being postponed, heart and diabetes sufferers are not being dealt with. The key point is that this dilemma of 'costing' a life would be reduced if there had been proper funding of health systems, sufficient to provide 'spare capacity' in case of crises.

Gourinchas modelled the impact of the pandemic on capitalist production. Without any action, the pandemic leads to a rising curve of cases and deaths. With action on lockdowns and social isolation, the peak of the curve can be delayed and moderated, even if the pandemic gets spun out for longer. This supposedly reduces the pace of the infection and the number of deaths.[53] What flows from this approach is that the quicker and more effective containment measures to deal with the pandemic led to a quicker and stronger economic recovery. China and some east Asian economies had low infection and casualty rates and stronger economic recovery while in the major capitalist economies slower and less coordinated containment led to deeper and longer slumps and slower and weaker recovery.

The capitalist economy is based on the private sector and the public sector operates as a support of the former. The private sector works for profit, so it engages into activities procuring profits and abstains and/or withdraws from non-profitable activities. Furthermore, the capitalist economy in order to surpass health and economic crises needs to mobilise primarily the private sector (as this is the dominant sector of the economy). This requires using the public sector in order to subsidise the private sector by giving to the latter sufficiently profitable incentives. So actions are slow and fuzzy in a capitalist economy.

On the contrary, the planned economy would operate on the basis of economic planning and its dominant sector is the public sector. Thus, it could have non-surplus producing activities and even loss-making activities if this were decided by social planning. Loss-making activities would also be viable since they would be designated as such by social planning and would be structurally subsidised by the other economic activities. Additionally, when faced with an urgent contingency, it could mobilise resources on time and in sufficient numbers. This would be a direct mechanism operated by the planning authority. Hence, it is certain that (a) it would take place and (b) be punctual. This holds for socialism where the private sector and a large public sector co-exist and if the latter is planned to produce not for profit but for the satisfaction of human needs (see Chapter 6 on socialism). In a capitalist economy, the planned sector is subordinated to the law of value.

For these reasons a planned economy is better equipped to face contingencies like a health crisis. As former President Donald Trump put it for the US economy, it is not built to be shut down. The fundamental reason is that capitalist enterprises operate for profit, or else they have no reason to exist. Consequently, they cannot operate at a low cost of production level and moreover with losses. Unless someone else subsidises them to keep operating, they are going to close. On the contrary, a socialist economy can survive without achieving surplus (profits) by simply covering production costs. For the same reasons it can survive longer even with economic losses.

Economic crises start with a supply deficiency not a demand one, and the COVID pandemic slump was no different. It was production, trade and investment that is first stopped when shops, schools, businesses were locked down in order to contain the pandemic. Of course, then if people cannot work and businesses cannot sell, then incomes drop and spending collapses and that produces a 'demand shock'. Indeed, it is the way with all capitalist crises: they start with a contraction of supply (due to profitability fall) and end up with a fall in consumption – not vice versa.

Around 2.7 billion workers worldwide were affected by full or partial lockdown measures to combat the COVID-19 pandemic – around 81 per cent of the world's 3.3 billion workforce. The world economy had seen nothing like this before. Cyclically, the world economy was already 'on the verge of falling into a new cyclical crisis because of the imbalances accumulated after the 2007–09 cyclical crisis.' Structurally, the major capitalist economies were not equipped to handle the pandemic because they had run down the health, medical and public services needed to cope. And systemically, the pandemic had shown that capitalism's drive for profit over need leads to recurring crises in humanity, the climate and nature.

Before the COVID-19 pandemic engulfed the world, the big pharmaceutical companies did little investment in vaccines for global diseases and viruses. It was just not profitable. Of the 18 largest US pharmaceutical companies, 15 had totally abandoned the field. Heart medicines, addictive tranquilisers and treatments for male impotence were profit leaders, not defences against hospital infections, emergent diseases and traditional tropical killers. A universal vaccine for influenza – that is to say, a vaccine that targets the immutable parts of the virus's surface proteins – has been a possibility for decades, but never deemed profitable enough to be a priority. So, every year, we get vaccines that are only 50 per cent efficient.

The impact of the pandemic slump has not been equal. While hundreds of millions lost their jobs, businesses and incomes and been forced to go to work; others stayed at home on full pay, saved money and became cash-rich. And a tiny elite made a 'killing' on the financial markets, fuelled by a huge injection of credit by central banks and direct financial support by governments, mainly in the richer 'global north'. In the year of the pandemic, billionaires' wealth soared by 27.5 per cent while 131 million people were pushed into poverty due to COVID-19.

Take Latin America. In its latest annual report, the UN's Economic Commission for Latin America and the Caribbean (ECLAC) estimates that the total number of poor people in the region rose to 209 million by the end of 2020, which is 22 million more people than in the previous year. In 2020, the 'extreme' poverty rate reached 12.5 per cent while the poverty rate affected 33.7 per cent of the population. 'Inequality in total income per person is expected to have grown in 2020, leading to the average gini index of inequality being 2.9 per cent higher than recorded in 2019. The pandemic has also brought a rise in mortality that could push down life expectancy in the region. Of every 100 infections last reported around the world, about 24 were reported from countries in Latin America and the Caribbean.

IMF chief Georgieva reports that by the end of 2022, cumulative per capita income will be 13 per cent below pre-crisis projections in advanced economies – compared with 18 per cent for low-income countries and 22 per cent for emerging and developing countries excluding China. 'Put another way, the convergence between countries can no longer be taken for granted. Before the crisis, we forecast that income gaps between advanced economies and 110 emerging and developing countries would narrow over 2020–22. But we now estimate that only 52 economies will be catching up during that period, while 58 are set to fall behind. ...There is a major risk that most developing countries will languish for years to come.'

The OECD goes on to say, 'despite the improved global outlook, output and incomes in many countries will still remain below the level expected prior to the pandemic at the end of 2022.' In other words, there looks like being permanent 'scarring' of most economies as a result of the pandemic slump of 2020, with most economies never returning to the pre-pandemic growth and trajectory – which was already lower than the trajectory before the Great Recession hit in 2008. The economic recovery will not be V-shaped or fast, but instead more like a 'reverse square root' shape when real GDP, investment and employment growth remain below previous rates indefinitely – suggesting another leg in the Long Depression that ensued after 2009.

And capitalist firms are getting ready to shed labour for more technology, such as robots and AI. Big Tech companies including Amazon, Alibaba,

Alphabet, Facebook, and Netflix are responsible for more than $2 of every $3 spent globally on AI (McKinsey Global Institute 2017). Workers will lose their jobs in many sectors because it will be the employers who decide, without any plan to use technology to reduce hours, retrain and create new jobs. 'The pandemic has certainly given employers more reasons to look for ways of substituting machines for workers, and recent evidence suggests they are doing so.' (COVID-19 and Implications for Automation | NBER. As Daron Acemoglu at MIT puts it: 'when employers make decisions about whether to replace workers with machines, they do not take into account the social disruption caused by the loss of jobs – especially good ones. This creates a bias toward excessive automation.'

Coronavirus vaccines made billions for the drug industry as they prove safe and effective. As many as 14 billion vaccines would be required to immunise everyone in the world against COVID-19. If, as many scientists anticipate, vaccine-produced immunity wanes, billions more doses could be sold as booster shots in years to come. And the technology and production laboratories seeded with the help of all this government largesse could give rise to other profitable vaccines and drugs. So while much of the pioneering work on mRNA vaccines was done with government money, the privately owned drugmakers will walk away with big profits, while governments pay for vaccines they helped to fund the development of in the first place!

The lesson of the coronavirus vaccine response is that a few billion dollars a year spent on additional basic research could have prevented a thousand times as much loss in death, illness and economic destruction. What better lesson can we learn from the COVID vaccine experience than that the multinational pharma companies should be publicly owned so that research and development can be directed to meet the health and medical needs of people not the profits of these companies? Sure, state-owned companies can also work for the interests of capital and profits, but within a democratically planned economy, they would work for social needs. In a planned economy, necessary vaccines can get to the billions in the poorest countries and circumstances rather than to just those countries and people who can afford to pay the prices set by these companies. 'This is the people's vaccine', said corporate critic Peter Maybarduk, director of Public Citizen's Access to Medicines program. 'Federal scientists helped invent it and taxpayers are funding its development. ... It should belong to humanity.'

Within a planned global economy, it would be possible to set up a programme to monitor wildlife, reduce spillovers, end the wildlife meat trade and reduce deforestation. Such a scheme could cost no more than $20 billion a year, a price tag that is dwarfed by the cost of the COVID-19 pandemic, which has wiped trillions of dollars from national economies round the world. Spending of about $260 billion over ten years could substantially reduce the risks of another pandemic on the scale of the coronavirus outbreak, which is just 2 per cent of the estimated $11.5 trillion costs of COVID-19 to the world economy. Furthermore, the spending on wildlife and forest protection would be almost cancelled out by another benefit of the action: cutting the CO_2 emissions driving the climate crisis. The New Nature Economy project, published by the World Economic Forum (WEF), says:

We are reaching irreversible tipping points for nature and climate. If recovery efforts do not address the looming planetary crises, a critical window of opportunity to avoid their worst impact will be irreversibly lost. And yet the cost of action to deal with these impending disasters would be not much more than the recent fiscal spending by governments to save jobs and businesses from the COVID-19 pandemic.[54]

2

Money, Prices and Value

2.1 MARX'S VALUE THEORY OF MONEY

In view of the controversies around and misinterpretations of Marx's theory of money, we shall start this chapter by letting Marx himself speak. To this end, we shall reproduce his analysis as closely as possible. The chief place to start from is Chapter 3 of Volume I of *Capital* (Money or the Circulation of Commodities).[1] It encompasses three sections.[2] In Section 1 (The Measures of Value) Marx focuses on the chief function of money, that of serving as a *measure of value*. Marx starts this section by assuming gold as the money-commodity. It follows that money-commodity does not mean that gold as a commodity is money. Quite the contrary, it means that gold has divested its commodity form to *become* money. Gold has become (is) money because it is a measure of value. If it is a measure of value it cannot have/be value, just as a metre is a measure of length and thus cannot have/be length. Otherwise, the question would arise: how long is a metre? Then the answer could only be: a metre – a tautology. As Marx puts it: 'Money itself has no price. In order to put it on an equal footing with all other commodities in this respect, we should be obliged to equate it to itself as its own equivalent.'

Immediately after this, Marx makes a remark of fundamental importance for some current debates.

It is not money that renders commodities commensurable. Just the contrary. It is because all commodities, as values, are realised human labour and therefore commensurable, that their values can be measured by one and the same special commodity, and the latter be converted into the common measure of their values, i.e., into money. Money as a measure of value is the phenomenal form that must of necessity be assumed by that measure of value which is immanent in commodities, labour-time.

Two points follow. First, by labour(-time) Marx does not mean the specific kinds of labour which go into the specific features of each commodity (as a use value) and which he calls concrete (maybe 'specific' would be better) labour. What is specific to a commodity cannot be immanent in all commodities. By labour, Marx means abstract labour, the expenditure of labour power in the abstract, disregarding the specific features of each type of labour.[3] This is of direct relevance for all those physicalist authors (as in the neo-Ricardian approach) who disregard abstract labour and focus only on commodities such as physical use value. But by negating abstract labour, which is the substance common to all commodities, they fall into the incommensurability problem: commodities lack a common, unifying element which alone makes addition, subtraction etc. possible. To escape this criticism, the physicalist economists resort to money (prices) as the element common to all commodities. Then supposedly money would perform the commensurability function. However, if money represents labour and if abstract labour is excluded, only concrete labour is left. Then money would represent concrete labour. But concrete labour is just that which differentiates, not homogenises, so money if it represents concrete labour cannot be the homogenising factor.

The attentive reader will have noticed that in the quotation above Marx speaks of value *realised*, and not of value *contained*. At this initial stage of the analysis, the assumption is that the value realised (price) *coincides* with the value contained. This is why value (value contained) and price (value realised) are used interchangeably. Marx is obviously aware of the difference but intends to explain it at a later stage. It is only in Volume III that this difference becomes relevant when the transformation of values into prices is dealt with.[4] Marx goes on: 'the magnitude of value expresses a relation of social production, it expresses the connexion that necessarily exists between a certain article and the portion of the total labour-time of society required to produce it.'

The socially necessary labour time is the value realised under conditions of average productivity. It exists *before* exchange because an average is something that pre-exists the elements that compose it.[5] But productivity refers to the same use value and the same use values do not exchange for each other. Exchange takes place between different use values. Then the socially necessary labour time refers to average profitability. Individual capitals realise through exchange more or less than that social average value by losing value to more productive capitals or gaining value from the less productive capitals.

All commodities as values – not as use values – are commensurable because they have a common substance, abstract labour. This holds also for gold and this is why the value of commodities can be gauged not only against each other but also against gold. It is in this act that prices, in gold, arise. Gold as gold, as a commodity, is (contains) value because it too is the product of human abstract labour. But gold as *money* is not, *has no value* and thus no price. If money is the 'socially recognized incarnation of human [abstract] labour', a certain quantity of money represents a certain quantity of gold and thus of labour. If money is the representation of value, it is an imaginary representation of value, and prices are *imaginary quantities of gold*. As Marx says: 'A price therefore implies both that a commodity is exchangeable for money, and also that it must be so exchanged ... Under the ideal measure of values there lurks the hard cash.'

The last point Marx mentions in this section is the following: 'Why does not money directly represent labour-time, so that a piece of paper may represent, for instance, x hours' labour?' This question is still asked nowadays by naive critics of capitalism. This question presupposes implicitly a society in which the producers make their own products and exchange them directly among themselves on the basis of their cost in labour time expressed in certificates of labour, improperly called money. But capitalism is different. In capitalism the producers work for the owners of the means of production and not for themselves. Then money represents labour time spent by the labourers for the owners of the means of production, it represents labour (time) within the context of capitalist production relations. In short, money expresses exploitation. Money has a class content.

In Section 2 Marx shifts perspective and focuses on money as *the medium of circulation*. In its turn, this section is subdivided into three subsections. In the first subsection 2A, Marx deals with *the metamorphosis of commodities*. He starts with an analogy:

For instance, it is a contradiction to depict one body as constantly falling towards another, and as, at the same time, constantly flying away from it. The ellipse is a form of motion which, while allowing this contradiction to go on, at the same time reconciles it.

A first point of clarification is needed before proceeding. Marx does not hold that in this form of motion a body is attracted and *at the same time* flying away from another. Rather that body is first attracted by and then repulsed by another. This is obvious and yet it must be mentioned in view of a similar mistake made both by critics and supporters of Marx when they hold that the same body (a commodity) is *at the same time* both the input and the output of the same production process. Time is an essential element in Marx.

This analogy is meant to introduce the notion of contradiction in exchange and thus in price formation. The ellipse is determined by two opposing and mutually contradictory forces.[6] Similarly, exchange in capitalism presupposes the differentiation of commodities into commodities and money (gold), that is,

(1) C-M-C

Commodities (I) and money (M) are two features of exchange that metamorphosise into each other. This is a *description* of the movement of exchange. There is nothing inherently Marxist in it. Any economic theory can (should) incorporate it. What is typical of Marx's analysis is that what makes exchange (the metamorphosis) possible is the common substance inherent in both commodities and money, abstract labour. Then a more complete notion of exchange can be depicted as

(2) $C(\lambda)$-M-$C(\lambda)$

where λ indicates not only abstract labour, but the socially necessary abstract labour because commodities exchange on the basis not of the labour time contained in them but of the socially necessary labour time (see above). Of course, $C(\lambda)$-M presupposes that $C(\lambda)$ does have a use value for the purchaser, otherwise the first metamorphosis would not take place and the producer of $C(\lambda)$ would suffer a loss.[7]

Another element missing in relation (1) is the difference between use values and value. If the use value of commodities is introduced, the commodities exchanged can be differentiated in A, the commodity sold, and B the commodity purchased. Then (2) becomes

(3) $A(\lambda)$-M-$B(\lambda)$

From the perspective of abstract labour, in the exchange of A for B, λ (the abstract labour of the seller) is exchanged for λ (the abstract labour of the buyer). From the perspective of use values, the use value of the commodity sold is metamorphosed into that of that bought, that is,

(4) $A(\mathbf{u})$ – $B(\mathbf{u})$

Commercial capital is unproductive. The reason is that if a commodity is always a use value containing value, productive labour is not only labour performed by labour for capital, but also labour transforming use values into new use values. In the act of exchange, the use values of A and B remain the same. The metamorphosis of use values in (4) does not affect the value exchanged λ as in (3). Relations (3) and (4) are unrelated.

Exchange as in (4) at the act of exchange is different from a real transformation, the change in the use value of A that takes place when it, as an input, is transformed into a different use value, (B) the output. Here the use value of the inputs does not remain the same but is transformed into a different use value, the output.

In the second subsection 2B, *the currency of money*, Marx considers again the act of exchange, the replacing of commodity A by commodity B (and vice versa). It appears that commodities circulate because of money acting as a means of circulation: in this case, commodities would be '*motionless*' and money would transfer them from the seller to the buyer. But, in reality, the movement of money is 'merely the expression' of the circulation of commodities. This is a fine example of Marx's dialectical method. Marx emphasises the change of form, the metamorphosis: commodity A changes its form (use value) from the commodity form to the money form and the money form changes into a new commodity form, the use value of B. Movement (exchange in this case) does not come from outside the exchange of commodities, money. Rather, the metamorphosis of commodities is their movement and the movement of money (which is external to this metamorphosis) is only the expression of this inner movement.

In the third subsection 2C, *coins as symbols of value*, Marx shifts his attention from value to the symbols of value. Due to their debasement, coins' wear and tear makes it possible for their nominal weight (nominal value) to part company from their real weight (real value). Metallic coins are replaced by symbols serving the same purposes as coins. 'Therefore, things that are relatively without value, such as paper notes, can serve as coins in its place.' Marx alludes to 'only inconvertible paper money issued by the State and having compulsory circulation'. But whether convertible or not, paper money is a symbol, a representation of value. As such it has purchasing power. So even if it has no value, *money has purchasing power in virtue of its being a symbol of value.* Purchasing power is often thought of as a symbol of the value contained. But actually, it represents the value contained after redistribution, that is, realised through exchange after the tendential equalisation of the rates of profit. Then (3) above becomes

(5) $A(\lambda r)\text{-}M\text{-}B(\lambda r)$

where λr is the value realised after the equalisation of the profit rates. Gold as a commodity (and not as money), and thus the gold industry, participates in the tendential equalisation of profit rates. We shall not delve into this point since it does not affect substantially our current analysis one way or another. The point here is that gold can be replaced by value-less tokens because and only inasmuch as they function as a circulating medium.

In the last section, Section 3, *Money*, Marx examines money from three different perspectives, as three distinct social functions.

The first function of money (subsection 3A) is *hoarding*. It happens when in (1) the first metamorphosis is not a prelude to the second one. Then money is petrified into a hoard. Hoarding has an important function. Money must be continuously attracted and repelled because changes in the circulation of commodities and in their prices imply continuous changes in the money in circulation. Hoarding can supply more money as a means of circulation and withdraw it if its demand falls. This is hoarding's social function.

The second function of money (subsection 3B) is as a *means of payment*, not only of present, but also of future obligation. A commodity can be sold but the payment can be delayed. Then the seller becomes a creditor and the buyer becomes a debtor. Two points follow.

First, 'The seller's commodity circulates, and realises its price, but only in the shape of a legal claim upon money', that is, as credit. Contrary to what is almost universally assumed (also by some Marxist authors), credit/debt is a legal claim upon money, not money. The fundamental difference is that money is a representation of value, of a productive activity (the real transformation of use values). Credit is a representation of debt. If more/less value is produced and comes into circulation, money as a means of circulation and thus as a representation of value follows the same movement. In this case, there is a change in the real economy reflected in the money in circulation. But if somebody's credit increases, somebody else's debt increases correspondingly and the real economy is unaffected. When a payment is due, credits and debts confront each other and cancel each other out as positive and negative quantities. No monetary measures can delete this fundamental difference.

Marx does use the expression 'credit-money'. By this Marx does not mean that credit is money. Rather, he focuses on one of the functions of money, that of delaying payments to the future. But it is mistaken to equate one of the functions of money (means of payment) with its nature (the representation of value). This mistake has a name: functionalism.

Second, the basic principle that money is the representation of value does not imply that the quantity of money in circulation and the value of the mass of commodities circulating must correspond. Here Marx sketches his theory of money:

> If we now consider the sum total of the money current during a given period, we shall find that, given the rapidity of currency of the circulating medium and of the means of payment, it is equal to the sum of the prices to be realised, plus the sum of the payments falling due, minus the payments that balance each other, minus finally the number of circuits in which the same piece of coin serves in turn as means of circulation and of payment. Hence, even when prices, rapidity of currency, and the extent of the economy in payments, are given, the quantity of money current and the mass of commodities circulating during a given period, such as a day, no longer correspond. Money that represents commodities long withdrawn from circulation, continues to be current. Commodities circulate, whose equivalent in money will not appear on the scene till some future day.

Finally, the third function of money (subsection 3C) is universal money, or world money. Every country needs a certain quantity of money not only for the internal circulation of commodities, but as a universal means of payment on international markets and as international reserves. Any commodity other than gold and silver, like oxen, does not serve the purpose because not all countries accept oxen as money, because each ox is qualitatively different from the others, and because an ox cannot be fractioned in smaller denominations. Gold and silver, on the other hand, are of uniform quality so that equal quantities represent equal quantities of value. There are also other advantages like their divisibility, durability, a relatively high value contained within a relatively small quantity etc. This is why all countries accept them as representations of international value.[8] And this is why in periods of crises gold and silver are safe havens to which other forms of money turn.

The above are the most salient features of Marx's theory of money. In the following two sections this theory will be the prism through which a new fashionable theory of money (the Modern Monetary Theory) and what is considered to be a new form of money, crypto and digital currencies, will be assessed.

2.2 MODERN MONETARY THEORY

For Marx, under capitalism money is the phenomenal form taken by the abstract labour, that is, by the value contained in commodities. But for Modern Monetary Theory (MMT), value plays no role in money. Money is a product of the functions of the state, namely, it arises from state spending and borrowing and taxing. MMT ignores value altogether as the foundation of the existence of money. So it ignores capitalism.

MMT has its base in the ideas of Chartalism. Georg Friedrich Knapp, a German economist, coined the term Chartalism in his *State Theory of Money*, which was published in German in 1905 and translated into English in 1924. The name derives from the Latin *charta*, in the sense of a token or ticket. Chartalism argues that generalised commodity exchange only came into being with the emergence of the state, which sought to raise funds by borrowing. By creating a sovereign currency, it could impose taxes on the population to cover its borrowing. The use of money as a unit of account for debts/credits pre-dates the emergence of an economy based around the generalised exchange of commodities. So Chartalism argues that money first arose as a unit of account out of debt and not out of exchange.

MMT supposedly supports the 'endogenous' money approach, namely, that money is created by the decisions of entrepreneurs to invest or households to spend, and from the loans that the banks grant them for that purpose. So banks make loans and so create money (as issued by the state). This confuses money with credit/debt. MMT rests on this confusion. Money is deposited by the receivers of loans and then they pay taxes back to the state. According to MMT, loans are created by banks and then deposits are destroyed by taxation, in that order. At a simple level, MMT merely describes the way things work with banking and money – and this is what many MMT authors argue: 'all we are doing is saying like it is'.

But MMT goes further. It argues that the state creates money in order to receive it for the payment of taxes. The state can force taxes out of citizens and can decide the nature of the legal tender that serves for money. So money is a product of the state. Thus, MMT has a circuit of money that goes:

state money – others (non-state entities) – taxes – state money

The state injects money into the private sector, and that money is then reabsorbed with the collection of taxes. According to MMT, issuing money and collecting taxes are not alternatives, but actions that merely occur at different times of the same circuit. So if a government runs a fiscal deficit and spends more than it receives in taxes, the non-state sector has a surplus which it can use to invest, spend and employ more. The state deficit can thus be financed by creating more money. Taxes are not needed to finance state spending, but to generate demand for money (to pay taxes!).

The Marxist theory of money makes an important distinction from MMT. Capitalism is a monetary economy. Capitalists start with money capital to invest in production and commodity capital, which in turn, through the expending of labour power (and its exploitation), eventually delivers new value that is realised in more money capital. The demand for money capital drives the demand for credit. Banks create credit as part of this process of capitalist accumulation, but not as something that makes finance capital separate from capitalist production. The Marxist theory of money reckons that *under capitalism* money is the *representation* of *value* and thus of surplus value. Marx argues that money emerges naturally as commodity production is generalised. The state merely validates the money form – it doesn't invent it, as MMT claims. Marx's theory of money is specific to capitalism as a mode of production while MMT and Chartalism is ahistorical. For MMT, money is a product of the state and before capitalism.

In the classic statement of Chartalism, Knapp argued that states have historically nominated the unit of account and, by demanding that taxes be paid in a particular form (sovereign currency), ensured that this form would circulate as means of payment. Every taxpayer would have to get their hands on enough of the state-defined money and so would be embroiled in monetary exchange. Joseph Schumpeter refuted this approach when he said:

Had Knapp merely asserted that the state may declare an object or warrant or token (bearing a sign) to be lawful money and that a proclamation to this effect that a certain pay-token or ticket will be accepted in discharge of taxes must go a long way toward imparting some value to that pay-token or ticket, he would have asserted a truth but a platitudinous one. Had he asserted that such action of the state will determine the value of that pay-token or ticket, he would have asserted an interesting but false proposition.[9]

In other words, Chartalism is either obvious and right; or interesting and wrong.

As we argued in Section 2.1, for Marx, money makes money through the exploitation of labour in the capitalist production process. In the circuit of money under capitalism (M-C-P-C'-M'), M can exchange with C because M represents C and M' represents C'. Money could not make exchange possible if exchangeability were not already inherent in commodity production, if it were not a representation of socially necessary abstract labour and thus of value.

The new value created is embodied in commodities for sale; the value realised is represented by an amount of money. Marx started his theory of money as a commodity like gold or silver, whose value could be exchanged with other commodities. So the price or value of gold anchored the monetary value of all other commodities. If the price of gold changed because of a change in the labour time taken for gold production, and thus a fall in its value, it would lead to a sharp rise in the prices of other commodities (Spain's gold from Latin America in the 16th century) – and vice versa.

The next stage in the development of money was the use of paper or fiat currencies fixed to the price of gold, that is, the gold exchange standard; and then finally to the stage of inconvertible fiat currencies. Contrary to the view of the MMT or of the Chartalists, this does not change the role or nature of money in a capitalist economy. Value is tied to the socially necessary labour time in capitalist production. Metallic money, inasmuch as it represents value, has no value. It costs so much labour to produce it, but this is not its value. It has value only as commodity when it is bought/sold to make ornaments. In this case, its value is given by the quantity of labour socially necessary to produce it. Paper money as money too has no value because it represents value. It acquires value when it becomes a commodity, that is, on the money market. Then its value is given by the labour it represents. Just as gold, the labour it has cost to make is unrelated to the value it represents.

Modern states are clearly crucial to the reproduction of money and the system in which it circulates. But their power over money is quite limited – and as Schumpeter said above (and Marx would have said), the mint can print any numbers on its bills and coins, but it cannot decide what those numbers deliver in purchasing power over commodities. Instead MMT echoes the ideas of French socialist Pierre Proudhon in the 1840s who argued that what was wrong with capitalism was the monetary system itself, not the exploitation of labour and the capitalist mode of production. Here is what Marx had to say about Proudhon's view in his chapter on Money in the *Grundrisse*: 'can the existing relations of production and the relations of distribution which correspond to them be revolutionised by a change in the instrument of circulation?' For Marx, 'the doctrine that proposes tricks of circulation as a way of, on the one hand, avoiding the violent character of these social changes and on the other, of making these changes appear not to be a presupposition but gradual result of these transformations in circulation' would be a fundamental error and misunderstanding of the reality of capitalism.

In other words, separating money from value and indeed making money the primary force for change in capitalism fails to recognise the reality of social relations under capitalism and production for profit. Without a theory of value, MMT enters a fictitious economic world, where the state can issue debt and have it converted into money by a central bank at will and with no limit, and without any connection to the world of capitalist production and accumulation.

MMT starts with the conviction that it is the state (not capitalist commodity relations) that establishes the value of money. Leading MMTer Randall Wray argues the money takes its value not from merchandise 'but rather from the will of the State to accept it for payment'. Chartalist founder Knapp says: 'money is a creature of the law ... The denomination of means of payment according to the new units of value is a free act of the authority of the State'; and 'in modern monetary systems the proclamation [by the State] is always supreme'. Thus, the modern monetary system 'is an administrative phenomenon' and nothing more.[10] Keynes also backed this Chartalist view. In his *Treatise on Money*, Keynes says: 'the Chartalist or state money was reached when the State assumed the right to declare which account money is to be considered money at a given moment'. So 'the money of account, especially that in which debts, prices and general purchasing power are expressed, is the basic concept of the theory of money'.

But deciding the unit of account (e.g. whether dollars or euros) is not the same as deciding its purchasing power in transactions as a measure or store of value. The MMT circuit of money fails to show what happens with the money that capitalists and households have. In MMT, M (in value) can be increased to M' purely by state dictat. For Marx, M can only be increased to M' if capitalist production takes place to increase value in commodities that are sold for more money. This stage is ignored by MMT. The MTT circuit starts from the state to the non-state sectors and back to the state. But this is the wrong way round causally. The capitalist circuit starts with the money capitalist and through accumulation and exploitation of labour back to the money capitalist, who then pays the state in taxes etc.[11] This shows that money is not exogenous to capitalist economic activity. Its value is not controlled by the state. MMT ignores this. In effect, given its confusion between credit and money, MMT argues that money can be created out of thin air.[12] MMT creates the illusion that this whole process starts and ends with the government when it really starts within the capitalist sector including the banking system. Taxes cannot destroy money because taxes logically occur after some level of spending on private output occurs. Taxes are incurred when the private sector spends and governments decide to use those taxes to mobilise some resources for the state. Private incomes and spending on resources precede taxes.

Actually, this is acknowledged by the Chartalist theory. According to it, the main mechanism by which the state provides 'value' to fiat money is by imposing tax liabilities on its citizenry and proclaiming that it will accept only a certain thing (whatever that may be) as money to settle those tax liabilities. But MMT admits that if the tax system breaks down 'the value of money would quickly fall toward zero'.[13] Indeed, when the creditworthiness of the state is seriously questioned, the value of national currencies collapses and demand shifts to real commodities such as gold as a genuine hoard for storing value.

Money only has value because there is value in production to back it. Government spending cannot create that value. Productive value is what gives money credibility. A productive private sector generates the domestic product and income that gives government liabilities credibility in the first place. When that credibility is not there, then trust in the state's currency can disappear fast, as we have seen in Venezuela or Zimbabwe.

Marx's theory of money concurs with the 'endogenous' approach in so far that it is the capitalist sector that creates the demand for money; to act as a means of exchange and a store of value. Banks make loans and create deposits, not vice versa. Indeed, Marx's theory of money is more *consistently* endogenous than MMT because it recognises the primacy of the capitalist accumulation process (with banks and markets) in deciding the purchasing power of money, not any 'exogenous' role of the state.[14] The state cannot establish at will the purchasing power of money that is issued for the very simple reason that in a capitalist economy, it is not dominant and all-powerful. Capitalist companies, banks and institutions rule, and they make decisions on the basis of profit and profitability. As a result, they 'endogenously' drive the value of commodities. Marx's law of value says a commodity's value is anchored around the socially necessary labour time involved in the overall production of commodities (goods and services), that is, by the average productivity of labour, and thus by technologies and intensity of work. The state cannot overcome or ignore this reality.

We can show this flaw in MMT more clearly by considering the macro model of MMT.[15] The MMT model is really a Keynes/Kalecki post-Keynesian macro model of aggregate demand. There are two ways of looking at an economy, by total income or by total spending and they must equal each other. This is simply an identity.

National Income (NI) = National Expenditure (NE)

Following the 'Keynesian Marxist' Michal Kalecki, we can break this down into:

(NI) Profits + Wages = (NE) Investment + Consumption. So now there are two sorts of income and two sorts of spending.

If we assume that all Wages are spent, we can delete Wages and Consumption from the identity. So

Profits = Investment

In the MMT version, the same macro identity is altered so that Investment is on the left side of the equality. Thus

Investment = Profits

Why? Because all post-Keynesian theory argues that it is Investment that leads Profits, not vice versa.

The MMT model then re-expands the parts on the right-hand side to look at flows, so that wages that are saved are added back with profits to get Private Saving (in other words, this assumes some household saving); and Government Saving (taxation less spending) and Foreign Saving (net imports or current account deficit) are also added. Profits as a separate category now *disappears* into Private Savings and we get:

Investment = Private Saving + Government Saving + Foreign Saving

But then MMT also dispenses with the separate category Investment and converts it into Private Saving less Investment or the *net* Private Sector Surplus. So now we have Private Sector Savings (Wages saved plus Profits less Investment). Thus:

Private Sector Surplus = Government Saving/Deficit + Current Account Balance

Or

Private Sector Surplus – Current Account Balance = Government Deficit

This is the key MMT identity. It argues that if the Government Deficit rises, then, assuming the Current Account Balance does not change, the Private Sector Surplus (Wages saved + Profits less Investment) rises. The MMT conclusion (assertion) is that increasing the Government Deficit will increase the Private Sector Surplus. And if we exclude Wages saved (the MMT identity does not) and the Current Account balance, then we have:

Net Profits (ie Profits after Investment) = Government Deficit

And we can conclude that Government Deficits determine Net Profits, that is, Profits less Investment.[16]

But is that how to view the causal direction of these macro identities? The post-Keynesians reckon that the causal connection is that Investment creates Profits or in the MMT version Government Deficits create Net Profits (private saving). But Marxian theory holds that profits determine investments. Which is right? Given a temporal cycle of profits and investment, we can start our observation either at the moment of investment or of the realised profit. This is our subjective decision. However, no matter when and where the analysis starts, in reality *the cycle begins always with profits*. This is evident if we consider investments as a form of expenditure and profits as the outcome of the process of production. Clearly something must first be produced (profits) before it can be spent (invested). Conversely, something cannot be spent (invested) if it hasn't previously produced. Temporally profits lead investments.

Let us go back to the basic Kalecki identity: Profits = Investment, with Investment back on the right-hand side. Investment (which disappeared in the MMT model) can be broken down into Capitalist Investment and Government Investment.

Profits = Capitalist Investment + Government Investment

Under the Kalecki causation, increasing government investment (by deficits, says MMT) will raise Profits (and for that matter, wages too through more employment and wage rates – the post-Keynesian identities just refer to Private Saving and (importantly) do not break that down into Wages saved and Profits). Thus:

Profits + Wages saved = Private Investment + Government Investment

But what if the Kalecki causation is back to front? What if Profits lead Investment, not vice versa? Then the identity is:

Profits (because Wages are spent) = Investment (comprising Capitalist Investment and Government Investment)

We can expand this to cover external flows so that:

Domestic Profits + Foreign Income = Capitalist investment + Government Investment + Foreign Inward Investment

Now assume both Domestic Profits and Foreign Income are *fixed*. What will happen if Government Investment rises? Capitalist Investment will fall unless Foreign Inward Investment rises.

How can Government Investment/spending be increased without Capitalist Investment falling (being 'crowded out')? By running budget deficits, say the post-Keynesians (and MMT). Borrowing could be done by issuing government bonds (orthodox Keynesian) or by 'printing money', that is, increasing cash reserves in banks (MMT). Issuing bonds may reduce Private Investment to boost Government Investment, but the credit created would stimulate overall Investment. Printing Money (MMT) would raise Investment without reducing Private Investment. MMT/Keynesians will say if Government Investment is not funded by taxes on Domestic Profits but by borrowing with bonds or printing money, then it will not affect profits.

But this conclusion is reached because the macro identities do not reveal causation and it is causation that matters.[17] For the Keynesians, it is the right-hand side of the equation (Investment) that causes the left-hand side (Profits); namely, that it is capitalist investment and consumption that creates profit. MMT is a variant of the same, but netted: Net Government Investment/Spending (deficits after taxes) causes Net Private Savings (Profits and Saved wages after Investment).

But *objectively*, profits lead Investment, not vice versa; and Net Private Savings enable Government Deficits, not vice versa. In other words, when capitalists hoard/save and won't invest, and that is particularly the case in recessions, then government deficits rise (through lower tax revenues and higher unemployment benefits). US government deficits reached peaks in all the post-war US recessions and were at their lowest in boom times.

Empirically, the evidence for the post-Keynesian/MMT causal connection is weak. For the US, between the government balance and net private savings, there is a very small inverse relation of 0.07; in other words, a larger government deficit is correlated (very weakly) with a net private savings surplus. But between the government balance and GDP growth, there is a small positive correlation. In other words, more government surplus/less deficit aligns with more

GDP growth, the opposite of the Keynes/Kalecki causation! This suggests that it is growth that leads government balances, not vice versa.[18]

Contrary to the Keynesian/post-Keynesian/MMT view, the Marxist view is that 'effective demand' (including government deficits) cannot precede production. There is always demand in society for human needs. But it can only be satisfied when human beings do work to produce things and services out of nature. In the perception of the capitalists (which is also the perspective of conventional economics), demand (the need for a commodity) precedes production because nothing is produced that is not supposed to be sold and thus to satisfy some need. But the need for a commodity is one thing: the capacity to satisfy that need by purchasing that commodity is another thing. It depends on the money available for that purchase, that is, on effective demand. The money needed to satisfy that demand follows production and thus the value generated by that production. Profits are created by the exploitation of labour and then those profits are either invested or consumed by capitalists. Thus, demand is only 'effective' because of the income that has been created, not vice versa.

Because the Keynesians/post-Keynesians have no theory of value, they don't see this and read their model the wrong way round. From a Marxist view, objectively, profits are the causal variable. If profits fall, then either investment, or capitalist hoarding or the government deficit must fall, or all three.[19] The more important question, however, is what drives a capitalist economy. It is the profitability of capitalist investment that drives growth and employment, not the size of a government deficit. The Keynes/Kalecki/MMT macro models hide behind identities and turn them into causes. But identities 'say nothing about causation' (Tobin, 1997). It's profits, not government spending, that calls the tune.

The most telling critique of MMT is that, because it has no recognition of the capitalist sector in its circuit of money and only the state and 'the non-state', it can tell us nothing about why and how there are regular slumps in production and investment in modern economies. On this issue, MMT has the same position as orthodox Keynesians: that it may be due to a lack of 'effective demand' or 'animal spirits' and it is nothing to do with any contradictions in the capitalist mode of production itself. But for MMT this issue is irrelevant. MMT takes the same view as orthodox Keynesian theory, namely, that it does not really matter what the cause of a depression is; the main thing is to get out of it with government spending – in the case of Keynesians with judicious government spending through bond issuance; in the case of MMT by government spending financed by the issuance of money.

If the Keynes/Kalecki causation direction is right, then all that we need to do to keep a capitalist economy going is to have more government budget deficits. What the orthodox Keynesians and the MMT disagree about is whether these deficits (of government spending over taxes) can and should be financed by issuing government bonds for banks to buy or by the central bank providing credit to commercial banks.

Where MMT also differs from Keynesian-type fiscal deficit spending is that its proponents see government deficits as *permanent*, in order to drive the economy up and achieve full employment of resources. In this way, the state becomes the 'employer of last resort'. Indeed, the MMT exponents claim that unemployment can indeed be solved within capitalism. So there is no need to change the social formations based on private capital. All that is needed is for politicians and economists to recognise that state spending 'financed' by money creation can sustain full employment.

The usual alternative comes from traditional Keynesianism, namely, that more government spending (by running deficits on annual budgets) can boost effective demand in the capitalist economy and create jobs and increase wages. And here is where MMT comes in. As leading MMT author, Randall Wray puts it, what MMT adds to Keynesian fiscal stimulus policy is a theoretical argument that 'a sovereign government cannot run out of its own currency'. Because the state has a monopoly over fixing the unit of account (dollars or euros or pesos), it can create as much money as it needs, distribute that money to 'non-state' entities, and so boost demand and deliver jobs and incomes.

MMT argues that 'money can be created out of nothing'.[20] If a central bank 'prints' money or deposits credits with the state accounts, that gives the state the money it needs to launch programmes for jobs, infrastructure etc. without taxation or issuing bonds. This is the policy conclusion of MMT. It is its 'way out' of the capitalist crisis caused by a slump in private sector production.

Running state budget deficits (and hiking up public sector debt) is not a problem. And because there is nearly always 'slack' in capitalist economies, that is, unemployment and underused resources, there is always room to boost demand, not just temporarily until the capitalist sector takes over again (as in Keynesian policies), but permanently. Here is a theoretical justification for unlimited government spending and budget deficits to achieve full employment without touching the sticky sides of the capitalist sector of the economy. All that is necessary is for politicians and governments to recognise the simple fact that the state cannot run out of money.

The key policy that MMT puts forward from that theoretical premise is a government job guarantee. Everybody will be guaranteed a job if they want or need it; the government will employ them on projects; or pay for them to get a job. Most people work for capitalist companies or the government, but unemployment remains and can engulf a sizeable section of the workforce. So the government should act as an 'employer of last resort'. It won't replace capitalist companies, but instead sweep up those of working age that capital has failed to employ. As Randall Wray puts it: 'I'd just operate a buffer stock program for labor.' You could call it a government backstop for capitalism.[21]

Guaranteeing a job for all sounds great. But apparently, it will not be a job paying a 'living wage' (a wage that people can live on). No, it will only be a 'minimum wage' to make sure that it is not 'in competition with the market-sector wage structure'.[22] In other words, the likes of Amazon or WalMart, or small retail and leisure businesses, will still be able to go paying their workers very low wages (at or near the minimum) without interference by any Job Guarantee, because such jobs will be paying less. So the Job Guarantee acts as a backstop for the private sector; it does not replace it.

Here is Bill Mitchell:

The Government operates a buffer stock of jobs to absorb workers who are unable to find employment in the private sector. The pool expands (declines) when private sector activity declines (expands). The JG [Job Guarantee] fulfils this absorption function to minimise the costs associated with the flux of the economy. The government continuously absorbs into employment workers displaced from the private sector. The 'buffer stock' employees would be paid the minimum wage, which defines a wage floor for the economy.

The Job Guarantee offers a minimum wage if you want to work. But the Job Guarantee does not threaten or replace capitalist sector wage structure or the decisions of capital over who to employ and under what conditions. As Mitchell says: 'To avoid disturbing the private sector wage structure and to ensure the JG is consistent with stable inflation, the JG wage rate is best set at the minimum wage level.'[23]

And what sort of jobs will there be? By definition, they won't be skilled jobs as the government will be 'hiring off the bottom'. But they will be in useful non-profit projects like building roads, bridges etc.: 'many socially useful activities including urban renewal projects and other environmental and construction schemes (reforestation, sand dune stabilisation, river valley erosion control, and the like), personal assistance to pensioners, and other community schemes. For example, creative artists could contribute to public education as peripatetic performers.'[24]

The other issue with MMT-inspired non-stop government spending is inflation. The state may control and issue the currency and governments may never run out of it, but the capitalist sector controls technology, labour conditions and the level of skills and intensity of the workforce. In other words, the productivity of labour (real value) is not in the control of the state with all its dollar printing. So an economy is limited by the productivity and the size of the labour force when fully employed. If the government then goes on pumping money in when output cannot be raised further, inflation of commodity prices will follow and/or inflation in speculative financial assets.

MMTers are aware of this problem. Bill Mitchell says: 'when the level of private sector activity is such that wage-price pressures form as the precursor to an inflationary episode, the government can manipulate fiscal and monetary policy settings (preferably fiscal policy) to reduce the level of private sector demand'. In other words, the government will cut spending or raise taxes and/or interest rates in traditional mainstream style. As Randall Wray puts it: 'The solution is to avoid spending more once full employment is reached; and to carefully target spending even before full employment to avoid bottlenecks.'

This begs the question of whether the private sector in an economy can be subjected to the fine manipulation of central bank and state policy. History has shown that it is not: there is no way governments can direct the capitalist production process and prices of production 'in such a finely managed' way.[25] We are back with traditional Keynesian macro management, something that abysmally failed in the 1970s when capitalist economies experienced stagflation, that is, rising inflation and unemployment at the same time. The reason for that was that inflation and employment are not under the control of the state in a capitalist economy but depend on the profitability of capital and the investment decisions of capitalists. MMT only offers a backstop to capitalist investment and employment, not an alternative.

If there is inflation domestically that curbs exports for a country, the MMTers propose to float the currency. So no capital controls and interference in currency markets? Randall Wray: 'I'd let the dollar float.' That might be ok for the US, where the currency, the dollar, is the international reserve currency and must be held by foreign states and companies to do business. But that is not the situation for smaller capitalist economies, particularly so-called emerging economies. If inflation takes hold because the government is printing pesos, lira or bolivars without stopping to try and maintain full employment while capitalist production is collapsing, the result will be hyper-inflation. And if those currencies are floating without any controls, then the value of the currencies will plummet – as in Turkey, Argentina, Venezuela etc.

Would it work in creating full employment anyway? Government spending in modern economies, particularly the ones that MMT considers, like the US or the UK or the G7, is around 30–50 per cent of GDP. Government investment is only about 3–5 per cent of GDP. This compares with capitalist sector investment of 15–25 per cent, while household spending varies between 55–70 per cent of GDP. According to MMT, you would expect that the higher the ratio of government spending in an economy, the lower the unemployment. The evidence shows the opposite. Government spending in France is over 55 per cent of GDP, while it is 39 per cent in Japan and 38 per cent in the US. But which of these three countries has the higher unemployment rate? France 9 per cent; Japan 2.4 per cent; the US 4 per cent. Most advanced capitalist economies with higher government spending ratios had higher unemployment rates. This shows that there are other reasons than the lack of state spending for the level of unemployment in capitalist economies.

The state may control the issuance of its national currency, but it cannot control its value relative to other currencies or to gold, the world money. If trust in a currency's value is lost by the holders or potential buyers of that currency, then its value will collapse, heightening inflation.

The answer to unemployment or the end of crises does not lie in the simple recourse of issuing money, as MMT claims. MMT relies on what Marx called 'the tricks of circulation' – 'the doctrine that proposes tricks of circulation as a way of, on the one hand, avoiding the violent character of these social changes and on the other, of making these changes appear not to be a presupposition but gradual result of these transformations in circulation'.

Labour leaders oppose austerity – the policy of the mainstream. But they do not want a policy that means the overthrow of capitalist economic relations – that is too frightening, risky and not 'realistic'. So they favour policies that they think can reverse austerity without threatening capitalism – like Keynesian deficit financing. MMT offers a novel theoretical justification for permanent deficit financing – the state controls money as the unit of account and so there is no limit on government spending and rising public debt is nothing to worry about. The only constraint is when resources run out and then inflation may ensue. Then it's time to tax. In this way, MMT acts as a backstop to capitalism – the state is the employer of last resort but not the main employer. It aims to compensate (patch up) the failures of capitalist production, not replace it.

MMT claims that it has an endogenous theory of money, but in reality, it has an exogenous one, based on state issuance of money. It claims that government spending can be expanded to any level necessary to achieve full employment through money issuance, without any reference to the productive activity of the non-state economy, in particular, the profitability of the capitalist sector. Indeed, according to MMT, capitalism can be saved and achieve harmonious growth and full employment by 'tricks of circulation'. MMT ignores or hides the social relations of exploitation of labour for profit. And by selling 'snake oil' (MMT) instead, it misleads the labour movement away from fundamental change.

2.3 CRYPTOCURRENCIES

In a paper published in 2009, Satoshi Nakamoto, whose identity is still unknown, remarked that: 'Commerce on the internet has come to rely almost exclusively on financial institutions [e.g. a bank] serving as trusted third parties to process electronic payments' (Nakamoto, 2009). As put by Nakamoto (2008, p. 1): 'What is needed is an electronic payment system based on cryptographic proof instead of trust, allowing any two willing parties to transact directly with each other without the need for a trusted third party.' The drawback is that 'completely non-reversible transactions are not really possible' (p. 1). The solution is the blockchain technology introduced by bitcoin, which 'simulates coin transfer, but in a different way – without centralized, hierarchical administration. It does this by creating public records of transactions, with copies of the blockchain existing on many computers, thus creating a hard-to-falsify record of who has title to each coin' (Beggs, 2018). With Nakamoto's paper, the bitcoin was born. While this initial motivation, the elimination of financial intermediaries and fees, was fairly modest, soon an additional reason for calling bitcoin into life was added, that it is a means to avoid the debasement of national currencies. Some have gone so far as to claim that bitcoins can threaten the life of banks and even the state or introduce a non-capitalist economy.

At present, bitcoins and other cryptocurrencies have become a global phenomenon known to most people but understood by few. A 2017 study reported that 'There are now more than 2,000 cryptocurrency ATMs across the globe, with the US (1,107), Canada (293), the UK (97) and Austria (91) leading the way' (den Haan et al., 2017). While one year later, 800 of these 2,000 cryptocurrencies had practically disappeared, by 2021 they had jumped to 8,000 (Gorton and Zhang, 2021).

Few people understand the technical intricacies of cryptocurrencies. But for our purposes it is sufficient to illustrate some of its basic technical features. Its simplest definition, which holds also for other cryptocurrencies, is 'a digital currency stored on an open and decentralised electronic payment system' (Huberman et al., 2017). Cryptocurrencies aim to eliminate the need for financial intermediaries by offering direct peer-to-peer (P2P) online payments. The main technological innovation behind cryptocurrencies has been the blockchain, a 'ledger' containing all transactions for every single unit of currency. It differs from existing (physical or digital) ledgers in that it is electronic and decentralised, that is, there is no central authority verifying the validity of transactions. Instead, it employs verification based on cryptographic proof, where various members of the network verify 'blocks' of transactions approximately every ten minutes. The incentive for this is compensation in the form of the newly 'minted' cryptocurrency for the first member to provide the verification.

The bitcoin's main innovation is the blockchain, a public transaction record of integrity without central authority. Blockchain technology offers everyone the opportunity to participate in secure contracts over time, but without being able to avoid a record of what was agreed at that time. So a blockchain is a transaction database based on a mutual distributed cryptographic ledger shared among all in a system. Fraud is supposed to be prevented through block validation, but fraud has been rife (Auer and Claessens, 2004; Foley et al., 2019; Twomey and Mann, 2020), mostly due to the fact that coins are held in the custody of unregulated middlemen (Kharif, 2020). The blockchain does not require a central authority or trusted third party to coordinate interactions or validate transactions. A full copy of the blockchain contains every transaction ever executed, making information on the value belonging to every active address (account) accessible at any point in history.

While Nakamoto's original intention was that of providing a safe system of payment on the internet, bitcoins and other similar cryptocurrencies have quickly become a means of speculation. The root cause is that the supply of bitcoin is limited to 21 million (although there is talk of 'forking' which would increase supply but at the expense of price). So their demand and price are due to rise while the supply is relatively static. This rise, in its turn, is basically determined by the bitcoin being a vehicle for tax evasion and other criminal activities, given that black-market and other illegal transactions are kept off credit-card statements and given the anonymity of the money with which bitcoins have been purchased. This is why they have become functional for speculation. And this is why the long-term price movement tends upwards and the short-term movement is made up of wild price fluctuations and booms and busts.

Bitcoin crises fit in the history of financial markets which are littered with asset price bubbles, from tulips in the early 1600s to more recent examples, such as internet stocks in the late 1990s and US house prices before 2008. The prices of bitcoin and other cryptocurrencies are driven by speculative investment with no immediate cause and effect in the real or financial economy. While economic and financial crises are separated by relatively long periods (several years), the time lag between cryptocurrencies crises is much shorter, sometimes two in a year. For example, the first bubble emerged in 2011 when the price of bitcoins went from $0.50 to $32 in about 60 days and over the course of a few months crashed to $2. Another bubble followed in April 2013 when the price went from $35 to $266 and in a few days crashed back to $50. November 2013 was the next one. The price went from $100 to $1,242, but then crashed to below the $400 level. But in spite of the ups and downs, over the last nine years, prices have showed a clear upward trend, particularly due to the spectacular increase from about $5,000 to almost $20,000 in about one month between 2017 and 2018. Since then, the movement has been again downward. Thus, the crises have been the *crises of individual speculators*, not of the economy, either financial or real. This is the real difference. According to a BIS (Bank for International Settlements) study of investors, 'cryptocurrencies are not sought as an alternative to fiat currencies or regulated finance, but instead are a niche digital speculation object'.[26]

In the subsequent hype, the price of bitcoin continued surging, exceeding $50,000 soon after the trading suspension, and peaking at over $63,000 several weeks later (Figure 2.1). Brought to the attention of many via widely read tweets by Elon Musk, the cryptocurrency Dogecoin saw an almost ten-fold price increase during this episode (Ossinger and Hunter, 2021). However, cryptocurrency prices collapsed during mid-May 2021, after renewed statements by Mr Musk and the announcement of a ban for financial institutions and payment companies from providing cryptocurrency services in China. As the end of the GameStop episode exemplifies, the narrative of cryptocurrencies as a censorship-resistant asset class does not always square with reality. Cryptocurrencies such as bitcoin that are sustained by costly computing ('proof-of-work') tend to be centralised (Huang and Mayer, 2022) and their basic security model might not be sustainable (Auer, 2019). There is ample debate on the censorship resistance, decentralisation and legal nature of other cryptocurrencies, as well (Froewis and Boehme, 2017; Walch, 2019).

Is bitcoin just a new means of speculation or is it a new form of money? In the first section we considered the nature of money in terms of the law of value. Gold as money is a means of exchange *not because it has an intrinsic value as a commodity, but because it represents value*. To this end, gold must have three functions. First, it has to be universally accepted as a medium of exchange. Second, it must be a unit of account with a fair degree of stability so that we can compare the costs of goods and services over time. And third, it must be a store of value that stays reasonably stable over time (but the length of time is variable). Inconvertible paper money, contrary to received wisdom, has a cost of production, but inasmuch as it is a representation of value, does not have value. Just as gold and silver as money, which inasmuch as they represent value do not have value. Besides being a medium of exchange and a store of value, incon-

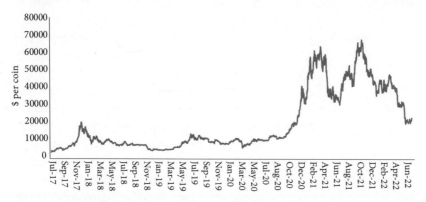

Figure 2.1   Bitcoin price $ (Coinbase)

vertible paper money is also a unit of account. But it is its nature as a store of value that is the most important. If it is not a reliable store of value, it is neither a means of exchange (people revert to barter) nor a unit of account. The currency ceases to be money. There are many examples in history of a national currency being replaced by another or by gold (even by cigarettes) when 'trust' in its stability is lost.

Let us now consider again the assertion above that inconvertible paper money has no intrinsic value. This is universally accepted, yet wrong. The reason is that supposedly it does not have a cost. However, the printing of a $100 bill requires paper with specific characteristics (e.g. it must be a special blend of 75 per cent cotton and 25 per cent linen), special printing machines, a special colour-shifting ink and qualified labour power, for example, the engravers. Each bill, regardless of its denomination, costs the US government about 3.8 cents to produce. Thus, inconvertible paper money does have a cost, even if minimal. If it has a cost, it has a (minimum) value. But the moment it represents value, its labour cost is not its value and thus it can represent any quantity of value. Just as in the case of gold, if gold functions as a commodity, it has value. If it functions as money, it has no value because it represents value.

Consider now the bitcoin. The driver of bitcoin and other rival cryptocurrencies has been the internet and the growth of internet-based trading and transactions. The internet has generated a requirement for low-cost, anonymous and rapidly verifiable transactions to be used for online barter and fast settling means of exchange has emerged as a consequence. This said, do bitcoin and other cryptocurrencies meet the criteria for money? Bitcoin too, like money, represents value, that is, it has purchasing power. But does this mean that it is money? We hold that to represent value is the main function of money, but also that to represent value is necessary but not sufficient for it to be money. Like inconvertible paper money, bitcoin has a cost and a very large cost at that. The energy and other costs are very high and vary from country to country. In Iceland, the mining of bitcoins consumes nearly as much energy as all of Iceland's households combined. A recent study reports that the production of one bitcoin costs $531 in Venezuela, $1,190 in Trinidad and Tobago, and $26,170 in South Korea (Cnbc.com).

But the speculative nature of cryptocurrencies impairs not only their function as stores of value, but also their function as units of account. For contracts to do what they are meant to – lock-in aspects of the future – the parties must have some confidence in the future meaning of the numbers written into them. Imagine what would have happened to anyone contracting for a wage set in terms of bitcoin, fixed for a year in advance. Maybe bitcoin's appreciation would mean the workers would now be rich – but more likely their employer would be out of business. Or imagine an annual wage struck in terms of bitcoin: already, the workers' living standards would have fallen by more than half. Clearly a currency subject to so much volatility cannot be adopted as a unit of account (Beggs, 2018).

However, these fluctuations can be locked in by financial 'instruments' as futures contracts. In 2018, the Chicago Mercantile exchange (CME), the world's largest futures exchange, has launched the bitcoins futures contracts. In the CME's own words: 'Now you can hedge Bitcoin exposure or harness its performance with a futures product developed by the leading and largest derivatives marketplace: CME Group' (advertisement by the CME).

Inasmuch as they function as a means of payment, bitcoin can be compared to money. But as a store of value and as a unit of account, it is a long way from fully having these two characteristic features because of its speculative nature. At present, it functions only in an extremely limited way as money. Bitcoins are not a very good store of value due to the very high fluctuations and because governments do not guarantee their price. For the same reasons, they are not a reliable unit of account. But the adoption of digital currencies by the central banks might change the role and nature of the bitcoin.

An international currency must meet at least four basic conditions: it must have a long-term stable value; there must be sufficient volume to meet the needs of international trade in goods, services and financial assets; transaction costs must be low, with small differences between bid and ask prices, and high liquidity; and there must be a stable issuer who guarantees the currency. Based on this, market participants choose which currency should be the most viable in world trade, and no supranational authority is needed. The conditions apply for both commodity and fiat money. For fiat, there must be an issuer, as the currency implies a commitment to the holder.

Bitcoin, however, meets none of the four conditions. First, it has greater volatility than any other predominant currency in history. Price changes of tens of per cent within days are commonplace. Second, there is a predetermined maximum amount that can be created. If it is to cover the needs of a growing international trade, the relative value of the currency must increase, which makes it even more unstable. Third, transaction costs are high; transactions take time and the system can only handle a limited number per time period. In 2021, El Salvador's president said he would make bitcoin legal tender in the country; but then explained that all bitcoin transactions would be pegged to the US dollar!

It is because of these reasons that at present cryptocurrencies can only be considered to be *an embryonic form of money*. It is still a long way before they will have the same reach as national currencies. In the short term, the obstacles are almost insurmountable. Bitcoin is limited to people with internet connections. That means billions are excluded from the process, even though mobile banking has grown in the villages and towns of 'emerging economies'. So far it is almost impossible to buy anything much with bitcoin. Globally, bitcoin transactions are at about three per second compared to Visa credit at 9,000 a second. And setting up a 'wallet' to conduct transactions in bitcoin on the internet is still a difficult procedure. However, specialised agencies could (and already do) offer their services. In the end, investors might not have to pay bank fees, but may have to pay the intermediaries' fees, thus defeating one of the supposed advantages to investors. Moreover, bitcoin and other crypto transactions can only reach 200 million a year which is only sufficient to let everyone on earth make two transactions in their entire life.

Also, bitcoin mining requires specialised equipment, as well as substantial electricity costs and miners thus have to balance their technology and energy investment. That means increasingly bitcoin could only work as an alternative replacement of global currency if mining became large operations. And that means large companies down the road, ones in the hands of capitalist entities, who may well eventually be able to control the bitcoin market. Also, if bitcoin were to become as viable tender to pay tax to government, it would then require some form of price relationship with the existing fiat money supply. So governments will still be there. Indeed, in 2021, China banned crypto mining outright.

Further, as above, energy consumption is huge. Bitcoin mining is already consuming energy for computer power more than the annual consumption of Ireland. Temperatures near computer miner centres have rocketed. Maybe this heat could be ecologically used but the non-profitability of such energy recycling may well 'block' the bitcoin expansion. Due to this huge waste of resources, the only rational option is to prohibit bitcoins altogether.

Cryptocurrency prices, aside from wild short-term fluctuations, have rocketed. On the one hand, this is due to their limited supply, and on the other, it is due to the rising demand as a speculative financial asset. But as investors tend to hold them rather than to spend them, this limits greatly their function as a means of exchange.

The cryptocurrency expansion has been remarkable. Capitalism is not ignoring blockchain technology. Indeed, like every other innovation, it seeks to bring it under its control. In spite of the above-mentioned disadvantages, mutual distributed ledgers (MDLs) in blockchain technology provide an electronic public transaction record of integrity without central ownership. The ability to have a globally available, verifiable and untamperable source of data provides anyone wishing to provide trusted third-party services, that is, most financial services firms, the ability to do so cheaply and robustly. Indeed, that is the road that large banks and other financial institutions are going for. They are much more interested in developing blockchain technology to save costs and control internet transactions.

Speculation is inherent in capitalism, but it increases, as other financial activities, in times of economic malaise and crises, that is, when profitability falls in the productive sectors and capital migrates to unproductive and financial sectors where the rate of profit is higher. We submit that this is the reason for bitcoin's tendential price and quantity increase since its birth in 2009. Nakamoto's *personal* intentions might explain why bitcoin was devised, but these intentions have been *socially determined*, that is, they are the personal perceptions of capital's need to find one more financial escape valve for falling profitability. It is this that explains its success and expansion.

In sum, there would be major disadvantages if the economy were to be based on cryptocurrencies instead of (or together with) inconvertible paper money. The state would lose one of its basic anti-crisis instruments, monetary policy, and the growth of the instability inherent in cryptocurrencies would spill over into the real and financial sectors proportionally to their increase. Given that they are not backed by anything and given the reasons mentioned above, bitcoins are not suitable to be (substitutes of) money. But it could be argued that 'stablecoins', which are backed with government currencies, could be made to morph into money.

The most popular one, Tether, launched in 2014, is pegged to the dollar with a market capitalisation of more than $60 billion. These Tether tokens are involved in half of worldwide bitcoin trades. But the stability of these stablecoins is seriously in doubt. Tether's accounts show that their reserves to back the dollar peg are only 4 per cent, with most of the rest in risky commercial paper. JP Morgan reported that the Tether stablecoin has not regulatory supervision or deposit insurance. So if people were unwilling or unable to use Tether tokens, 'the most likely result would be a severe liquidity shock to the broader cryptocurrency market', which could lead to everyone trying to sell at once. A fundamental issue for all stablecoins is their resilience to conventional speculative attacks, analogous to attacks on fixed exchange rates. Even if the stablecoins are much closer to 'narrow banks' than conventional bank accounts, they can still be vulnerable in the same way as money market funds.[27]

One way to make Tether unnecessary is to create a digital dollar, and some US lawmakers seem to be warming to the idea, including Senator Elizabeth Warren (DMA). (China's doing something like this already.) A digital dollar would drive out all the dollar-pegged stablecoins, because that would mean zero counterparty risk, Mizrach says. 'That's the biggest risk to Tether', he says. The conditions necessary for this to happen, as well the many economic and juridical aspects involved, are discussed in Gorton and Zhang (2021). The point of interest is why would central banks recur to stablecoins, either side by side with national currencies, or in their place. Which are the advantages of stablecoins vis-à-vis national currencies? Gorton and Zhang mention the following: 'The benefits of implementing a central bank digital currency are to increase the convenience yield, reduce the costs of payment systems, and maintain monetary sovereignty' (p. 36). In short, 'a central bank digital currency ... would be more efficient than paper currency and coins' (p. 36). This argument is rather thin.

Central banks have maintained monetary sovereignty even before their own stablecoins. As for the reduction of the costs of payment systems, this is not a negligible factor, but it is certainly not a decisive one. The reasons should be sought elsewhere. Very likely, we are witnessing a new phase of imperialist struggle in the monetary arena. As Section 2.5 below argues, one of the ways US imperialisms is strangling Venezuela and other dominated countries is through the monopoly of the international currency, the US dollar. The US induced shortage of dollars in Venezuela impedes the import of many essential goods (from medicines to machinery). To obviate this, Venezuela has launched the Petro (see below), its version of a stablecoin as a way to evade the monetary blockade.

Also, some small countries, seeking to overcome the dollarisation of their economies and to find a hedge against devaluation of their national currencies, have made attempts to make bitcoin legal tender. In September 2021, El Salvador became the first country to do this – with mixed success. And Nigeria has also done the same, having failed to stop the spread of cryptocurrencies as citizens flee from the national currency.

2.4 DIGITAL CURRENCIES

One way to undermine this strategy is for the US to introduce its own digital currency as a competitor of the Petro and of all other central banks' stablecoins. They would then become less attractive than the US competitor, thus limiting their anti-imperialist usefulness. Related to this is that a US cryptocurrency would mop up huge quantities of international currencies, which could then be profitably invested. The other countries, if sufficiently strong, would introduce their own cryptocurrencies as a way both to rake in international currencies (especially strong ones) and of limiting the US financial supremacy.

This seems to be behind the move of the Chinese government to introduce a Digital Currency Electronic Payment (DC/EP), a payment arrangement for digital renminbi (RMB), also called e-CNY (or e-yuan). The e-CNY is issued by the People's Bank of China (PBC), operated and exchanged by authorised operators including commercial banks, payment service providers and other private sector institutions.

For some, cryptocurrencies might be the embryo of a post-capitalist world without states and even the first step towards socialism. But can technology in and of itself, even a technology that apparently is outside the control of any company or government, really break people free from the law of value? Certainly not. In a capitalist economy, money is the representation, a symbol of value. Thus, it is a socially determined representation of the social relations of production, of the private ownership of the means of production (and thus it is a representation of exploitation). As such, money cannot represent socialist production relations. Even if exchange on the basis of bitcoins were to become universal, bitcoins would be used only to purchase capitalistically produced commodities and by capital to purchase labour power. They would become a new representation of exploitation.

In principle, any digital currency ought to make payments for goods and services simpler and cheaper so that people do not need to carry wads of cash about (e.g. flying to a country with a suitcase). But a digital currency poses issues. Who controls this currency and what about people who want to hold cash and do not want to be forced to have a bank account or a digital 'wallet' to buy things? Take Libra. Libra is the name that Facebook, the global social network company, called its planned international digital currency. What is Facebook's purpose with this planned new currency?

Its professed aim is to provide a currency for everybody using the internet to buy and sell goods and services to each other across the world, seamlessly and with near-zero transaction costs. International banks and national currencies would be bypassed and all their costs and fees would be avoided. Moreover, all transactions would be private and not viewable by the authorities or banks. And supposedly over one and half billion people without bank accounts would be able to carry out transactions globally on their phones and laptops, not using cash.

Libra is the Latin word for pound in weight of silver or gold. It was a universal measure of value in Roman times. But Facebook's Libra will be no such thing. It is not the future people's currency controlled by the people. It is a privatised currency for commercial gain for Facebook and its investment backers. It will be owned and controlled by a board of multinational corporate investors who will pledge capital to get it going. The US dollar currency is owned by the US government. This is the same for other national currencies. As such, there are regulations and laws on how national currencies are issued. None of that will apply to Libra. Holders of Libra will have to trust Facebook and the investing board, not any government, that nothing will go wrong with their money.

Facebook is not a pioneer here – already a digital payments service operates in China with WeChat and Alipay. The issue here is the sheer size of Libra's global grasp, with the billions of Facebook users and the number of large multinationals that have pledged to back and take the new currency. But Libra does not even have the ambition of bitcoin to be a universal decentralised digital currency for people. It will be a private currency designed to extend Facebook's control over the purchasing power of its four billion users and make money.

Indeed, Libra's setup may make international transactions a little faster, but actually not nearly as fast as traditional payments processors. It looks like Libra can do about 1,000 transactions per second. A traditional payments processor like Visa can do about 3,000 transactions per second.

Libra is really, in financial jargon, an exchange traded fund (ETF), where the value of Libra is based on a 'basket' of five national currencies (dollars, euros, yen, sterling and Swiss franc) according to a weighted ratio. Libra is not a true international digital currency in its own right but dependent on the value of these major national currencies. It's a private currency for Facebook users. It will be similar to the Special Drawing Rights (SDR) used by the IMF for the settlement of contributions and payments by national governments to the IMF. SDRs are also tied to the value of national currencies like the dollar.

If you buy some Libra and hold it in your Facebook Libra 'wallet' for future purchases, you won't get any interest as you would if you held dollar deposits in a bank. But this Libra sitting in wallets around the world will be invested by the multinational board in financial assets to make money for them. The board can convert Libra into financial assets that yield interest, but none of this is passed on to Facebook Libra holders. In effect, all interest goes to the owners of this private currency – it's a form of seignorage, previously only available to national governments and central banks for the use of their currencies. As Facebook's white paper puts it: 'Interest on the reserve assets will be used to cover the costs of the system, ensure low transaction fees, pay dividends to investors who provided capital to jump-start the ecosystem, and support further growth and adoption ... Users of Libra do not receive a return from the reserve.'

Indeed, the huge amounts of Libra that build up in Facebook users 'wallets' would become available for the board to speculate in financial assets globally, thus adding a new dimension to the possibility of credit bubbles and financial crashes that could come back to hit billions of Libra users. The regulation of the banks and other financial institutions has not worked, as the global financial crash proved. And the huge rise of private sector debt continues alongside the rise in public sector debt that mushroomed to bail out the global banking system. With a successful Libra, there would be another new layer of credit-fuelled debt created, with repercussions for billions of people and this time without any deposit insurance from governments!

What is worrying from global capital's view is that if a large section of a country's population were to use Libra instead of the sovereign currency, central banks could be left powerless or unable to stop the rapid conversion of currency into Libra during periods of financial distress. Now you might say that's good news for people, if not for capital. People need to break away from the control of central banks, commercial banks and governments and 'free up' the currency and reduce the cost of our transactions. But Libra will not deliver on this aim.

Libra's claim that the currency will be designed and operated 'as a public good' with 'decentralised governance' is hard to tally with an operating structure comprised of unaccountable and highly centralised global corporations such as Facebook, Uber and Paypal. With cash use increasingly restricted, we're already reliant on a handful of big banks to manage our money and make payments, while Visa and Mastercard have achieved almost total dominance of the card market. Visa now accounts for 98 per cent of debit cards issued in the UK. Libra is really a corporate attempt to assert even greater control over money supply (Figure 2.2).

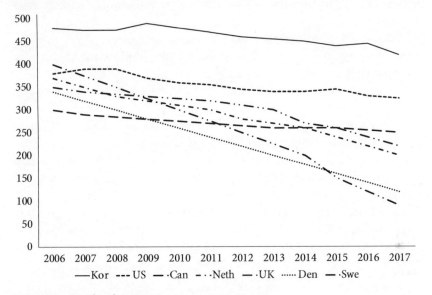

Figure 2.2   Retail cash transactions per person per year

A digital currency should be transparent in its operations and preserve privacy with your data – Facebook's Libra is the mirror opposite of that. What we really need is democratic control of financial institutions and the takeover of mega-tech companies like Facebook, Google and Amazon. Governments should then use technological innovation to develop an international digital currency controlled and run in the public interest. But such a public digital currency would require common ownership and control of financial institutions and digital monopolies In the meantime, it will be the US dollar. For the time being Libra has not got off the ground.

2.5 INFLATION

Inflation is paramount in any discussion of money. In our opinion neither conventional mainstream nor previous Marxist theories of inflation have adequately explained changes in price inflation in modern fiat currency economies. In particular, there is no satisfactory explanation for the overall secular decline in the US inflation rate in the post-war period, or for the period of disinflation after 1980 in spite of a first inflationary period before 1980.

In contrast, we argue that changes in inflation rates depend on *primarily*, a tendentially decreasing fall in the relative combined purchasing power of labour and capital, that is, wages and profits, as a percentage of total value; and *secondly*, on the injection of money by the monetary authorities. By combining the purchasing power in value terms and money quantities, we can obtain a value rate of inflation, which can explain inflation of prices over the medium to long term. Let us explain.

A theory of inflation should address the following question: why do prices of goods and services rise or fall; or more specifically in the modern context, why does price inflation accelerate or decelerate?[28]

There has been a long-term secular decline in the US consumer price index (CPI) inflation from 1960 to 2019 (Figure 2.3). But that period of 60 years can be divided into two sub-periods: a 20-year period from 1960 to 1979 when price inflation accelerated; and a 40-year period from 1980 to 2019 when price inflation decelerated (disinflation). What determines the long-term secular decline in post-war US consumer inflation and, in particular, the change from the first sub-period of acceleration to the second sub-period of deceleration? Mainstream economic theory is unable to answer these questions.

In conventional economics, there are two major theories of inflation: the cost-push approach and the demand-pull approach.[29] Both look at supply and

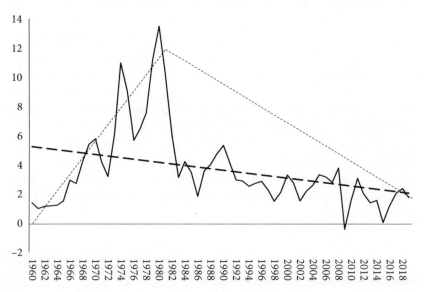

Figure 2.3 US CPI (% yoy)

demand but from different ends. The cost-push theory focuses on the increase in the input costs for companies, that is, means of production and labour power. The argument is that higher input prices are passed onto other producers and eventually to consumers in higher prices for finished goods. This leads to the idea that higher wages can lead to higher inflation and that therefore wages should be restrained in order to contain inflation. This is an attractive argument for the interests of capital over labour.

In the demand-pull theory, prices rise/fall if there is increased/decreased demand for goods across the economy. If demand rises, prices increase and vice versa. What is lacking here is the objective cause for changes in demand. Moreover, this theory leaves out the impact of changes in money supply.

The basic proposition of the demand-pull theory of inflation is that if wages grow less than the output of wage goods, this will lead to 'insufficient demand' and thus disinflation. Conversely, if wages grow faster, 'excess demand' for goods will rise and there will be accelerating inflation. This theory disregards a fundamental point, that not only wages but also profits exert pressure on prices. And the data do not support it. From 1960 to 2019, average wage growth in the non-financial sector was 6.1 per cent annually, while output growth averaged 6.3 per cent.[30] And in the two (dis)inflation sub-periods, wage and output growth rates are also similar. So CPI inflation should have been virtually stable over the 60-year period, but instead the CPI data show a long-run disinflationary trend, first an inflationary sub-period and then a second disinflationary one.

In the post-World War II period, US wage growth accelerated in the first sub-period up to 1979 and decelerated afterwards (Figure 2.4), just as CPI inflation did. This would seem to support the wage-push inflation view. Once the inflationary process has been set in motion, it can be argued that wage growth determines inflation and/or disinflation through its effect on consumer prices.

But this cannot be taken as evidence that rising wages are the cause of inflation. The line of causation could be reversed, namely, that it is accelerating inflation that provokes labour's higher demands (in wages) as its line of defence against capital. Capital triggers an upward movement of prices in its unrelenting search for higher profits as a way to depress real wages. Labour reacts to this by claiming higher wages. As Marx put it in *Value, Price and Profit*, when debating with the trade unionist Weston who argued that wage rises would cause inflation, rising wages are 'reaction of labour against the previous action of capital'. In Marx's view, wages rise/fall and profits fall/rise, while prices can remain unchanged. So the focus should be not only on wages but also on profits, that is, on the combined effect of wages and profits on prices. Changes in the distribution of new value cannot affect inflation. As Marx remarked: 'A general rise in the rate of wages would result in a fall in the general rate of profit, but broadly speaking not affect the prices of commodities.' If there is no change in

77

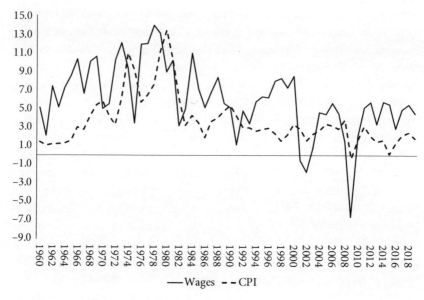

Figure 2.4 US wage and CPI annual growth (% yoy)

new value, higher wages mean lower profits, not higher prices. The distribution of new value will not affect price inflation. If new value grows, both wages and profits can grow. Wages can grow more than profits or vice versa.

It is not just wages that can exert pressure on prices: it is wages plus profits that represent society's total purchasing power. And total purchasing power is what exerts pressure on prices. Given that the capitalists purchase not only means of production, but also (luxury) means of consumption, any pressure on prices is due to the *combined* pressure of wages and profits, not on wages only. The ideological roots of 'forgetting' the role of profits in examining the cause of inflation are clear: labour is condemned and capital is acquitted. The wage-push theory is not only analytically wrong, it is also ideologically biased.

The Keynesian inflation theory is fundamentally a 'cost-push' theory, namely, that companies push up their prices when their costs of production rise, particularly wages, the largest part of costs of production. In effect, Keynesian theory is a wage-push theory. Inflation depends on the relative demand for and supply of labour forcing up wages. So the argument goes: the lower the unemployment rate and the higher the demand for labour relative to the available supply, the more wages and then prices will be forced up. Keynesian theory sees inflation as being caused by workers getting too high wage increases (and eventually losing out in real terms as price rises eat into wage increases).

The usual Keynesian way to estimate likely changes in inflation is to use the so-called Phillips curve: the curve of the statistical relation between unemployment rate and the price inflation rate. Again, however, this theory has proven to be false. The 'curve' does not hold or is so 'flat' as to provide no guide to inflation. Indeed, since the Great Recession of 2008–09, unemployment rates in the major economies have dropped to near all-time lows and yet wage rises have been relatively moderate and inflation rates have slowed. This is the mirror image of the 1970s when unemployment rates rose to highs, but so did inflation and we had what was called 'stagflation'. Both examples show that the Keynesian cost-push theory is wrong. In Figure 2.5, based on monthly data, the solid line shows where the Keynesian Phillips curve *should be* if it works; and the dashed line shows where it *actually is*. Indeed, the dashed line shows that falling unemployment leads to slowing inflation, at least since 2010!

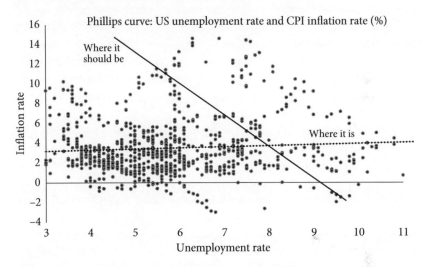

Figure 2.5   US unemployment rate and CPI rate since 2010 (%)

As mentioned above, in his speech to trade unionists in 1865, Marx argued against the view that wage rises cause inflation. In his view, a rise in wages will generally lead to a fall in profits, not a price rise. That is why capitalists oppose wage rises vehemently. And there is no wage push inflation. Indeed, over the last 20 years until the year of the COVID, real weekly wages rose just 0.4 per cent a year on average, less even that the average annual real GDP growth of around 2 per cent. It's the share of GDP growth going to profits that rose (as Marx argued in 1865).

In addition to the cost-push and demand-pull theories, there is the monetary theory of inflation. This holds that inflation and disinflation are purely monetary phenomena, that is, that inflation is determined by changing money quantities.[31] Leading monetarist Milton Friedman argued that 'Inflation is always and everywhere a monetary phenomenon in the sense that it is and can be produced only by a more rapid increase in the quantity of money than in output' (Friedman, 1970, p. 6). The Friedman thesis has been challenged by many.

Indeed, the order of causation could be reversed: namely, that it was an economic downturn and falling prices or slowing inflation that then causes a reduced money supply. Moreover, the empirical evidence for the monetarist view is weak. For the US, the correlation between the M2 money supply growth rate and CPI inflation in our 60-year period is only 0.18. The monetarist theory has been proven wrong, particularly during the COVID slump. During 2020, money supply entering the banking system rose over 25 per cent and yet consumer price inflation hardly budged and even slowed.

Monetarist theory has been proven wrong because it starts from the wrong hypothesis: that money supply drives prices of goods and services. But the opposite is the case: it is changes in prices and output that drive money supply. Take the monetarist formula: $MV = PT$, where M is the money supply; V is the velocity of money (the rate of turnover of money exchanges); P = prices of goods and services and T = transactions or actual real production activity. Monetarist theory also assumes that the velocity of money (V) is constant, but this is just not true, especially during slumps and the COVID slump, in particular (Figure 2.6).

In the COVID slump, the huge rise in money supply (M) was dissipated by an unprecedented fall in the velocity of money (V). So MV, the left-hand side of the monetarist equation, did not move up much at all. Contrary to monetarist theory, prices of goods and services have not been driven by the money credit injections. But has this money disappeared then? No, it's still there, but the money injections by the Federal Reserve and other central banks, mainly achieved by 'printing money' and purchasing huge quantities of government and corporate bonds, as well as making loans and grants, have ended up, on

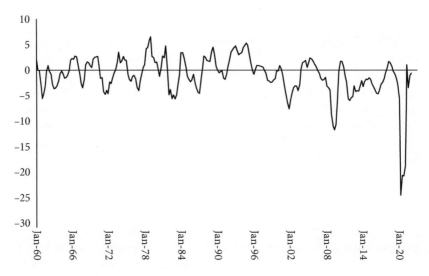

Figure 2.6   Velocity of M2 money stock

the whole, not in the hands of businesses and households to spend, but in the deposits of banks and other financial institutions. This money has been hoarded or used to fund speculation in financial assets (a booming stock market and investment in hedge funds etc.). So the velocity of money (V) in goods and services transactions has plummeted.

In another variant of the cost-push theory, it is argued that inflation is caused by monopolies and by their power to impose market prices above (mythical) free competition prices.[32] There are Marxist versions of this view. For example, Kotz (1982) argues that monopolies can set market prices that exceed prices of production. This holds also even if the monopolised commodity is a wage good.

Paul Sweezy argued similarly that 'Keynesian theory assumed free competition; under oligopoly, increased demand leads to rises in prices ... and ultimately (as a result of the rising cost of living) to higher wages rather than an expansion of output. The result is general inflation.' However, in Marxist theory, market prices can be above or below their tendential level, that is, the production prices. At any given level of output (value) if the market price of a commodity rises, the market price of other commodities must fall. Rising prices in the monopolised sectors simply imply lower prices in the non-monopolised sectors. So monopolies cannot account for a *general* level of inflation. Moreover, monopolies have existed both during the rising inflation period (1960–79) and the disinflation period (1980–2019). And concentration and centralisation of US industry increased in the second period. So inflation must be explained aside from monopolies.

Mainstream economics has turned to theories emphasising inflation expectations as a major determinant of (dis)inflation. This is a variant of the demand-pull theory. Inflation expectations supposedly reflect the psychology of the economic agents. If an economy goes well, inflation expectations rise; and expectations fall if the economy slackens.

Here is how one mainstream economic paper argued for the inflation expectations theory:

> Over the longer-term, a key determinant of lasting price pressures is inflation expectations. When businesses, for example, expect long-run prices to stay around the Federal Reserve's 2 percent inflation target, they may be less likely to adjust prices and wages due to the types of temporary factors discussed earlier. If, however, inflationary expectations become untethered from that target, prices may rise in a more lasting manner.[33]

The IMF also presents this view:

> It is possible that changes in current and expected inflation are both driven by changes in expectations about the future state of the economy. For example,

if firms and households expect that the economy will be in a recession in the near future and inflation will be lower than today, they will start cutting their consumption and investment expenditures now, putting downward pressure on inflation today. In that case, both inflation expectations and inflation would decline, but this would be driven by a third factor (expectations of future slack), rather than a causal link from inflation shocks to inflation expectations – especially on short-term horizons.[34]

But expectations must be based on something. People are not stupid; businesses and households' expectations of whether prices are going to rise (faster) depend on some guesses or estimates of how prices are moving and why. Moreover, expectations of price rises do not explain the price rises themselves. What comes first, the chicken or the egg? Do expectations trigger inflation or is it the other way around? In and of itself, this mutual interaction says nothing about causation.[35]

Expectations theory has been dubbed by Goodhart as a 'bootstrap theory of inflation': that, as long as inflation expectations remain anchored, inflation itself will remain anchored. Goodhart calls this 'a very weak reed' because in reality inflation expectations are backward looking as people tend to extrapolate their recent experience into the future. A review of the relevant theoretical and empirical literature suggests that this belief rests on extremely shaky foundations.[36] Rudd finds that the theoretical case for expectations determining actual inflation was always weak ('surely for example firms and workers care more about short term inflation when setting prices and bargaining for wages and yet the theoretical case, in policy circles, has usually rested on long term expectations') and he goes on to demonstrate that the empirical case has also always been weak.[37] Goodhart concludes: 'the world at the moment is in a really rather extraordinary state because we have no general theory of inflation'.[38]

Unfortunately, in our view, Marxism has also not offered a satisfactory theory of inflation. Paul Mattick Snr argues that: 'Inflation is an expression of inadequate profits that must be offset by price and money policies ... If prices rise faster than wages, then what could not be extracted from the workers in production is taken from them in the circulation process' (1977, chapter 3). But this does not *explain* inflation. If prices rise faster than wages, there is a pro-capital redistribution at the cost of wages. And if prices grow less than wages, there is a pro-labour redistribution at the cost of profits. But neither case affects the *general* price level. Inter-class redistribution might change relative prices, but not the general price level.

Jim Devine (2000) finds a 'rough correlation between the fall of the rate of profit ... and a rise in the SPF, where the SPF is 'the sum of the official inflation and unemployment rates' (p. 400). Devine's profit rate is the 'rate of return of domestic non-financial corporations divided by the manufacturing rate of capacity utilization' (p. 404). This is not Marx's frame of reference for the rate of profit. If the rate of profit is properly defined and computed, the inverse relation between profitability and inflation fails. The rate of profit falls tendentially throughout the whole post-World War II period (Carchedi and Roberts, 2018). On Devine's hypothesis, this should mean a secular *rise* in inflation, but the opposite is true.

Chris Harman (1979) correctly rejects the wage-push inflation approach. Like Devine, Harman stresses profitability as the cause of inflation. However, for Harman the rate of profit falls because of the rise in the capital/output ratio and not, as in Marx, because the ratio of constant capital to variable capital (the organic composition of capital) rises. But changes in profitability cannot be *explained* in terms of changes in the capital/output ratio even if a correlation between this ratio and profitability can be found.

This ratio disregards value because its denominator is output and not variable capital, and thus labour, which is the only source of value. It follows that Harman's account of the link between profitability and inflation, lacking the anchor to the fundamental and objective role of labour and thus value, rests on the subjectivity of capitalists' behaviour. Harman (1979, p. 39) submits that 'in a boom, capitalists feel confident that their goods would sell, even if they increased their prices. ... Once the recession sets in, capitalists have to respond ... [by] contracting markets [and] have to slash prices.' So (dis)inflation is explained more in terms of the capitalists' perceptions and behaviour, like the expectations theory above, than in terms of capitalism's objective laws of motion.

Ernest Mandel (1990) correctly states that for Marx: 'A strong decrease in the average productivity of labour in gold mining (as a result for example of a depletion of the richer gold veins) will lead to a general depression of the average price level, all other things remaining equal.' Thus, Mandel argues that the value of gold (money) determines the level of prices. But in a modern system of inconvertible paper money, Mandel argues that if 'paper money circulation has doubled without a significant increase in the total labour time spent in the economy, then the price level will tend to double too'. So it is the quantity of fiat money in circulation relative to the value produced and not the value of gold that determines prices.

However, Mandel makes clear that 'this does not mean that in the case of paper money, Marx himself has become an advocate of a quantity theory of money'. The reason is that Marx rejects '*any mechanical automatism* between the quantity of paper money emitted on the one hand, and the general dynamic of the economy (including on the price level) on the other'. For Mandel, there is no automatism because the quantity of money is 'always combined with given ups and downs of the rate of profit, of the productivity of labour, of output, of market conditions (overproduction or insufficient production)'. This might be true, but this is no theory of inflation because it leaves us with an indefinite approach. Which are the key variables, how do they relate to each other and how does this interaction affect or cause inflation?

Differently from other Marxist authors, Anwar Shaikh (2016) makes no attempt to connect inflation to value theory. Here the key variable is not value, but output as use values. As Shaikh (2016, p. 90) puts it, 'if for any reason the gap between the actual growth rate and the "throughput limit" narrows, there will be less and less room for output growth and consequently more and more pressure on prices'. This is no theory of inflation. The gap between the actual growth rate and the 'throughput limit' is not the cause of inflation, but the consequence of 'any reason' that narrows this gap. The reason for inflation can be 'any reason'. What is needed here is a necessary cause, not any undetermined cause. And even if we were to accept that this gap is the cause of inflation, this would be a new version of the old-fashioned scheme of price determination based on the interplay of demand and supply of use values, with the added feature of the technical specification of the cause of the restriction of supply. Labour is missing and with it any connection to Marx's value theory.

In spite of their useful insights, these theories fail to answer adequately the fundamental question: how value determines prices and thus inflation under a regime of non-convertible paper money. In other words, the theories above fail to develop a value theory of modern inflation. A Marxist theory of inflation must connect inflation to the production of value. Marx states clearly the relation between prices and money: 'If the velocity of circulation is given, then the quantity of the means of circulation is simply determined by the prices of commodities. Prices are thus high or low, not because more or less money is in circulation, but there is more or less money in circulation because prices are high or low'.[39] This is Marx's critique of the monetarist theory: namely, that the prices of commodities, that is, their value, determines the quantity of money in circulation and not vice versa.

To be properly understood, this critique should be placed within its historical context. If the value of gold is kept constant, the price of commodities can increase only because their value has increased. Then more gold is needed to circulate that greater quantity of value, that is, for its realisation. Conversely, if value and thus prices decrease, less gold is needed and the difference is hoarded.[40]

But what if the value of gold falls? Marx answers:

the fall first shows itself in a change in the prices of the commodities which are directly exchanged with the precious metals at their source. The greater part of all other commodities, especially at the less developed stages of bourgeois society, will continue for a long time to be estimated in terms of the former value of the measure of value, which has now become antiquated and illusory. Nevertheless, one commodity infects another through their common value-relation so that their prices, expressed in gold or silver, gradually settle down into the proportions determined by their comparative values, until finally the values of all commodities are estimated in terms of the new value of the monetary metal. (Marx, *Capital*, Vol. I, Section 2)

This is how changes in the value of gold cause ripples in the structure of prices until the value/price of all commodities adjusts to the new value of gold. But nowadays the origin of the ripple effect cannot be due to changes in the value of gold because of gold's negligible incidence as the circulating medium. In the modern system of non-convertible paper money, the *basic factor* affecting prices and thus inflation is the new *value created* by labour power in the form of wages and profits or what is the combined purchasing power of capital and labour (CPP).[41] Since money is the manifestation of value, a certain quantity of new value, to realise itself, needs and determines a certain quantity of money, in the spirit of Marx's analysis.[42]

Total value in an economy is constant capital plus new value created by labour (subdivided between wages and profits). Under Marxist theory, due to the labour-shedding nature of technological innovations, the share of constant capital in total value (C/TV) tends to grow. So, the share of the combined purchasing power (CPP) in total value (CPP/TV) tends to fall, as in Figure 2.7, where gross value added is taken as a measure of total value (TV).[43] The assumption is that the decrease in wages is not more than compensated by the increase in profits. This is indeed the case, given that the increase in constant capital and thus the decrease in wages, that is, the increase in the OCC, is the tendency and the increase in the rate of surplus value is the counter-tendency. This, in its turn, is confirmed by the tendential fall in the average rate of profit: if the rate of profit falls, both profits and wages fall (labour power is shed). The theory of inflation is thus tied to the theory of the tendential fall in the profit rate.

The falling share of the CPP in total value is *objectively determined* by the increase of constant capital in total value, itself due to the basic law of movement of capitalism, that is, technological competition and the concomitant replacement of labour by means of production. So, technological competition determines the percentage decrease of the CPP in total value and this determines the falling rate of growth of the CPP and thus of the rate of inflation for the whole post-World War II period. But within this period, there are two sub-periods: a first inflationary one where the rate of inflation rises, and a second disinflationary one in which the rate of inflation decelerates.

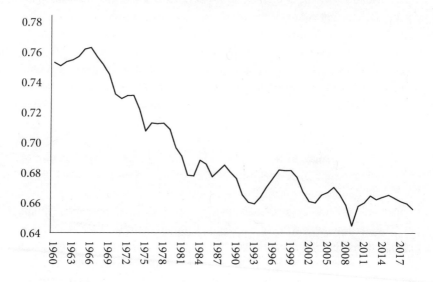

Figure 2.7 CPP-GVA ratio
Source: Appendix 2.

In the first sub-period total value rises at 8.7 per cent, constant capital grows by 19.2 per cent and the CPP by 8.5 per cent (Table 2.1). Thus, the CPP falls as a percentage of total value, but given that total value grows strongly, the CPP rises percentage-wise. This explains inflation. In the second sub-period, total value slows to 5.1 per cent. Constant capital growth accelerates to 22.3 per cent (from 19.2 per cent), so there is less space for the CPP to grow and the CPP growth decelerates from 8.5 per cent to 4.7 per cent. This explains disinflation. For the whole period, total value falls percentage-wise, constant capital rises also per-centage-wise and consequently the CPP falls relative to total value. The CPP grows, but at a decreasing rate. The fall of the CPP relative to total value is a constant tendency in the whole 1960–2019 period. This explains the long-run falling rate of inflation.

Table 2.1 Total value, constant capital and CPP percentage changes

	First sub-period (%)	*Second sub-period (%)*
Total value	8.7	5.1
Constant capital	19.2	22.3
CPP % growth	8.5	4.7
CPP as % of total value	75.4 to 70.9	69.7 to 65.6

However, in the world of non-convertible money, besides the CPP, there is a *second* factor affecting inflation: the money quantity in circulation. *Inflation is the result of the interplay between these two factors.* But they do not have an equal weight in determining inflation. The quantity of new value is the principal, objectively determined factor and the quantity of money is the secondary, subjectively determined factor. Together they compose the *value theory of inflation* (VTI). We define the *value rate of inflation* (VRI) as the percentage change in the CPP (the value factor) *plus* the percentage change in M2 (the money factor).

VRI = CPP % change plus M2 % change

This is the general formula for the VRI. The calculation of the VRI requires some adjustments. First, we compute the VRI for the productive sector of the economy only, defined as non-financial corporate sector (NFC). For this we only need the quantity of money used for the realisation for the combined purchasing power in the NFC, thus leaving aside that used for finance and speculation. So we adjust M2 by the ratio of financial assets to total assets in the non-financial business sector.[44] Then we adjust the M2 stock by the share of constant capital in total NFC value to find the M2 required for realising the CPP in the NFC. The VRI can now be calculated. Over the whole 1960–2019 period, both M2 growth and CPP growth fall tendentially. So the VRI falls tendentially. In the two sub-periods, the VRI exhibits rising inflation (up to 1979) and then disinflation (1980–2019) (Figure 2.8).

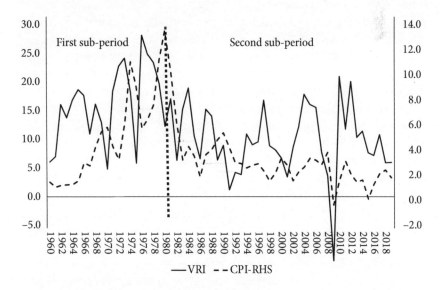

Figure 2.8   NFC VRI-CPI annual percentage change

Table 2.2   Correlations between CPP, M2 and CPI

	CPI% correlation with VRI%	CPI% correlation with CPP%	CPI% correlation with M2%
1960–2019	0.31	0.34	0.18
1960–1979	0.23	0.33	0.05
1980–2019	0.23	0.22	0.12
1993–2019	0.32	0.38	0.17

When comparing the VRI with the official CPI rate, we find that for the whole period 1960–2019, more than a third of the variations in the CPI (0.37) is explained by changes in the VRI (Table 2.2). Also, the weight of the CPP is five times more (0.50) than that of M2 (0.10) in the determination of CPI inflation. Similar results are reached for each of the two sub-periods. This confirms the greater role of the CPP in the determination of inflation for the economy as a whole, as well as for the productive sectors.

The value theory of inflation (VTI) explains why monetary policies have failed to control inflation, particularly disinflation. It's because monetary policies cannot stop the percentage fall in the production of new value, which is objectively determined by the movement of the economy and in turn is the objective determinant of inflation. This is why so-called *fine tuning* – a very short-term alternation of expansive and restrictive monetary policies around a moderate inflation target of 2 per cent per year – has not worked. What the monetary authorities lack is a view filtered through the prism of value. Disinflation is due to the shrinking share of new value (wages and profits) within slowing total value growth. There is nothing money manipulation can do to halt this decreasing trajectory. This is what the monetary authorities do not understand, thus being unable to solve the puzzle. Indeed, for the last 20 years, central banks have failed to achieve their target rate of inflation of around 2 per cent a year with their monetary zig zags on interest rates and monetary controls.

There has been a general pattern of the labour share of income falling during the early phase of recoveries that has characterised most of the post-World War II recoveries, though it has become more extreme in recent business cycles. By 2019, labour's share was at an all-time low. The decade of the 2010s saw basically a stagnation of average real wages in most major economies.

The Bank for International Settlements (BIS) makes the point that

in recent decades, workers' collective bargaining power has declined alongside falling trade union membership. Relatedly, the indexation and COLA clauses that fuelled past wage-price spirals are less prevalent. In the euro area, the share of private sector employees whose contracts involve a formal role for inflation in wage-setting fell from 24% in 2008 to 16% in 2021. COLA coverage in the United States hovered around 25% in the 1960s and rose to about 60% during the inflationary episode of the late 1970s and early 1980s, but rapidly declined to 20% by the mid-1990s.[45]

Since the COVID slump, labour's share of income and real wages have been falling sharply even as unemployment falls. This is the complete opposite of the Keynesian inflation theory and the so-called 'iron law of wages' proposed by Weston against Marx. The rise in inflation has not been driven by anything that looks like an overheating labour market – instead it has been driven by higher corporate profit margins and supply-chain bottlenecks. That means that central banks hiking interest rates to 'cool down' labour markets and reduce wage rises will have little effect on inflation and are more likely to cause stagnation in investment and consumption, thus provoking a slump.

Prices of commodities can be broken down into the three main components: labour costs (V = the value of labour power in Marxist terminology), non-labour inputs (C = the constant capital consumed), and the 'markup' of profits over the first two components (S = surplus value appropriated by the capitalist owners). $P = V + C + S$.

The Economic Policy Institute reckons that, since the trough of the COVID-19 recession in the second quarter of 2020, overall prices in the producing sector of the US economy have risen at an annualised rate of 6.1 per cent – a pronounced acceleration over the 1.8 per cent price growth that characterised the pre-pandemic business cycle of 2007–19. Over half of this increase (53.9 per cent) can be attributed to fatter profit margins, with labour costs contributing less than 8 per cent of this increase. This is not normal. From 1979 to 2019, profits only contributed about 11 per cent to price growth and labour costs over 60 per cent. Non-labour inputs (raw materials and components) are also driving up prices more than usual in the current economic recovery.

Current inflation is concentrated in the goods sector (particularly durable goods), driven by a collapse of supply chains in durable goods (with rolling port shutdowns around the world). The bottleneck is not labour asking for higher wages, it is the lack of shipping capacity and other non-labour shortages. Indeed, in the current inflation spike, US weekly earnings growth has been decreasing month by month. It's profits that have been spiralling upwards. Firms that did happen to have supply on hand as the pandemic-driven demand surge hit have had enormous pricing power vis-à-vis their customers. Corporate profit margins (the share going to profits per unit of production) are at their highest since 1950.

The BIS study finds similarly:

Firms' pricing power, as measured by the markup of prices over costs, has increased to historical highs. In the low and stable inflation environment of the pre-pandemic era, higher markups lowered wage-price pass-through. But in a high inflation environment, higher markups could fuel inflation as businesses pay more attention to aggregate price growth and incorporate it into their pricing decisions. Indeed, this could be one reason why inflationary pressures have broadened recently in sectors that were not directly hit by bottlenecks.

Does this mean that companies can raise prices at will and are engaged in what is called 'price-gouging'? Marx, arguing with Weston in 1865, did not think that was the case in general. The power of competition still ruled. George Pearkes, an analyst at Bespoke Investment, pointed to Caterpillar, which recorded a 958 per cent profit increase driven by volume growth and price realisation between 2019 and 2021's fourth quarters. Eliminating price increases may have dropped the company's 2021 quarter four operating profits slightly below the $1.3 billion it made in 2020. 'This isn't price gouging … and it shows pretty concretely that there's a lot of nuance here', Pearkes said, adding profiteering is 'not the primary driver of inflation, nor the primary driver of corporate profits'. Indeed, companies that push prices as hard as the current environment allows to maximise profits in the short run may find themselves paying a price in market share down the road as others get into the game. It is clear, however, that the greater the concentration of capital in any sector, the greater ability to hike prices. 'When you go from 15 to 10 companies, not much changes', one analyst argued. 'When you go from 10 to six, a lot changes. But when you go from six to four – it's a fix.'

Recently, the UK's Competitions and Market Authority (CMA) published an important report.[46] The CMA found a mixed picture. Profit persistence has increased as measured by markups over marginal costs and the return on capital but not when measured by profits before tax.

And the CMA also found that the more international competition there was, the less ability for firms to increase prices and markups. 'This highlights the important role that international trade plays in contributing to keeping UK markets competitive.' The BIS summed up this debate:

In product markets, the degree of competition comes into play. Firms with higher markups – an indication of greater market power – could raise prices when wages increase, while those without such pricing power may hesitate to do so. Strategic considerations in price-setting are also relevant. Firms may feel more comfortable raising prices if they believe their competitors will also do so. Price increases are more likely when demand is strong. With less concern about losing sales and less room to adjust profit margins, even firms with less pricing power could pass higher costs through to customers.

The Fed and other central banks cannot 'manage' inflation as it depends on what is happening in capitalist production. If profitability rises and thus business is good, capitalists need more money (money proper and credit) to support capital investments and accumulation. The central bank complies. Mainstream economists interpret this as if rising inflation were determined by the growing quantity of money. They call for restrictive monetary policies. In contrast, in the value theory of inflation the quantity of money plays a subordinate role. (Dis)inflation in the prices of consumer goods is accounted for principally in terms of the production of value, itself a consequence of the decreasing profitability.

Inflation in the productive sectors determines inflation in the economy as a whole and thus also in the unproductive sectors. This is empirically shown by the correlation between the two value rates of inflation, for the non-financial sector (VRI) and for the economy as a whole (the VRI*). One important observation for our theory is that the VRI and the VRI* are consistently higher than CPI inflation (see Table 2.1). So labour should be aware that claims for wages sufficiently high to catch up with the rise in the CPI will continually be insufficient to compensate for the loss of purchasing power in value terms, as measured by the VRI and the VRI*. In wage negotiations between capital and labour, labour should not use the official CPI but an alternative indicator (e.g. the VRI) that would preserve labour's purchasing power.

3

Crises and Value

3.1 MARX'S THEORY OF CRISES

Marx's theory of crises under capitalism is composed of various elements and levels of causation that must come together to explain slumps in production, investment and employment, which is the definition of a crisis. Before capitalism, crises were products of scarcity, famine and natural disasters. Now they are products of a profit-making money economy: they are man-made and yet appear to be out of the control of man. Above all, crises show capitalism as a failing system despite the great strides in the productivity of labour that this mode of production has generated in the last 200 years or so.

Marx's theory of crises was not fully developed or explained by Marx during his lifetime. Unfortunately, Marx was not able to complete his great work on the capitalist economy as he had outlined it in his *Contribution to the Critique of Political Economy* in 1859. Therefore, we do not find an elaborate and systematic presentation of the theory of crisis in his writings. But it can be claimed that all the elements of such a theory are to be found in various works by Marx and especially in all three volumes of *Capital* and in the *Theorien über den Mehrwert* [Theories of Surplus Value], posthumously published by Kautsky. As the different aspects of this complicated problem are treated by Marx in various contexts, his ideas have been interpreted in different ways by Marxists, which has made it difficult to connect the links in one consistent chain of thought.[1]

In making this argument, Marx finds that the determinant cause of crises in the capitalist production process is the production for profit and specifically the tendential fall of the profit rate. In Marx's view, this is the 'most important law of political economy'.

> The declining profit rate is in every respect the most important law of modern political economy, and the most essential for understanding the most difficult relations ... Beyond a certain point, the development of the powers of production [productivity of labour] become a barrier for capital [the decreased production of surplus value]; hence the capital relation becomes a barrier for the development of the productive powers of labour.

Typically, productivity is raised through new technologies, which are productivity-increasing, but also labour-shedding. When new technologies are brought into the production process to increase productivity, as a rule, assets replace labour. Given that only the exertion of labour power creates value, if labour declines relatively in each unit of production, the new value of that unit falls. This raises the ratio of the capital invested in the means of production (technology, equipment and structures) relative to the investment in the employment of labour power. Marx called this ratio the organic composition of capital. Tendentially, due to the application of new technologies, the number of labourers per unit of capital invested falls, that is, the organic composition rises.[2] As that ratio rises, so the rate of profit falls, *ceteris paribus*. This is the barrier: the contraction of capital's vital lymph relative to the capital invested as the result of the development of the productivity of labour. Marx continues:

> The growing incompatibility between the productive development of society [i.e. the development of productivity] and its hitherto existing relations of production [i.e. production for profit] expresses itself in bitter contradictions, crises, spasms. The violent destruction of capital not by relations external to it, but rather as a condition of its self-preservation [i.e. the destruction of the weakest and less productive capitals], is the most striking form in which advice is given it to be gone and to give room to a higher state of social production.[3]

Marx's law of the tendential fall in the profit rate is framed in terms of tendencies and counter-tendencies.[4] The general tendency is for the organic composition of capital (OCC) to rise.[5] There might be capitalists investing in less efficient and thus lower-productivity means of production, which implies a lower organic composition of capital. But if they persist in this choice, they are doomed to bankruptcy because they become unable to compete with more efficient capitalists.

But there are powerful counter-tendencies to Marx's tendential law. These counter-tendencies temporarily dampen or reverse the tendency of the rate of profit to fall. When they have exhausted their action, the tendency emerges again. In particular, Marx mentions the following counter-tendencies:

- The increasing intensity of exploitation of labour, which increases the rate of surplus value.
- The relative cheapening of the elements of constant capital lowering the organic composition of capital.
- The lowering of the wage rate below the normal value of labour power, thus raising the rate of surplus value.

- Profits from foreign trade into a national economy.
- Investment in the stock and bond markets for financial gains (i.e. fictitious profits).

Many Marxists would add as another counter-tendency the shortening of the turnover time in circulating capital. In our view, a shorter turnover time increases the absolute quantity of surplus value created in a given time. But contrary to longer working days and higher intensity of labour, it does not increase the rate of surplus value, *ceteris paribus*.[6]

However, Marx's law of profitability also has a 'double-edge'. As the rate of profit falls, it is perfectly possible, indeed likely, that the mass of profit will rise. This can keep investment and production rising. But a persistently falling rate of profit must eventually slow and reverse the rise in the mass of profit.

> The two movements not only go hand in hand, but mutually influence one another and are phenomena in which the same law expresses itself ... there would be absolute over-production of capital as soon as additional capital for purposes of capitalist production = 0 ... at a point, therefore, when the increased capital produced just as much, or even less, surplus-value than it did before its increase, there would be absolute over-production of capital; i.e., the increased capital $C + \Delta C$ would produce no more, or even less, profit than capital C before its expansion by ΔC.[7]

When the rate of profit falls to the point where the mass of profit falls, Marx called this point 'absolute over-accumulation', the tipping point for crises. Henryk Grossman explains:

> Not only does the rate of profit fall but the rate of growth of the mass of profit ... also falls behind the rate of growth of the total value of production. So a point is eventually reached when the increase in mass of profit is not large enough to cover the projected increase in investment, which is growing at a higher rate. The rate of profit cannot, therefore, fall indefinitely. Whatever the rate of accumulation assumed in the model, the rate of profit eventually declines to a level at which the mass of surplus value is not great enough to sustain that rate of accumulation. (Grossmann, 1992, p. 103, 1971, pp. 331–2)[8]

And as Marx put it: 'the so-called plethora (overaccumulation) of capital always applies to a plethora of capital for which the fall in the rate of profit is not compensated by the mass of profit ... and 'overproduction of commodities is simply overaccumulation of capital'.

Let us consider a real example.

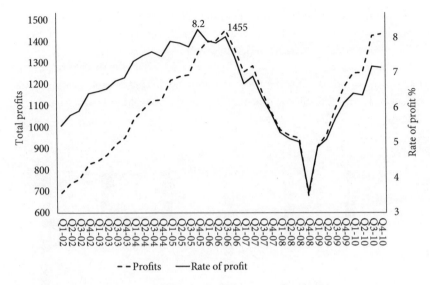

Figure 3.1   US corporate profits ($ billion) and the rate of profit (%)

In Figure 3.1, we show the mass of US corporate profits and the rate of profit on the capital of that sector on a quarterly basis. We find that both the rate and mass of profit rises from 2002. However, the rate of profit peaks at the end of 2005, but the mass goes on rising for another year. From the end of 2006, both the rate and the mass of profit fall in unison, with a turning point upwards for both at the end of 2008. This shows that the falling rate of profit eventually takes the mass of profit down.

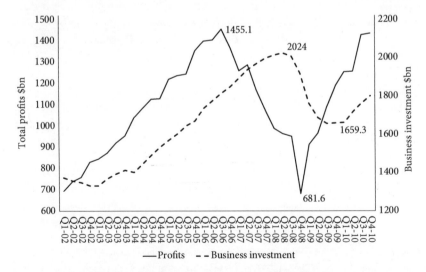

Figure 3.2   US corporate profits and business investment ($ billion)

The fall in the mass of profits from the end of 2006 leads eventually to an investment collapse and a slump in capitalist production in 2008. This is a real example of absolute over-accumulation (Figure 3.2).

And in every US recession since the war, it is broadly the same. The rate of profit falls before and during each recession by 4–18 per cent and the mass of profit drops by 6–26 per cent (with the exception of early 1990s recession (Figure 3.3).

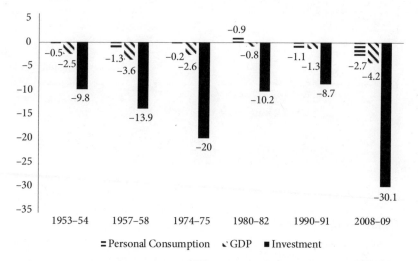

Figure 3.3   Recessions: percentage change of US rate of profit and mass of profits

This leads to an 'investment strike' by capital. It can be held that if company management see profits or earnings slowing or falling, they reduce their investment expansion and stop hiring workers and even start to lay off employees. But even in a period of crisis, there are also firms whose profitability rises and with them investments. So, this view is unsatisfactory. The reason why investments fall following falling profitability is that if profits fall, less is left for investments. This excludes the individuals' motivations as the macroeconomic cause of the fall in investments. Tapia shows the close connection between the changes in the mass of US corporate profits and investment, leading to successive crises.[9] As Tapia concludes:

> the evidence is quite overwhelming that profits peak several quarters before the recession. Then profits recover before investment does, as illustrated by the investment trough that occurs around the end of the recession or the start of the expansion, but following the profit trough for at least a few quarters.

And Carchedi shows that, when total new value (mass) starts to fall along with a fall in the rate of profit (CE-ARP) and employment, a slump in production follows[10] (Figure 3.4).

Figure 3.4 Crises: percentage fall from pre-crisis to last crisis years, 1949–2009
Source: Authors' calculations.

In short, Marx's law of profitability goes as follows: as capitalism develops, new labour-saving but productivity-increasing new technologies replace the old ones and the amount of constant capital rises in relation to variable capital. Because labour power hired with variable capital is the only part of capital that produces value and thus surplus value, the amount of value and thus *ceteris paribus* of surplus value falls relative to total capital invested and this depresses the rate of profit – unless there is a faster increase in the rate of surplus value, among other counter-tendencies. But Marx contends that the law will assert itself sooner or later, that is, when the counter-tendencies cannot counter the tendency any longer.[11] For example, if profitability falls in the productive sectors, less surplus value can be appropriated by the financial sectors. These sectors, by lending less, see their profits fall. The crisis is born in the productive spheres and extends itself into the unproductive ones. When the speculative bubble explodes, financial firms go bust and the crisis moves from the financial and speculative sectors to the productive ones. Thus, the financial crisis is a catalyst of the crisis of profitability, but the origin of the crisis is not in finance and speculation.

The counter-tendencies introduce cyclical trends in the long-term trend of the downward rate of profit. The operation of these counter-tendencies transforms the breakdown into a temporary crisis, so that the accumulation process is not something continuous but takes the form of periodic cycles. A crisis or slump in production is necessary to correct and reverse the fall in the rate and eventually any fall in the mass of profit. But each new high point in profitability is lower than the previous one: the long-term tendency is downwards. In a period of slump, some capitalists close down. They are usually the low OCC capitals; those who invest percentage-wise more in labour power and less in means of production. Thus, they produce less *use* values but more surplus value than their higher productivity competitors. But upon the (tendential) equalisation of the profit rates, they lose surplus value to the more productive capitals through price formation. So, their mass, as well as their rate, of profit falls. Their finances deteriorate, pushing them to bankruptcy. Investments as well as employment collapse. Both the capitalists and the labourers purchase less. The crisis of realisation follows in the footsteps of, and is determined by, the crisis in the production of surplus value. Given that unproductive capital (commerce, finance and speculation) rests on the surplus value produced by productive capital, also unproductive capital collapses.

In the slump, the productive capitals which have weathered the storm fill the vacant economic space. They buy the means of production, raw materials, semi-finished products of the bankrupt capitalists at deflated prices. Due to these lower prices, the purchasers appropriate value from the sellers, which they capitalise. Initially, they invest in the existing technologies. Due to extended reproduction, more labour power is employed at lower wages so that a larger mass of (surplus) value is produced. The rate of profit rises. But at a certain point, the surviving capitals introduce new technologies with higher OCC. The fall in the rate of profit asserts itself again. However, within this falling tendency for the economy as a whole, the rate of profit rises for the more productive companies because they appropriate more value due to their higher technology and thus higher OCC, but falls for the less productive capitals because of the loss of surplus value. The former appropriate an increasing share of the total surplus value. The innovators become the engine of the economic recovery even if they are the cause of the fall in the average profitability. Rising employment due to enlarged reproduction increases labour's purchasing power and rising profitability for the technological innovators increases their purchasing power. Both factors facilitate the realisation of the greater output. Moved by rising profitability and by reduced problems of realisation, new capitalists and those who had set aside capital during the crisis join the race. The unproductive sectors can appropriate more surplus value from the productive ones.

Credit becomes abundant. It is also more easily accessible because the danger for the unproductive sectors to lend to the productive ones recedes due to the latter's economic upswing. So the downward profitability cycle generates *from within*, first the crisis, and then the upward cycle. Accumulation and growth accelerate. However, the upswing, in its turn, generates from within the *next* downward profitability cycle. In fact, the new means of production of the innovators will start to reduce the average rate of profit because of their higher OCC. Eventually, this hurts the low profitability capitals and the downward movement sets in again. In short, the crisis is expressed in the fall in the average rate of profit and the concomitant bankruptcy of the weakest capitals, and thus reduced reproduction and higher unemployment. The recovery and boom is the opposite: it is expressed in rising profitability, expanded reproduction and growing employment. Each cycle generates its opposite from within itself.

Each crisis has the same ultimate cause, falling profitability, but has its own specific features, that is, modes of manifestation, including its own counter-tendencies. For example, the trigger of the 2008–09 Great Recession was the huge expansion of fictitious capital (mortgages given to households that became insolvent and the mountain of debts built upon these debts). This eventually collapsed when the ratio of house prices to household incomes reached extremes. This is the specificity of this case. But the ultimate cause is a consequence of the need of capital to counter falling profitability. Critics hold that the theory above is mono-causal and is thus obviously wrong because all crises are different and thus cannot have the same cause. They do not see that the same cause can and does manifest itself in different forms depending on the continuously changing effects of falling profitability on the socio-economic relations and processes.

3.2 MARX'S THEORY OF CRISIS IS BOTH CYCLICAL AND SECULAR

Marx's law of profitability predicts regular and recurring crises and slumps followed by recovery and booms for a while. It foresees that, as the organic composition of capital rises globally, the rate of profit will fall despite counteracting factors and despite successive crises (which temporarily help to restore the conditions for rising profitability). But Marx's law suggests also an inexorable decline over decades (and longer) in the profitability of capital accumulation, possibly suggesting an end to capitalism (Figure 3.5).[12] This is shown in Figure 3.5 and supported by a large number of empirical studies.

Some Marxists reckon that the law of profitability only applies to the secular long term. Rosa Luxemburg was one of these, dismissing any role for the law in explaining recurrent crises under capitalism. Instead, she looked for a different explanation based on a surplus of output beyond that which could be realised in the imperialist economies, thus forcing capital to be exported to countries which were not yet incorporated into capitalism. It was Rosa Luxemburg's view that the law of profitability was such a very long-term tendency that the 'sun would burn out' before a falling rate of profit would play a role in pushing capitalism into crises. When the Russian Bolshevik economist Isaakovich Nakhimson

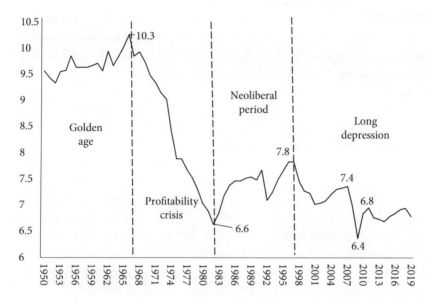

Figure 3.5   G20 rate of profit (%)

(now forgotten by history)[13] challenged Luxemburg on her rejection of Marx's law of profitability as an explanation of crises, she responded sarcastically.

> How the dear man envisages this – whether the capitalist class will at a certain point commit mass suicide in despair at the low rate of profit, or whether it will somehow declare that business was so bad that it simply wasn't worth the trouble, whereupon it will hand the key to the proletariat? However, that may be, this comfort is unfortunately dispelled by a single sentence by Marx, namely in the statement that, 'large capitals will compensate for the fall in the rate of profit by mass production'. Thus, there is still some time to pass before capitalism collapses because of the falling rate of profit, roughly until the sun burns out.[14]

But we have seen above that the fall in the mass and in the rate of profit are two sides of the same movement occurring at different times in the cycle and that the increase in the former cannot compensate for the fall in the latter. Contrary to Luxemburg, Marx did apply the law of profitability as an explanation of periodic crises. His understanding of the recurrence of crisis integral to capitalism was already spelt out in the Communist Manifesto written in March 1848, just before the revolutions in Europe broke out.

> It is enough to mention the commercial crises that by their periodical return put the existence of the entire bourgeois society on its trial, each time more

threateningly. In these crises, a great part not only of the existing products, but also of the previously created productive forces, are periodically destroyed ... And how does the bourgeoisie get over these crises? On the one hand by enforced destruction of a mass of productive forces; on the other, by the conquest of new markets, and by the more thorough exploitation of the old ones. That is to say, by paving the way for more extensive and more destructive crises, and by diminishing the means whereby crises are prevented.[15]

Marx commented further that: 'Once the cycle begins, it is regularly repeated. Effects, in their turn, become causes, and the varying accidents of the whole process, which always reproduces its own conditions, take on the form of periodicity.'[16] He wrote to Engels at the end of May 1873 about 'a problem which I have been wrestling with in private for a long time'. He had been examining 'tables which give prices, discount rate, etc. etc'. As he said: 'I have tried several times – for the analysis of crises – to calculate these ups and downs as irregular curves and thought (I still think that it is possible with enough tangible material) that I could determine the main laws of crises mathematically.'

Marx saw the turnover of fixed capital as a part of the explanation of the periodicity of the cycle. Engels told Marx that it was normal to set aside 7 ½ per cent for depreciation, which implied a replacement cycle of 13 years, although he noted 20- and 30-year old machines still working. Marx concluded that:

The figure of 13 years corresponds closely enough to the theory, since it establishes a unit for one epoch of industrial reproduction which *plus ou moins* coincides with the period in which major crises recur; needless to say their course is also determined by factors of a quite different kind, depending on their period of reproduction. For me, the important thing is to discover, in the immediate material postulates of big industry, *one factor* that determines cycles. (emphasis added)[17]

The key point for Marx was that

the cycle of related turnovers, extending over a number of years, within which the capital is confined by its fixed component, is one of the material foundations for the periodic cycle [crisis] ... But a crisis is always the starting point of a large volume of new investment. It is also, therefore, if we consider the society as a whole, more or less, a new material basis for the next turnover cycle.[18]

So Marx connected his theory of crisis to cycles of turnover of fixed capital. The accumulation of capital, including fixed assets, under capitalism depends on its profitability for the owners of capital. From that fundamental premise, if there is a replacement cycle of some duration, there is likely to be a cycle of profitability.

3.3 ALTERNATIVE MARXIST THEORIES OF CRISES

There are alternative 'Marxian' theories of crises that ignore and/or reject Marx's law of profitability as being relevant. They fall into three camps:

1. Crises are caused by instability and reckless anarchy in the banking and financial sector.
2. Crises are caused by underconsumption of the working class, inherent in capitalism, so that slumps occur when demand for consumption goods falls.
3. Crises are caused by the disproportional expansion of the sector producing capital goods (for other capitalists) compared to the expansion of the sector producing consumer goods (for workers and capitalists). This inherent disproportion leads to a collapse in demand for consumer goods that feeds back into the demand for capital goods.

In the first view, crises originate in the financial/speculative sphere due to extremely high levels of debt, rampant speculation, a permissive monetary policy, the loosening of rules governing borrowing and lending due to deregulation etc. In short, crises are the outcome of policy mistakes. The obvious question follows: if crises are merely due to the policymakers' mistakes, why would these mistakes be recurrent and constant? Why cannot policymakers learn from their mistakes? Obviously, there must be some structural reasons that prevent them from learning from their past mistakes, that is, that force them to continue making these very mistakes. Some Marxist authors argue that there has been a structural change in the capitalist mode of production that makes finance dominant in the accumulation of capital and the appropriation of surplus value. This is the financialisation theory.

For example, Jack Rasmus proposes a thesis that the world economy is engulfed in a 'systemic fragility' not seen before.[19] Rasmus cites nine fundamental economic trends that underlie what he considers caused this growing fragility. Basically, they consist of a massive injection of liquidity (money and debt) starting with central banks worldwide and spreading as debt through the financial system, households and government. In short,

key variables of liquidity injection, debt, a shift to financial asset investing, a slowdown in real asset investment, disinflation and deflation in goods and services trends, financial system restructuring, labour market restructuring, and declining effectiveness of central bank monetary policy and government

102

fiscal policies on historical multipliers and interest rate elasticities all together constitute the major trends underlying the long run deepening of fragility within the system.

These trends now interact with each other, creating a new 'systemic fragility' in modern capitalism. Obviously, this list is far from being comprehensive. Almost anything could be added. Moreover, a list of causes without an internal structure of causality is not an explanation. It does not reveal the direction of determination but rather is a chaotic whole which cannot specify the weight of each cause and its relation to the other causes. What is lacking is an ultimately determining cause. In fact, if each crisis has its own specific causes which characterise only that crisis, then these causes cannot determine other crises, so that the recurrence of crises is not explained. Or perhaps some causes are permanent. But then one needs a theory of why those causes are permanent and how they relate to each other.

Rasmus calls those Marxists who hold to Marx's law of profitability as the underlying cause of crises as 'mechanical Marxists'. Supposedly, 'mechanical Marxists' fail to see that crises now originate in the financial/credit sector and flow into production, not vice versa. So he concludes that 'Marxists should focus more on capital accumulation as such and not on the determinants of investment like profitability.' The 'mechanical' Marxist law of the tendency of the rate of profit to fall is out of date, Rasmus holds, or only 'half-correct', as a cause of crises because of 'fundamental structural changes that have occurred in the global financial system and in labour markets in the 21st century'. Supposedly, Marx's law of profitability does not incorporate financial instability and the expansion of debt, so it cannot be a full and coherent explanation of crises – and indeed of the current long depression. One is left with the impression that Rasmus did not read the third volume of *Capital*, which contains detailed analyses of commercial, financial and speculative crises, and of their relation to the production of value, which are amazingly modern and relevant to the analysis of modern crises. Rasmus ponders: 'A correlation [between profitability and crises] exists in the data, but what is the direction of causation? One could just as clearly argue that the acceleration of finance forms of capital is a causation of the decline of profitability from real production.' This argument does not stand. In finance (surplus) value is distributed. But before it can be distributed it must have been produced. Thus, whatever changes in finance, it must originate in production.

One counter-argument is that finance capital is itself productive of (surplus) value. This obliterates Marx's distinction between productive and unproductive capital. This position too is untenable. Take two financial capitalists. If A lends money (M) to B, the value represented by M shifts from A to B. When B returns M to A, the initial situation is restored. The value represented by M has simply been shifted, it has neither increased nor decreased. To hold the opposite implies that the act of lending M creates value. If one is willing to pursue this train of thought, there are two alternatives. First, when A lends M to B value would be created. But then, when M is returned to A, value is destroyed. No new value is created. Or one could argue that value is created both if M is lent and if M is returned. Recurrent financial transactions would increase the value created. The fact that crises explode when this 'value' is greatest should be sufficient to see that what bourgeois economic theory (and many Marxists with it) sees as value is in fact debt. In the real world, crises take the form of collapse (not an increase) in value. Indeed, wherever the fictitious expansion of capital has developed most is where the crisis begins, for example, tulips, stock markets, housing debt, corporate debt, banking debt, public debt etc. The financial sector is often where the crisis starts; but one thing is the cause of crises, another is their trigger.

Marx was clear that the possibility of breakdown in the circulation of capital was inherent in commodity production. The possibility of crises existed in the separation of sale and purchase in commodity circulation and in the role of money as means of payment. But this only raised the possibility of crises not their cause and even less their regular occurrence. That was the barrier set up by 'capitalist profit, which was the basis of modern overproduction'.[20] The underlying cause of crises is to be found in the law of tendency of the rate of profit to fall, while the actuality of crises can 'only be deduced from the real movement of capitalist production, competition and crises'.[21] The financial sector (and particularly the size and movement of credit) does play a role in capitalist crisis. Indeed, the growth of credit and speculative investment in stocks, bonds and other forms of money assets, or 'fictitious capital', functions as one of the counteracting factors against the downward tendency on profitability for those capitalists who shift their investments to the more profitable financial sphere. But for the economy as a whole, the growth of finance and speculation inflates the financial bubble and weakens the productive sectors which must provide surplus value when finance tries to claim real profits (money) in exchange for its paper profits.

There has been a massive increase in the weight of the financial sector in the global capitalist economy. But this does not mean that the financial sector is replacing the productive one as the new motor of capitalism. Rather, the growth of the former is a consequence of the fall in profitability in the latter. The share of US gross domestic income accruing to finance and insurance rose dramatically from 2.3 per cent in 1947 to 7.9 per cent by 2006. But can we say that the growth of the financial sector was the cause of the Great Recession if it had been expanding for six decades without a crisis of the proportions of 2008?

Movements in the rate of profit have their effect on the financial sector. ... Bubbles tend to begin as profits revive after a downturn. ... As crisis [in the productive sector] impends, capital panics and takes flights [in the financial and speculative sectors]. The bursting of the bubbles seems an accidental affair, but accident is the manifestation of necessity.[22]

A fall in the rate of profit promotes speculation. If the capitalists cannot make enough profit producing commodities, they will try making money betting on the stock exchange or buying various other financial instruments. Capitalists experience the falling rate of profit almost simultaneously, so they start to buy these stocks and assets roughly at the same time, driving prices up. But when stock and other financial asset prices are rising everybody wants to buy them – this is the beginning of the bubble, the lines of which we have seen over and over since the infamous Tulip crisis of 1637. If, for example, the speculation takes place in housing as in 2008–09, this creates an option for workers to borrow (mortgages) and spend more than they earn (more than the capitalists have laid out as variable capital), and in this way the 'realization problem' (sufficient money to buy all the goods produced) is solved.[23] But sooner or later, such bubbles burst when investors find that the assets (mortgage bonds) are not worth what they are paying for them or when mortgages cannot be repaid. The 'realisation problem' reoccurs in an expanded form compared with before the bubble. The result is even greater overproduction than was avoided temporarily in the first place.[24]

Thus, 'a crisis must evidently break out if credit is suddenly withdrawn and only cash payment is accepted ... so *at first glance* [emphasis added] the entire crisis presents itself as simply a credit and monetary crisis'.[25] In analysing the crises of 1873 and 1882, Marx commented that loanable moneyed capital increases after a crisis, since there is more money seeking investment opportunities that are no longer available. This is the main reason why crises are always preceded by a wave of optimism in financial markets, since there is a super-abundance of loanable capital during prosperous periods, which causes a reduction in interest rates. Marx concluded: 'Altogether the movement of moneyed capital (as it expresses itself in interest) is the contrary of productive capital.' But the crucial moment lies in the movement of productive capital.[26]

As Paul Mattick Snr pointed out: 'The crisis characteristic of capital thus originates neither in production nor in circulation taken separately, but in the difficulties that arise from the tendency of the profit rate to fall inherent in accumulation and governed by the law of value.'[27] And as Carchedi put it in referring to the Great Recession, 'the ultimate cause of crises resides in the productive (of surplus value) sphere, that is, in the shrinking productive basis of the economy and in the attendant falling profit rate in this sphere, even though this downwards movement has manifested itself at first in the financial and speculative sectors'.[28] It is not possible to separate crises in the financial sector from what is happening in the production sector. The financialisation theory and its theory of crises would have been rejected by Marx with a wave of the hand. As he put it: 'That is to say, crises are possible without credit'.[29]

The second thesis, one that enjoys a wide currency with Marxists, is underconsumption. Among Marxists, it has gained much support from the work of Rosa Luxemburg. Luxemburg argued that there was an inherent tendency for capitalist accumulation to overreach the market for buying the goods and services being produced. In her view, that showed that capitalism could and would get into crises; and moreover, it also explained imperialist expansion. To avoid crises of overproduction at home, capitalism was forced to search for new markets overseas and find buyers for its goods in the non-capitalist sectors of the world. She argued that Marx's analysis of crises fell short here. Marx had failed to see in his reproduction schemas in Volume Two of *Capital* that this was the ultimate cause of crises: namely, the overproduction of capital goods relative to demand (both from capitalists and workers in the imperialist countries), forcing capitalism to find that demand from the colonial non-capitalist peasants.

There are many effective critiques of Luxemburg's thesis. As Anton Pannekoek remarked:

> there is actually no unresolved theoretical problem, and we don't need to look for any external source of demand. What she [Luxemburg] calls an absurdity from the capitalist point of view because it would represent an aimless circular motion – to produce more and more means of consumption in order to feed more workers, who would produce more and more means of production that serve for the production of those means of consumption – only appears to be absurd because the decisive factor was left out of consideration. The goal of producing more and more is to extract and accumulate more and more surplus value, but those accumulated masses of capital can only fulfil their goal of producing new surplus value by being thrown again and again into the whirlpool of production. The self-valorisation of capital in the creation of profit, the transformation of profit into new capital, is the driving force giving sense and a goal to that alleged absurdity: the apparently aimless, always expanding circuit of production.[30]

Modern versions of the underconsumption thesis argue that crises are caused by a long-term fall in wages against a rise in labour's productivity. In the words of Ollman, the workers 'can buy ever smaller portions of what they themselves produce … leading to periodic crises of overproduction/underconsumption'.[31]

As for the Great Recession in 2008, the underconsumptionist thesis holds that the cause was a long-term fall in wages. Lower wages, it is submitted, instead of increasing the rate of profit, cause it to fall because of failed realisation, first, in the consumer goods sector and from there to other sectors. This is so because the capitalist economy is driven in the last instance not by the movement of the average rate of profit but by 'aggregate demand'. Aside from the obvious point that here Marx is substituted by Keynes, the question is whether this substitution holds its own in the face of theoretical and empirical data. 'Demand' is actually demand for consumption goods by consumers, for investment goods by the capitalists and for both types of goods for public expenditure by the state. But the crucial element in the underconsumption argument is the demand for consumer goods. A fall in the demand for consumer goods provokes a chain-reaction, because the demand for the means of production needed to produce those consumer goods also falls. This fall, in its turn, provokes the fall in the demand for means of production needed to produce those means of production. If wages decrease, a part of the consumption goods and thus of the investment goods, cannot be sold and capital suffers a loss. Consequently, the average rate of profit falls. Lower wages are thus the determinant cause of the crisis.

Marx and Engels repudiated this theory of underconsumption with empirical arguments. Marx points out that 'crises are precisely always preceded by a period in which wages rise generally' and that this 'relative prosperity' of the working class occurs always only 'as a harbinger of a coming crisis'.[32] Engels stresses the point that underconsumption of the masses, that is, the limitation of their consumption to the bare minimum, existed thousands of years before capitalism emerged, but only with capitalism does the new phenomenon of overproduction emerge. Underconsumption is a chronic fact in capitalist society while crises recur periodically.

Marx invalidated the underconsumption thesis in the second volume of *Capital*:

It is sheer tautology to say that crises are caused by the scarcity of effective consumption ... That commodities are unsaleable means only that no effective purchasers have been found for them. ... But if one were to attempt to give this tautology the semblance of a profounder justification by saying that the working-class receives too small a portion of its own product and the evil would be remedied as soon as it receives a larger share of it and its wages increase in consequence, one could only remark that crises are always prepared by precisely a period in which wages rise generally and the working-class actually gets a larger share of that part of the annual product which is intended for consumption. From the point of view of these advocates of sound and 'simple' common sense, such a period should rather remove the crisis.[33]

Marx was obviously aware of the possibility that not all the output produced could be sold:

> The entire mass of commodities … must be sold. If this is not done … the labourer has been indeed exploited, but his exploitation is not realised as such for the capitalist. … The conditions of direct exploitation, and those of realising it, are not identical. … The first are only limited by the productive power of society, the latter by the proportional relation of the various branches of production and the consumer power of society.

If commodities are unsold, capital suffers a loss and the rate of profit falls. Could lower wages, then, reduce workers' consumption and thus the rate of profit and act as the cause of crises, *ceteris paribus*? The rate of profit rises with a rise in surplus value and falls with a rise in the organic composition of capital (the ratio of constant to variable capital). If wages are reduced, profits increase and the rate of profit rises. This is always the case for the individual capitalist. If wages are reduced, profits increase. But this is only a temporary situation. It ignores the smaller production of surplus value due to the increase in the organic composition of capital. Thus the rate of profit rises due to lower wages, given a certain level of employment, but falls due to the higher organic composition of capital and thus due to the lower level of employment per unit of capital invested. Which weighs more?

Let us consider three facts. The first is that workers' consumption is not the largest sector of 'demand' in a capitalist economy; it is productive capital consumption. Gross domestic product or expenditure is a measure of annual demand for 'wants, needs and desires'. In the US, consumption constitutes 70 per cent of GDP in value-added. However, if you look at 'gross product' which includes all the intermediate value-added products not counted in GDP, then consumption is only 45 per cent of the total product; the rest constitutes demand from capital for parts, materials, intermediate goods and services (Figure 3.6). It is investment by capitalists that is the swing factor and driver of demand, not consumption by workers.

This is also shown in the second fact. If we analyse the changes in investment and consumption prior to each recession or slump in the post-war US economy, we find that consumption demand has played little or no leading role in provoking a slump (Figure 3.7). In the six recessions since 1953, personal consumption fell less than GDP or investment on every occasion and does not fall at all in 1980–82. Investment fell by 8–30 per cent on every occasion.

Figure 3.6 Share of consumption in US production (%)

Source: BEA Gross Output KLEM series Composition of Gross Output by Industry, authors' calculations. See also https://theplanningmotive.com/?s=gross+product

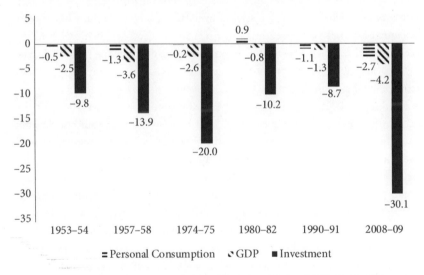

Figure 3.7 Percentage changes in consumption, investment and GDP in the US, one year prior to a slump

In every US recession since 1945, it has not been a fall in household consumption levels that has emerged before a slump, but a fall in business investment levels. Consumption may be 70 per cent of US GDP on official accounts, but it is the 15–20 per cent of GDP in capital investment that is the swing factor in causing slumps. Consumption hardly drops – because households must go on paying for energy, food and basics, running up debts and running down savings although, of course, a fall in personal consumption affects much more the poor and low-income groups.

The third fact relates directly to wages and the claim that raising them would avoid crises. Carchedi finds that of the twelve post-World War II crises, eleven have been preceded by *rising* wages (as Marx suggested) and only one by falling wages (the 1991 crisis).[34]

A related argument to low wages being the cause of crises is rising inequality. Rising inequality of income (and wealth) in the major capitalist economies since the early 1980s has been presented as the main cause of crises and, in particular, the Great Recession of 2008–09. This remains the dominant view not only among left economists of the Keynesian or post-Keynesian variety, but also among many Marxists.[35] The argument goes that the great financial crisis was caused by debt – mostly in the private sector. As wages were held down in the US, households were forced to borrow more to get mortgages to buy homes or loans to buy cars and maintain their standard of living. They were encouraged to do so by reckless lending from banks even to 'subprime' borrowers. And as we know, eventually the sheer weight of this debt could not be supported by rising home prices or by the chicken legs of average incomes and the whole house of cards eventually came tumbling down.[36] So the credit crunch, the banking collapse and the Great Recession had nothing to do with the classic Marxist explanation of the downward pressure on profitability. It was down to the rapacious speculative lending of the too-big-to-fail banks.[37]

Leading post-Keynesian economist Engelbert Stockhammer argues that the economic imbalances that caused the Great Recession crisis should be thought of as the outcome of the interaction of the effects of financial deregulation with the macroeconomic effects of rising inequality. In this sense, rising inequality should be regarded as the root cause. Rising inequality creates a downward pressure on aggregate demand since poorer income groups have high marginal propensities to consume. Higher inequality has led to higher household debt as working-class families have tried to keep up with social consumption norms despite stagnating or falling real wages, while rising inequality has increased the propensity to speculate as richer households tend to hold riskier financial assets than other groups.[38] For Stockhammer, capitalist economies are either 'wage-led' or 'profit-led'. A wage-led demand regime is one where an increase in the wage share leads to higher aggregate demand, which will occur if the positive consumption effect is larger than the negative investment effect. A profit-led demand regime is one where an increase in the wage share has a negative effect on aggregate demand. The post-Keynesians reckon that capitalist economies are wage-led. So when there is a decline in the wage share as there has been since the

1980s, it reduces aggregate demand in a capitalist economy and thus eventually causes a slump. The banking sector increases the risk of this with its speculative activities.

There are several problems with this argument. First, surely, no one is claiming that the simultaneous international slump of 1974–75 was due to a lack of wages or rising debt or banking speculation? Or that the deep global slump of 1980–82 can be laid at the door of low wages or household debt? Every Marxist economist reckons that the cause of those slumps can be found in the dramatic decline in the profitability of capital from the heights of the mid-1960s; and even mainstream economists look for explanations in rising oil prices or technological slowdown. Nobody reckons the cause was low wages or rising inequality.

It could be argued that in the 1970s, capitalist economies were 'profit-led' but now they are 'wage-led'; so, each crisis has a different cause. But how did a profit-led capitalist economy become a 'wage-led' one? Yes, wages were held down and profits rose. But why? Surely the answer lies in the attempts of the strategists of capital to raise the rate of exploitation as a counteracting factor to the fall in profitability – the classic Marxist explanation. Rising inequality is really the product of the relatively successful attempt to raise profitability during the 1980s and 1990s by raising the rate of surplus value through unemployment, demolishing labour rights, shackling the trade unions, privatising state assets, 'freeing' up product markets, deregulating industry, reducing corporate tax etc. – in other words, the neoliberal agenda.

Second, the empirical evidence for a causal connection between inequality and crises remains questionable. Michael Bordo and Christopher Meissner from the Bank of International Settlements analysed the data and concluded that inequality does not seem to be the reason for a crisis. Credit booms mostly lead to financial crises, but inequality does not necessarily lead to credit booms.

Our paper looks for empirical evidence for the recent Kumhof/Rancière hypothesis attributing the US subprime mortgage crisis to rising inequality, redistributive government housing policy and a credit boom. Using data from a panel of 14 countries for over 120 years, we find strong evidence linking credit booms to banking crises, but no evidence that rising income concentration was a significant determinant of credit booms. Narrative evidence on the US experience in the 1920s, and that of other countries, casts further doubt on the role of rising inequality.[39]

Edward Glaesar also points to research on the US economy that home prices in various parts of the US did not always increase where there was the most income inequality.[40] That calls into question the claim that income inequality was inflating the housing bubble. Glaesar refers to Atkinson on this: 'Atkinson

111

and Morelli's international data also suggest little regular connection between inequality and crises. Looking at 25 countries over a century, they find ten cases where crises were preceded by rising inequality and seven where crises were preceded by declining inequality. Inequality was higher in two of the six cases where a crisis is identified, which is exactly the same proportion as among the 15 cases where no crisis is identified.

As argued above, the problem of underconsumption theory is two-fold. First, it clashes with the empirical observation that wages rise before crises. Second, underconsumption locates the source of aggregate demand in the spending decisions of workers, in effect ignoring the other, and more important, source of aggregate demand, capitalist expenditure. As John Weeks puts it: 'one cannot simultaneously explain crises in terms of underconsumption and employ the labour theory of value as a tool of analysis. In so far as one identifies 'Marxian theory' as a theory based on the labour theory of value, 'Marxian theory' so defined excludes the underconsumption hypothesis.'[41]

Underconsumption is not only wrong. Its policy consequences are far-reaching. First, if lower wages and lower consumption were indeed the cause of crises, in principle, the economy could exit the crisis through higher wages. As just argued, higher wages may increase the realisation by labour of commodity purchases, but it also decreases profits. Second, if the economy could exit the crisis through higher wages, crises would be due to harmful distributional policies, and could thus, in principle, be avoided. If crises can be avoided, the economic system does not tend towards depressions and crises, as Marx holds, but tends towards recovery and booms and prosperity. Crises then could only be temporary hurdles on this path. And the consequences for labour are disastrous. If the system tends (or can be made to tend) towards prosperity and growth, the system is rational. But if the system is rational, the struggle to replace it with a different system becomes irrational, because it is a fight against a rational system, at most a pure act of will, not based on an objective movement. Labour is deprived of the theoretical basis upon which to base its struggle for a better system. Underconsumptionism is not only irreconcilable with Marxism and is not only disproven by facts: it is also inimical to labour.

The third alternative to Marx's crisis theory is disproportionality. In Volume II of *Capital*, Marx derives a formula which gives the technically determined relations which must obtain between the two main departments of social production, the production of means (MP) and the production of means of consumption (MC), to make simple or expanded reproduction of capital possible. These are physical quantities containing value and surplus value. As long as commodities are produced and exchanged in these proportions, production can continue on the same or an ever-enlarged scale, according to whether profits are consumed unproductively by capital or are reinvested, accumulated. According to the disproportionality theory of crises, crises arise if the commodities exchanged between the two sectors do not match the technically necessary quantities. This approach too is problematic for a number of reasons. A first common misinterpretation is to consider the quantities exchanged only as physical quantities, use values, as the product of concrete, specific labour. In this case, prices are the money representations of use values. But this is untenable. Use values are, by definition, different. If money is made to represent something different, it cannot represent that which unifies commodities and makes them comparable, that is, measurable and exchangeable. Then, money has to represent abstract labour and the quantities in the reproduction schemes must represent use values containing value and surplus value.

Consider an initial situation. Sector 1 produces means of production (MP) investing 80c and 20v with which it produces 20s and 120MP (use values). A value of 120 is contained in 120MP. Sector 2 produces means of consumption (MC) by investing 60c and 40v with which it produces 40s and 140MC. A value of 140 is contained in 140MC. The above implies that, for the sake of simplicity, the total values produced ($V_1 = 120$) and ($V_2 = 140$) are equal to the physical outputs, 120MP and 140MC.[42] Consider simple reproduction.

Table 3.1 Simple reproduction with values contained

Sector 1: 120MP	80MP + 20MP + 20MP =120MP	$80c_1 + 20v_1 + 20s = 120V_1$
Sector 2: 140MC	60MC + 40MC + 40MC =140MC	$60c_2 + 40v_2 + 40s_2 = 140V_2$

In Table 3.1, sector 1 produces 120MP, for which it needs 80MP plus 20MC. The 120MP are not exchanged for the 140MC produced in sector 2. Rather, 80MP are consumed within sector 1 and 40MC + 40MC are consumed by capital and labour within sector 2. It follows that for physical reproduction to be possible, 60MC (subsector 2) must be exchanged against 40MP (subsector 1). In terms of the values contained, the condition for simple reproduction is $60c_2 = (20v_1 + 20s_1)$. But this is the case only fortuitously. In fact, in the example above $60c_2 \neq (20v_1 + 20s_1)$. However, in Marx's price theory commodities are not exchanged on the basis of the value contained. Rather, they are exchanged at their production prices, that is, on the basis of the equalisation of the rates of profit into an average. Second, the average rate of profit (ARP) to be applied to capitals invested for inter-sectoral exchange is not that holding for the whole economy (given that only a share of the total output in each sector is exchanged) but that emerging from the inter-sectoral exchange. Then, if 120MC require an investment of 80 + 20 = 100, a value of 40 (the value of the MP to be exchanged for MC) requires an investment of 40x100/120 = 33.33. This is subdivided into constant capital, variable capital and surplus value. Similarly, for 60MC (to be exchanged with 40MC), which require an investment of 60x100/140 = 42.8.

This too can be subdivided into constant capital, variable capital and surplus value. Then, on the basis of these data, the inter-sectoral ARP can be computed. What is lost by one subsector is gained by the other. However, a value of 33.3 must be exchanged for a value of 42.8.

Exchange seems to be impossible. Does this mean that Marx's reproduction schemes collapse if the condition of an average profitability is taken on board? No. Marx did not link the reproduction schemes to a theory of crises. He sought the proportions within which the two subsectors must exchange their product for the economy to reproduce itself on the same or an enlarged scale. He disregarded crises *within* this context, and with good reason. *Crises occur when a country's average ROP falls and not when only one of its sectors' profitability falls.* The profitability emerging from inter-sectoral exchange is only a part of the profitability for the whole economy, which encompasses also the profitability of the sector producing for internal production or consumption. Thus, for a theory of crisis the rate of profit (ROP) must be computed for the whole economy, and not only for the inter-sectoral trade.

That the fall in the ROP in one subsector cannot cause a generalised crisis has been challenged. It is argued that if the crisis initiates in one subsector, it is not absorbed within that sector but expands to the other ones. A local crisis would become generalised. But consider the following. We know that in the equalisation of the rates of profit some sectors gain and the others lose surplus value. If the loss is considerable, say in sector 1, the crisis might emerge in that sector. But actually, what is lost by sector 1 is gained by sector 2 and there is no reason to assume that gaining surplus value is a reason for crises. True, if sector 1 cannot deliver its output to sector 2, the latter might experience difficulties. But then capital moves to sector 2 and proportionality is re-established. There is no reason for disproportionality to be the cause of crises. And even if disproportionality were the cause of crises, it could not explain their recurrence.

A more articulated version of disproportion theory was expounded by Bolshevik activist Pavel Maksakovsky.[43] We consider it here because of the attention it has drawn in recent discussions and because this is an attempt to explain the recurrence of booms and slumps.[44] Maksakovsky refers to Marx's law of profitability, but only to dismiss it as irrelevant to the cycles of boom and slump and, instead, focuses on Volume II of *Capital* with its reproduction schema. His is a physicalist and an equilibrium theory. His personal take is that 'the "proportionalities" of social reproduction ... only exist in the form of a law-governed *tendency*' (p. 140; emphasis added) even if 'the tendency towards equilibrium is never one hundred per cent realised' (p. 142). The movement 'excludes any final equilibrium' (p. 140). We agree. But we disagree that crises are due to the disruption of this proportionality, that they are hurdles on the movement towards equilibrium (p. 140). In essence, in Maksakovsky's theory, the starting point of the cycle, the recovery, is 'a massive renovation of fixed capital' (p. 144) following the mass destruction of capital during the crisis. Moreover, 'because of the high organic composition of the capital it uses, Department I is not immediately able to expand in accordance with the rapidly increasing tempo of demand' (p. 149). Demand for fixed capital rises. Market prices rise more than the production prices.

This 'disrupts both the 'harmony' between market 'demand' and 'supply' and 'proportionality' in the distribution of capitals' (p. 150). The demand for the means of production spills over to the demand for the means of consumption. The economy expands. However, if the rising profits are capitalised, 'The result is overcapitalisation, with social production growing more rapidly than effective demand' (p. 150). Falling demand ushers in the period of depression and crisis. Basically, for Maksakovsky, after the crisis, capitalists increase their demand for capital because of higher market prices. Profits rise and production rises too. Here the prevailing tendency is towards expansion rather than contraction of production. Proportionality is restored.[45]

But does disproportionate investment growth compared to consumption lead to overproduction and periodic crises? Historically, business investment always grows faster than workers' consumption – that is the result of capitalist accumulation, that is, of the tendential increase in the organic composition of capital. But this does not create a chronic slump or permanent stagnation because investments create their own demand (capitalist demand). Indeed, investment drives the productivity of labour and thus drives economic growth. The problem is when investment collapses, not when it grows 'too fast'.

For Maksakovsky, the reason why recovery turns into depression and crisis is lower demand and falling market prices: demand falls behind production and production slows down. Here the prevailing tendency is towards contraction of production rather than expansion. So the recovery and crises are caused by movements in demand and prices rather than by profitability. The expansion or contraction of production is the basic feature of Maksakovsky's cycle, not profit rates. But why should capitalists as a whole increase their demand for capital and production if they cannot increase their profits, or better said, if the average rate of profit does not rise? In and of itself, higher demand and prices cannot spur the recovery. Rather, the massive renovation of fixed capital is due to rising profit rates just as the massive destruction of capital is due to falling profit rates.

Some Marxist authors reject what they see as 'mono-causal' explanations, especially that of the tendential fall in the rate of profit. Instead, they argue, there is no single explanation valid for all crises, except that they are all a 'property' of capitalism and that crises manifest in different forms in different periods and contexts. However, if this elusive and mysterious 'property' becomes manifest as different causes of different crises, while itself remaining unknowable, if we do not know where all these different causes come from, then we have no crisis theory. If crises are recurrent and if they have all different causes, these different causes can explain the different crises, but not their recurrence. If they are recurrent, they must have a common cause that manifests itself recurrently as different causes of different crises. There is no way around the 'mono-causality' of crises.

Mono-causality must be tempered with a modification: namely, a Marxist theory of crises must look beneath the appearance of events, beneath the proximate causes to the essential or ultimate cause. We need to identify the underlying or ultimate cause of crises in the same way that Newton identified the underlying cause of motion of earthly bodies in the law of gravity and in force and counter-force. But we must also recognise that the 'trigger' for each crisis can be different: it could start from a collapsing stock market (1929) or a bursting housing boom (2007), or a sharp jump in commodity prices (oil in 1974). This is where each 'conjunctural' event can be different (Roberts, 2016). Capital starts with the 'general', or should we say with the 'abstract', and proceeds step by step to the concrete (Grossmann, 2015; Rodolsky, 1977). This is vital to understand because the biggest sin committed by the method of mainstream bourgeois economics is to look only at the appearance of things and not see the essence. But, of course, you cannot stay with the essence and must proceed to flesh out any critique of an economy so that the appearances can be explained.

In sum, Marx's tendency of the rate of profit to fall (TRPF) remains integral to any Marxist theory of crises under capitalism. The law of the tendency and the counter-tendencies offers a causal explanation of the cyclical nature of capitalist accumulation, with an increasing body of empirical evidence to back it up. Nothing offered as an alternative is as compelling.

4

Imperialism and Value

In this chapter, we look at the modern economic aspects of imperialism through the prism of value. We define imperialist exploitation as a persistent and long-term net appropriation of surplus value by the high-technology imperialist countries from the low-technology dominated ones. This process is placed within the secular tendential fall in profitability, not only in the imperialist countries but also in the dominated ones. We identify four channels through which surplus value flows to the imperialist countries: currency seignorage; income flows from capital investments; unequal exchange through trade; and changes in exchange rates.

One of the specific features of this work is the theorisation and quantification of international unequal exchange (UE) of value in trade. We do this by extending Marx's transformation procedure to the international setting. We use two variables in the analysis of UE: the organic composition of capital and the rate of exploitation; and we measure which of these two variables is more important in contributing to the systemic international transfer of value.

This chapter does not offer a general or complete theory of imperialism. Nor do we review or assess present and past debates on imperialism.[1] The aspects of modern imperialism dealt with here are far from being comprehensive. Our focus is on some key new economic and financial traits of modern imperialism.

We do not deny the continued existence of colonialism, for example. Colonialism and modern imperialism do not exclude each other. Colonialism is the appropriation of natural resources, military occupation, the direct state control of colonies, the stealing by the imperialist countries of commodities not produced capitalistically and the brutal exploitation of labour in the colonies. But colonialism contains in itself the germs of modern imperialism. Modern imperialist exploitation is the appropriation by capitals in the imperialist countries of the surplus value produced by capitals in the colonies through the trade of the commodities with high technological content produced in the imperialist countries for the capitalistically produced industrial goods (including raw materials) produced with lower technological content in the dominated countries. The result is unequal exchange, that is, the appropriation of international surplus value through international trade. This modern form of appropriation of international surplus value is not absent in colonialism. But it is not the most important one. Modern imperialism penetrates and develops within colonialism until it becomes the dominant form. Under modern imperialism, technology has become the new battlefield.

The above could be misinterpreted as economism. But this charge would be unwarranted. We focus on the economy's *determining* features, which make possible the existence of other extremely important, but *determined* traits, like military and political domination, as well as cultural and ideological pre-emi-nence.[2] These other features are not simply added to the economic ones to get a more complete picture. Their interrelation is dialectical. Particularly important, military and ideological supremacy is not simply an appendage of economic power. Rather, economic power is *determinant* because it is the condition of existence of the military and ideological power and the latter is *determined* because it is the condition of reproduction (or supersession) of the former. Military, political and ideological power are determined by superior technology and economic power in the sense that they are essential for economic power's reproduction.[3]

4.1 GLOBAL GROWTH AND PROFITABILITY OF CAPITAL

The production and appropriation of international surplus value should be framed within the context of the post-World War II tendential long-term fall in world profitability. This fall affects both the imperialist countries (hence-forth IC) and the dominated countries (DC) even if in different measures.[4] Official statistics focus on GDP rather than on profitability figures. Neverthe-less, they are telling. They show the tendential fall of the world GDP growth rate (Figure 4.1).

The falling rate of GDP growth for the G20 countries is puzzling to con-ventional macroeconomics. Usually, the culprit is found in falling consumer spending and investment growth. This simply means that GDP falls percent-age-wise because of the fall of its components, which in its turn is made to depend on a silly psychological motive such as 'animal spirits'. This is hardly an explanation in the absence of the objective reason why rate of growth of the components falls. The reason is as follows. If investments rise, a greater portion is invested in assets than in labour power (as determined by new technologies). As seen in the previous chapter, the rate of profit falls because the labour power employed and thus the surplus value produced per unit of capital falls. If the rate of profit falls, less profits are available to invest in each unit of new invest-ments. It follows that new investments grow at a slower pace. Labour power falls. Output increases, but at a lower rate, as shown in Figure 4.2.

This is not a linear movement; it is the tendency. There are many coun-ter-tendencies to falling profitability, especially the rising rate of surplus value. But empirical research shows that the latter cannot hold back the former. The slowdown in real GDP growth is particularly notable for the imperialist bloc of countries.[5] This slowing trend in real GDP growth is matched by the secular decline in the profitability of capital in the imperialist bloc. The pie is growing ever more slowly. In the wake of this long-run persistent economic deterioration in both output growth and profitability, the imperialist countries are like

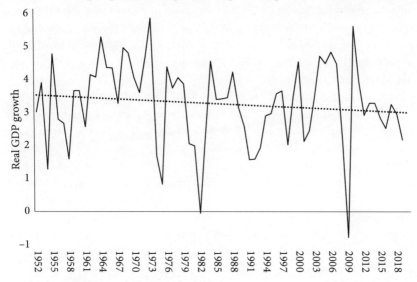

Figure 4.1   G20 countries annual real GDP growth rate 1950–2019 (%)
Source: Penn World Tables 10.0, authors' calculations.

Figure 4.2   G20 rate of profit (%)
Source: Penn World Tables 10.0, authors' calculations.

hungry wolves, which when the game gets scarcer, not only take an extra chunk out of the weaker prey, but also increasingly cut each other's throats. The inflow of surplus value into the imperialist countries from the rest of the world has helped to slow down the deterioration in output growth and profitability but has not reversed it. The imperialist countries get a larger share of the shrinking quantity of surplus value at the cost of the dominated countries. But this larger share cannot reverse the fall in profitability. Nevertheless, the imperialist appropriation of surplus value through unequal exchange in trade (see below) is an important counter-tendency to the decreasing growth of surplus value in the imperialist countries.[6]

Marx focused mainly on the falling rate of profit within a nation. Within it, the national rate of profit falls because sectors compete by introducing labour-saving and productivity-increasing new technologies, thus raising the organic composition of capital (OCC henceforth). In this chapter, we extend Marx' analysis and apply it to international trade and investment between the imperialist and the dominated bloc. Our empirical research reveals the *specificity of the law of profitability under imperialism*. The downward movement in profitability is because (a) *both* blocs' rates of profit fall; (b) the dominated countries' profitability is *persistently above* that of the imperialist ones because of their lower OCC; and (c) the dominated countries' profitability, while persistently higher than in the imperialist countries, *falls more* than in the imperialist bloc.

Since 1974, the rate of profit of the imperialist (G7) bloc has fallen by 20 per cent, but the higher rate of the dominated bloc has fallen by 32 per cent. This leads to a *convergence* of the two blocs' profit rates over time (Figure 4.3).

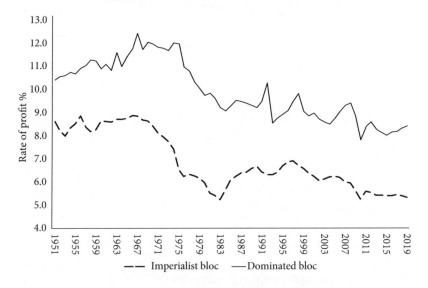

Figure 4.3   Rate of profit in imperialist and dominated blocs (%)

Development economics argues for a convergence upward, that is, the 'under-developed' or 'emerging market' economies approach the level of wealth of the 'developed' ones. As Figure 4.3 shows, the two blocs do converge, but *downwards in profitability*. In spite of the different pace at which the rate of profit tends to fall in the imperialist and the dominated countries, the cause is the same, namely, the inability of the counter-tendencies, especially of the increase in the rate of surplus value, to counter sufficiently the rise in the organic composition of capital, as Marx's law of profitability argues.[7]

4.2 PRODUCTIVITY AND IMPERIALISM

In the Marxist analysis of modern capitalism, the focus is on competition through technological development. As mentioned above, capitals compete basically by introducing new techniques, which are incorporated into new means of production, or non-financial assets. New techniques, on the one hand, shed labour so that less value and surplus value is produced. On the other hand, due to greater productivity, less labour produces a bigger output of use values. New technologies are both labour-shedding *and* productivity-increasing. The primary role of technological competition holds, both within and between nations.

But between nations there is a new factor on the scene: the different countries' rates of exploitation. Here Marx introduces an important difference. While within a nation we can assume a tendential equalisation of the different sectors' rates of exploitation, 'On the universal market ... the integral parts are the individual countries. The average intensity of labour changes from country to country; here it is greater, there less. These national averages form a scale, whose unit of measure is the average unit of universal labour.'[8] So, if countries are considered, what counts is the average intensity etc. of labour *within* each country. These national averages form a scale and thus do not aggregate in an international average because the factors that make possible the formation of an average within a country (labour's freedom of movement, trade unions etc.) are relatively inoperative across national boundaries. *There is no tendential equalisation of the rates of surplus value in the universal economy*. This bears directly on the notion of productivity.

Productivity is usually defined as GDP per unit of labour. However, the numerator (GDP) can rise both because more advanced technologies increase the quantity of use values per unit of labour *and* because of an increase in the rate of exploitation, that is, by raising the length of the working day and the intensity of labour. But only the former measures productivity. The latter measures exploitation. This is stressed by Marx: the productivity of labour 'is expressed in the relative extent of the means of production that one worker ... turns into products' (Marx, 1976, p. 773). There is no mention of the effect of exploitation on output. Since in the measurement of the GDP the rate of exploitation plays a part, assets must replace GDP in the numerator of the productivity ratio. This is the ratio of the mass of assets per unit of labour. This is what Marx calls the technical composition of capital (TCC). Since new technologies are productivity-increasing but labour-shedding, the TCC tends to grow.

However, if assets are considered as use values, the productivity ratios cannot be compared: use values are by definition non-quantitative and non-commensurable. For the TCC to be quantified and compared, assets must be expressed in value and thus money terms. Then productivity is the value of assets divided by labour units. This applies both between and within sectors, that is, for the economy as a whole, as shown in Figure 4.4.

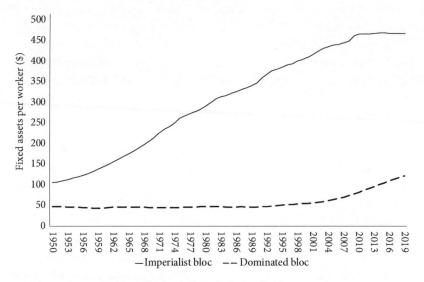

Figure 4.4   Technical composition of capital in the imperialist (IC) and dominated bloc (DC) $ billion per employee

Source: Penn World Tables 10.0, authors' calculations.

The TCC in the imperialist bloc has a consistently much higher productivity than the dominated bloc and the gap has tendentially widened from 1950 up to the 2007–08 crisis, at which point the TCC has started to rise faster in the dominated bloc. The narrowing of the gap from 2008 has probably to do with the fact that around that time China's investments in fixed new capital (and thus in assets with a higher TCC) started to close the gap with those of the US.

Productivity ratios are meaningful only if they indicate profitability. But for the rates of profit to be computed, labour units must be expressed as wages. This is the *value composition of capital*, that is, total value divided by the mass of wages. Marx calls the value composition of capital as determined by the TCC, the *organic composition of capital* (from now on, OCC). The OCC is affected by the value of both the assets and of labour power. So productivity can be measured either directly by using the TCC or indirectly by means of the OCC, given that the OCC is determined by the TCC through the value composition. The difference between the TCC and the OCC resides in the denominator: it is units of labour in the former and wages in the latter.

The OCC of the IC has been consistently higher than that of the DC (Figure 4.5). Since 1970, the OCC of the IC has risen 50 per cent while the OCC of the DC has risen 20 per cent. Up to the early 2000s, the OCC of the DC was closing the gap with the IC. But after that there was a significant decline in most DC countries (excepting China).

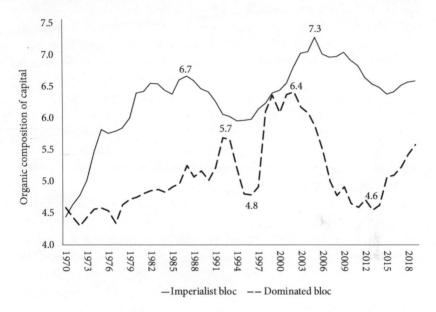

Figure 4.5   The organic composition of capital in the imperialist and dominated blocs
Source: Penn World Tables 10.1, authors' calculations.

4.3 LENIN AND MODERN IMPERIALISM

Before we analyse some of the various methods of transfer of surplus value from the dominated economies to the imperialist ones, let us reconsider Lenin's notion of economic imperialism, as summed up in five well-known points from his 1916 work. They are:

1.   The concentration of production and capital, developed to such a high stage that it has created monopolies, which play a decisive role in economic life.

2. The merging of bank capital with industrial capital and the creation, on the basis of this 'finance capital', of a 'financial oligarchy'.
3. The export of capital, which has become extremely important, as distinguished from the export of commodities.
4. The formation of international capitalist monopolies, which share the world among themselves.
5. The territorial division of the whole world among the greatest capitalist powers is completed.

These features are still relevant now.[9] However, a list of features does not constitute a theory. Lenin's five points should be subsumed under a unifying theoretical frame from which they can be derived. In our view, *economic imperialism* is a system of international social relations *basically* founded on long-term technological differentials in which the high-technology, high-productivity imperialist countries (and thus with higher OCCs) persistently capture in a variety of ways the surplus value generated in the low-technology and low OCC dominated countries. Persistent unequal levels of technology are the necessary condition for the persistent appropriation of surplus value in a variety of ways. In this sense, they are determinant. We stress 'basically' because there is another great source of loss of surplus value by the DC, namely, their higher rate of exploitation. But as we shall see below, this too is determined by the OCC differentials.

Economic imperialism is in the first instance the appropriation of surplus value by high-technology *companies* from low-technology *companies* in different countries. Moreover, companies with headquarters located in the imperialist countries can invest in subsidiaries in the dominated countries. The profits repatriated are an appropriation of surplus value generated by labour in the dominated countries. So, the *imperialist countries* can be defined as those countries with a *persistently* higher number of high-technology companies and thus *with persistently higher national average OCC*. Their average technological development is persistently higher than the national average of other countries. The latter are thus technologically and economically dominated.

On this basis, we can refine our definition of the two blocs: the bloc of the imperialist high-technology countries (from now on, HTC) with a persistently higher average OCC and lower average rate of surplus value and the bloc of the dominated low-technology countries (LTC) with a high average rate of surplus countries and a persistently lower average OCC. The OCC differentials and rates of surplus value differentials determine the appropriation of surplus value by the imperialist countries not as an *accidental* occurrence or for short-term periods, but for *long, multi-decennial periods*. Even so, this is not an immutable situation. A country can change from a non-imperialist or dominated status to an imperialist position and vice versa (e.g. Japan in the late 19th century). But these changes not only can take decennia to happen. Also, and most important, they do not change the unidirectional flow of surplus value between the two blocs, irrespective of their changing composition.

As pointed out above, within both the LTCs and HTCs, there are low- and high-technology companies. If the profit rates are equalised among countries, companies with a predominance of high technology and average lower rates of exploitation cause a net inflow of surplus value into their country (or bloc). Conversely, low technology and average high rate of exploitation companies cause a net outflow of surplus value from their countries (bloc).

Due to their technological superiority, some countries are *hegemonic* or *leading* in the sense that they impose their policies (economic or otherwise) both on other imperialist countries and on countries of the dominated bloc in order to pursue their own interests. This is accepted by other imperialist countries because in fostering their own economic interests, the hegemonic countries also foster the interests of the capitalists in the other countries within that bloc, even if in a contradictory way. Marx spoke of the capitalists as 'hostile brothers' (1968, p. 29). The US is the hegemonic country within its bloc and Germany within the European Union. In the EU, one common bond is the euro, which is advantageous both to German and to the other European countries' capitals and disadvantageous for labour. The hegemonic imperialist countries become regional powers and gain spheres of political influence within their blocs.

Economic blocs complicate the flow of value. Value flows among (a) hegemonic and non-hegemonic imperialist countries, (b) among imperialist and dominated countries and (c) among dominated countries. This complex movement results in the flow of value between blocs. Outsourcing complicates further this picture. Companies, usually high-technology companies, can commission segments of their production process (from design to the production and to the delivery of the finished product) to firms in foreign countries, possibly in other blocs. Due to their higher technology, the outsourcing companies can appropriate surplus value from the foreign suppliers. But this international value chain does not bring about any substantial change in the nature of imperialism.

4.4 THE ECONOMICS OF IMPERIALISM: THE EVIDENCE

Let us now consider the empirical evidence. First, the official data. They are not value quantities, yet they are telling. Conforming to our analysis, we would expect the imperialist countries to have net cross-border *inflows* of income and for non-imperialist countries to have net *outflows* over time. The IMF defines 'primary income flows' in a country's balance of payments as the net cross-border flows of rent, bank interest and financial asset returns (as well as workers'

125

remittances). This provides a partial but important picture of the level and direction of 'tribute' flows.[10]

We define the imperialist countries as the G7 and the dominated countries as the rest of the G20. The imperialist G7 countries run a persistent and rising annual net primary income surplus that reached over half a trillion dollars in 2019, or 1.4 per cent of G7 GDP. That's a sizeable contribution to the surplus value of the G7 economies. In contrast, the DC countries are leaking large amounts of net primary income – nearly up to $250 billion a year. Even the strongest of the so-called emerging economies are forced to remain in a dominated role – paying out much more than they receive in primary income. And the trend is worsening.

UNCTAD also finds a similar transfer of financial flows (Figure 4.6). Between 2000 and 2017, there were annual transfers of net capital inflows and net income payments to foreign capital, including net changes in international reserves of $200 billion in 2000 and reaching $970 billion in 2012, before dropping back to $500 billion in 2017. When estimated data on net illicit financial flows – available up to 2015 for country aggregates – are added to the (official) data on net financial resource transfers, overall net resource transfers from developing countries are even steeper. Net transfers of financial resources from developing to developed countries far exceed any compensation by net overseas development aid (ODA) flows to developing countries, which averaged less than $100 billion a year.

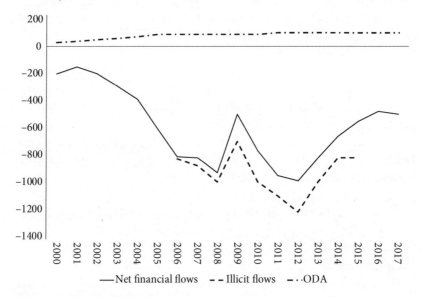

Figure 4.6 Net financial resource transfers from developing economies to developed economies ($ billion)

Source: UNCTAD, https://unctad.org/system/files/official-document/presspb2020d2_en.pdf

Another measure of persistent imperialist domination is the stock of foreign investment. The G7 imperialist countries' stock of investment abroad has persistently outstripped such investment by the larger dominated economies. If China were excluded, the gap would be even larger (Figure 4.7).

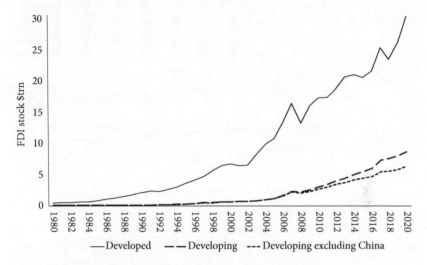

Figure 4.7 Outward foreign direct investment stock ($ trillion)
Source: UNCTAD, authors' calculations, see Appendix 1.

Another important source of value appropriation is seignorage. It is the privilege accruing to the countries whose currency is the international one, most notably the US. The typical case is the US dollar. A substantial quantity of US dollars is used by other countries as (a) international reserves, (b) money circulating within those countries, and (c) a means of payment on the international markets. US imperialism is able to appropriate surplus value thanks to the international use of the dollar, which has become the international currency of trade, investment and store of value.[11] Basically, value (imported foreign commodities) is exchanged for a representation of value (dollars) which is not converted for the imports of US products value. This is international seignorage (Figure 4.8).

The euro is the only possible challenger to the dollar's dominance in seignorage. But so far that has proved illusory as more than two-thirds of all FX reserves globally are still held in dollars. Whether and when the Chinese renminbi will emerge as a real challenger of the US dollar is a matter of debate. But this is unlikely to happen as long as the US retains its technological superiority together with its absolute military predominance.

Unequal exchange (UE) is another important way that imperialism appropriates international surplus value through international trade.[12] We rely on Marx's

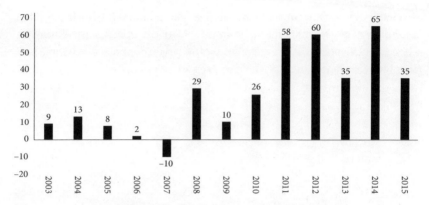

Figure 4.8   Net transfer of US dollar notes to rest of world ($ billion)

Source: J. Louwerse, International Seigniorage The US Dollar and the American Trade Deficit, Thesis, May 2017.

transformation procedure to theorise and compute it. The guiding principle is the difference between value before realisation, or *unrealised* value, and value after realisation, or *realised* value. The value contained in a commodity is its value before that commodity is sold. It is the value right after that commodity exits the ports of the factory. But if that commodity is sold a second time, its unrealised value is the value it realised after the first sale and its realised value is its value when it is sold the second time. The general principle, then, is that given two consecutive periods of purchase/sale of a commodity, the value of a commodity is unrealised before sale at the end of the first period. It becomes realised when that commodity is sold at the moment of sale. When that commodity is resold, the realised value at the end of the first period becomes the unrealised value at the beginning of the second period. This becomes its realised value at the end of the second period. This is the temporalist approach.[13] At the moment of sale, the value of the output is modified because a share of its surplus value is lost to/gained from other commodities due to different OCCs and different international rates of surplus value (RSVs). The tendential result is the formation of an average rate of profit (ARP). This is the value *tendentially* realised. In short, in quantitative terms, realisation is redistribution. Let us provide an example.

Table 4.1   International trade in value terms between two economies

---

Sector A: 80c + 20v + 20s = 120; PP = 130; output 200a; UE = +10, OCC = 4
Sector B: 60c + 40v + 40s = 140; PP =130; output 100b; UE = −10; OCC = 1.5

In Table 4.1, sectors A and B produce a certain physical output (200a and 100b) with a certain value (120A and 140B). At the end of the period of production, the two sectors sell their output to each other and realise the value of their products. But this is not the value before realisation (120 and 140). If this were the case, sector A would not have sufficient purchasing power to buy 100b and sector B would have an excess of purchasing power. Exchange at value contained, or unrealised value would make trade impossible. So both sectors have to sell at an *average* value (price) of 130.[14] This is the production price (PP), which is based on the average rate of profit on the capital invested, and not only actually used. UE is the difference between the surplus realised on the basis of the tendential equalisation of the profit rates versus the surplus value contained before sale. In Table 4.1, UE is 130 − 120 = +10 for sector A; and 130 − 140 = −10 for sector B. *Ceteris paribus*, the positive or negative UE depends on the relative size of the organic composition of capital (OCC) in each sector. In the exchange upon sale, the higher OCC sector (A) gains surplus value from the lower OCC sector (B) because the latter produces more surplus value, a part of which, upon redistribution, is gained by the former.

UE is *not* exploitation. Exploitation is the relation *between capital and labour*, between surplus value and variable capital. UE is a relation *between capitals*, namely, the appropriation of surplus value when a higher OCC capital trades with a lower OCC capital. UE hinges on the formation of an average rate of profit (ARP), exploitation does not.

The existence of the ARP is pivotal for Marx's price theory and thus for UE. Yet is often disputed. A first objection is that supposedly the formation of an ARP is incompatible with monopolistic reality.[15] It should be pointed out that monopolies are an exception; what impedes inter-capitalist competition are oligopolies. The argument is that oligopolies ward off competition through barriers to capital entry because of the sheer size of capital investments needed for the development and application of new technologies. Large investments are thus unavailable to non-oligopolistic capitals. Note that we do not use the term 'free competition', which comes from neoclassical theory; rather, we refer to those capitals that can compete with each other but cannot compete with oligopolies because of insurmountable economic barriers. Thus, supposedly, oligopolies prevent the emergence of *one* average profit rate; instead, there would be one for the oligopolistic and the other for non-oligopolistic sectors.[16]

However, oligopolies too do engage in technological innovation. This is the opposite of the held view that oligopolies slow down the introduction of innovations (Kalecki; see Sawyer, 1988, p. 54). If an oligopoly applies a productivity-increasing new technology, its greater output is exchanged for the output of other monopolies with a lower OCC. So a transfer of value takes place from the latter to the former, just as in the non-oligopolistic sectors. Moreover, oligopolies invest in each other's activities (as in conglomerates). So, an average rate of profit can arise even within an oligopolistic market.

It could be argued that *within a country* there are two tendencies towards two national average profit rates, one for each of the two sectors (the oligopolistic and the non-oligopolistic one). Supposedly, this would undermine Marx's theory. However, this would be consistent with the theory because the prerequisites for the formation of the ARP would be lacking in the monopolistic sector. But this conclusion changes if countries are considered not in isolation, but as elements of the *international* economy. For Marx, 'on the universal market the integral parts are the individual countries'. The profitability determining the transfer of surplus value necessary for the formation of an international ARP is *the profitability of the whole country, the average of the profitability of all capitals within a country, both monopolistic and not.* All capitals, both monopolistic and not, contribute to the inter-country transfer of surplus value and thus to the formation of *a national average rate of profit which is an aliquot part of the international ARP.* So, from the perspective of the 'universal market', in each country there emerges only one ARP.[17]

A second objection is whether the ARP is a real quantity or simply a statistical average devoid of economic substance. In the latter case, it could not be argued that the transfers of surplus value (through UE) computed on the basis of the ARP are real. If empirical observation, it is held, does not show a convergence towards an empirically observable average, then this is proof that there is no such (real) average. Only the scatters are real and the ARP is imagined, unreal.[18] The answer depends upon whether we hold a static view or a dynamic one. But reality is not static: 'all that is solid melts into air' (Marx and Engels, 2010, p. 487). If reality is considered dynamically, as constantly changing, it is clear that due to capitals in competition, the different rates of profit constantly overtake each other *and in so doing* create a tendential average (something that becomes the more evident the higher the speed of the overtaking), whether that average is represented by a specific capital or not. Then the statistical average depicts the tendency.

The international UE is an application of the procedure above to the international economy. Basically, countries replace sectors within a country. If their output is sold directly on the international markets, that value is the international realised value. If that output is first sold on the national market and then resold abroad, the value (of which the GDP is a proxy) is realised national value, but it is also the unrealised international surplus value as long as it is not sold on the international market. At the moment of sale on the international market, the surplus value contained in the GDP is redistributed through an international ARP. Then the international production prices are the values tendentially realised due to the international equalisation of the national rates of profit. The *difference between the international production prices (international realised surplus value) and the national GDPs (internationally unrealised surplus value)* is the *international UE*. There is nothing mysterious about the GDP being the *realised* national value and the *unrealised* international value. It is a matter of the scope of the analysis, that is, whether the scope is intra- or international.

UE should not be confused with the deficit or surplus of the trade balance. In Table 4.1, let us substitute sector A with the US and sector B with China. Both the US and China export at the international price of 130 and import at a price of 130. *The balance of trade is in equilibrium. Yet the US books a positive UE and China a negative one.*

4.5 ALTERNATIVE VIEWS OF UE

Let us now consider some alternative ways of measuring UE in international trade. Cockshott (2019) holds that UE is not actually a redistribution of surplus value through trade, but comes from the production of surplus value: 'A ton of US maize contains a lot less labour than a ton of Mexican maize. But once imported to Mexico the US maize sells at the same price under Nafta as the domestic variety.' The effect is that 'one hour by a US farmer creates more value than one hour by a Mexican one'. This is incorrect. One hour is one hour and it creates the same quantity of value, no matter where. Cockshott can think differently because he deletes the difference between value created and value realised. If a ton of US maize requires less labour than a ton of Mexican maize, a ton of US maize has a lower value contained because of the higher productivity of US farmers. The lower quantity of US labour which has gone into a ton of maize does not change just because it is exported. Once exported, and if the US and the Mexican maize of a certain quality are sold at the same price, the US agricultural farmers appropriate through UE a share of the surplus value generated in the production of the Mexican maize.

Köhler (1998) identifies UE through the exchange rate mechanism and measures it as the difference between the GDP valued at PPP (purchasing power parity) and at current exchange rates. In the PPP approach, the same basket of goods is identified in all countries. They can be aggregated in the goods making up the GDP. Consider a limited example: the US and Colombia. One computes how many commodities $1 can buy in the US and how many pesos are needed to buy the same commodities produced in Colombia. Suppose an American spends $1 on some commodities produced in the US. If a Colombian spends 4.64 pesos to purchase the same commodities in Colombia, the PPP ratio is $1 = 4.64 pesos. Suppose now that the actual exchange rate (ER) is $1 = 5.52 pesos. An American who exchanges $1 for 5.52 pesos and spends them in Colombia can purchase more Colombian commodities. The measure of this difference is the exchange rate deviation, $d = ER/PPP$. In the example above, $d = 5.52/4.64 = 1.23$. Then, $T = X^*d - X$ where T is unequal exchange and X is the volume of exports from a low-wage country to high-wage countries.

There are two critical objections to this measure of UE. First, seen from the perspective of the US, if the US appropriates goods from Colombia, it is *both* US capital and US labour that benefit from it. Then it becomes possible to argue that capital in the IC 'exploits' labour in the DC (whereas it is capital in the DC that exploits labour in the DC). Worse, it can be argued that labour in the IC exploits labour in the DC. The interests of the US and Colombian labour are objectively contradictory. Köhler's theory is inherently anti-labour. Second, there is a logical contradiction here. On the one hand, it is argued that both capital and labour in the IC profit from UE. But on the other, only *capitals* engage in international trade. So it cannot be held that both capital and labour appropriate use value through international trade.

Hickel et al. have also used exchange rate differentials to quantify unequal exchange since 1960. The authors find the IC (or Global North, or 'advanced economies') appropriated from the South commodities worth $2.2 trillion in Northern prices. Over the whole period, drain from the South totalled $62 trillion (constant 2011 dollars), or $152 trillion. This amounts to unequal exchange representing up to 7 per cent of 'Northern' GDP and 9 per cent of 'Southern' GDP.[19] This procedure can be subjected to the same criticisms as Köhler's.[20]

Emmanuel's UE (1972) thesis is that 'The capitals invested can themselves be equalized, yet the transfer of value from one country to another will take place nonetheless' (p. 61). This transfer of value, or UE, is caused by 'the institutionally determined wage levels ("rates of surplus value") in the presence of an internationally equalised rate of profit' (p. 64). In the discussion that followed the publication of Emmanuel's works, it became customary to distinguish between 'broad UE' – due to differences in the OCC – and 'narrow UE' – due to differences in wages and rates of exploitation.[21] It can be remarked right away that if by 'capital equalized' Emmanuel means 'rates of profits equalized', then the transfer of value takes place not 'nonetheless' but just 'because' of that equalization. But let us consider Emmanuel's argument in some detail.

Emmanuel submits the following example as in Table 4.2, where K is the total capital invested and c is the constant capital (value) actually used.

Table 4.2   Emmanuel's UE

Country	K	c	v	S	V	PP	UE	RSV	OCC
A	240	50	100	20	170	210	+40	20%	2.4
B	240	50	20	100	170	130	−40	500%	12.0

Note: K = stock of fixed assets; c = depreciation of stock of fixed assets; v = wages; S = surplus value; V = total output in value; PP = production in prices; UE = unequal exchange of value; RSV = rate of surplus value; OCC = organic composition of capital.

In Emmanuel's computation, country B loses value to country A even if B has a higher OCC than A. This is contrary to Marx, but not because Marx is wrong. Rather, it is Emmanuel's computation which is based on incorrect assumptions. First, Emmanuel computes the ARP on the constant capital used (50) rather than on that invested (240) for each capital. This is contrary to Marx but also to the logic followed by the capitalists.

If we correct Emmanuel's computation and use the total capital invested, B still has a negative UE in his example, again a result that seemingly contradicts Marx. The reason is that the inter-sectoral transfer of value is due to both the different OCCs (productivity) and to the different RSVs (exploitation). Productivity ratios must be kept separate from exploitation rates. This becomes evident if the RSV is controlled for and we equalise the two rates of exploitation. Then UE depends only on productivity differentials and B has a positive UE, as in Marx. But if we allow different rates of exploitation, then while B gains surplus value due to its higher OCC, it loses more due to the equalisation of its much greater RSV. The ratio between the two RSVs (500/20 = 25) is greater than that between the two OCC (12.0/2.4 = 5). *If the RSV is taken into consideration together with the OCC, the transfer of value depends on whether the ratio between the two RSVs is greater or smaller than the ratio between the two OCCs.* If the former ratio is greater than the OCC ratio, a country loses surplus value due to exploitation even if its OCC is greater.

Another way to compute UE is through Input-Output analysis. These tables have the advantage of identifying which sectors within different countries are responsible for a positive or a negative transfer of value. From this perspective, this method is not an alternative but complementary to ours. However, the input-output tables do not compute prices on the basis of the equalisation of the profit rates and thus of the production prices derived from such an equalisation. But this is an essential step before the market prices can be accounted for. Instead, these tables depict and analyse the dependence of one industry or nation on the others through a set of linear equations connecting market prices only. Within this framework, there is no room for tendential values. However, in spite of this, several authors using the input-output tables have reached many important conclusions broadly consistent with ours (Herrera et al., 2020; Mavroudeas and Seretis, 2018; Nakjima and Izumi, 1995; Ricci, 2018; Tsaliki et al., 2018).

On a different line, Gibson (1980) holds that the labour theory of value has nothing to do with UE. The author mentions two reasons. First, the IC can sell their commodities below their value. But 'buy cheap, sell dear' has nothing to do with UE. Second, 'a transfer of value ... is meaningless if commodities are exchanged at their prices of production'. But UE originates precisely because commodities are exchanged at their production prices.

Finally, Norfield (2014b) challenges that different OCCs are key to understanding flows of value: 'how corporations and countries appropriate surplus value may have little to do with their 'C + V' investment or production! It may have more to do with their commercial and financial power in the world economy! ... It is more important to analyse forms taken by capitalist exploitation today than to waste time refining C, V, S data.' For Norfield (2014b) the OCC differentials are not the determining factor of the international appropriation of surplus value: 'this has nothing to do with imperialism as something special in a new phase of capitalism! It is a normal feature of the capitalist market. Instead, the economic content of imperialism should show how the more powerful countries exert economic power over the oppressed.' We agree that the (international) appropriation of surplus value is a normal feature of capitalism, but what Norfield disregards is the specificity of this appropriation within modern imperialism.

4.6 SUPER-EXPLOITATION

A more recent critique of Marx's UE as a key explanation of how imperialism appropriates value from the dominated economies is that of 'super-exploitation' in the dominated countries. This thesis was first developed by Marini in the 1970s.[22] It is argued that super-exploitation is a *third* type of exploitation, in addition to the production of absolute and relative surplus value, as in Marx. By super-exploitation is meant the reduction of workers' consumption beneath its 'normal' limit.[23] Recently, this view has been embraced by some contemporary authors.[24] But it is problematic.

First, against what should super-exploitation be measured? What is the 'normal' minimum consumption? Within a nation, the term of comparison is the average quantity and value of the wage goods, that is, the average value of labour power. So if sections of the labour force are paid less than this value, they are super-exploited. There is nothing new in this.

In a national economy, there can be different levels of exploitation, that is, different wage levels, different intensities of labour and different lengths of the working day. In this case, super-exploitation comes with lower wages relative to those segments of labour that are paid the wage deemed socially necessary for the reproduction of the working class in that national economy. Hundreds of millions of workers everywhere, not just in in the 'Global South', are paid below the value of the labour power, the cost of its reproduction – in the US, Germany, Italy, Spain; a large portion of this falls upon the migrant workers in those 'advanced' countries.

Problems arise if the term super-exploitation is extended to comparisons between nations. A national average is a meaningful concept because, within the national borders, labour power is relatively free to move from lower paid (higher rates of exploitation) to higher paid jobs or sectors (or lower rates of exploitation). This movement – plus the action of other factors, like trade unions and legislation for a minimum wage etc., gives rise to a tendential average.

But what holds within a country does not necessarily hold between countries. Different countries have different socially accepted such parameters. It is incorrect to talk of 'super-exploitation' internationally, of labourers in the 'North' relative to labourers in the 'South', simply because wages in the latter are lower than in the former. There is no level of wages socially accepted as 'normal' by all nations. It is not only possible but a general rule that the levels of wages in many DC are lower than in the IC. But this does not mean that the former are lower and the latter are higher than an average *international* level. The term 'super-exploitation' indicates a wrong theorisation. Indeed, the formation of an international wage level would bring irreparable damage to the super-exploitation thesis. The formation of an average presupposes necessarily a redistribution from 'more' to 'less'. So, value would flow from high-wage to low-wage countries, contrary to the super-exploitation thesis. In reality, there is a hierarchy of national average wages and rates of exploitation, some higher than others; on this basis, there is little 'flow'.

'The reduction of workers' consumption below its normal limit' presupposes the same normal limit (e.g. 200 grams of rice per person per day) in different countries. So, workers receiving 150 grams of rice in a country could be said to be super-exploited relative to workers in another country who receive 200 grams. But what is the normal limit of consumption of rice in one nation is not normal in another nation, and comparison becomes impossible if the workers in the other country consume potatoes instead of rice. There is no internationally valid normal limit to consumption if consumption refers to use values.

So we need to theorise exploitation in terms of value. To this effect, we need Marx's basic assumption that *ceteris paribus* one hour of work produces one unit of value *no matter where it is carried out*. It follows that the international comparison of wage levels must rely on the *value* of wage goods (the number of hours of necessary labour) relative to surplus value, irrespective of the wage goods' quantity and physical features.

Having clarified this, the point of dispute is whether the rates of exploitation are higher in the DC than in the IC or vice versa. The higher the productivity, the lower the necessary labour time to produce wage goods, and *ceteris paribus*, the higher the rate of surplus value. So labour is more exploited in the IC on this basis. Vice versa, the lower the productivity, the higher the necessary labour time and the lower the rate of surplus value. Exploitation is lower in the DC and higher in the IC. But this is only a first, provisional, conclusion.

To contain the loss of value, the DC reduce wages, lengthen the working day and increase the intensity of labour; in short, they increase the rate of exploitation. A share of this extra surplus value is lost through UE to the IC and another share is retained by the DC. This is what interests capital. What interests labour is that the RSV in the DC increases due to capitalist competition and that it increases above that of the IC. When the effects of capitalist competition are taken into consideration, labour is more exploited in the DC than in the IC. In what follows, we explain these points one by one.

We can measure the contribution of the differential of the OCCs and the rate of surplus value between the IC and DC blocs. We find that an average of 64 per cent of the value transfer was due to the higher OCC differential of the IC over the DC and 36 per cent due to the higher rate of surplus value differential of the DC to the IC (Figure 4.9).

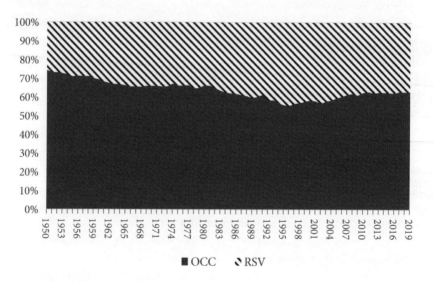

Figure 4.9   Relative contribution of OCC and RSV to value transfer between IC and DC (%)

Source: Penn World Tables 10.0, Appendix 2.

The super-exploitation thesis too holds that labour in the DC is more exploited than in the IC. But differently from our theory, it rejects Marx's value perspective. It stresses the workers' miserable living and working conditions in many dependent countries of the 'Global South' as evidence that labour is more exploited in those countries than in the imperialist ones. However, exploitation and poverty are not the same. Exploitation is in terms of (surplus) labour and thus value; poverty is in terms of use values. Even if the effects of international capitals competition are disregarded, in the DC the rate of surplus value is lower, but the productivity of labour can be so low that relatively few wage goods (use values) can be produced in the same labour time. So, poverty is greater even if the rate of surplus value is lower. *In the DC workers are poorer and yet can be less exploited.* But for the super-exploitation thesis in the DC labour is more exploited because it is poorer.

Indeed, the substitution of categories such as North/South, or East/West, or centre/periphery for imperialist versus dominated is a gigantic step backward in the analysis: it suggests that the fundamental contradiction 'capital versus labour' is replaced by 'rich versus poor' and contributes to the confusion between exploitation and poverty. It is on the basis of this confusion that the super-exploitation theory denies that the workers in the DC are less exploited than in the IC, thus leaving behind Marx's value theory. Workers in the DC are indeed more exploited, but *not* for the reasons adduced by the super-exploitation thesis.

Marx's approach to UE must be extended because it ignores the appropriation of surplus value by the IC capitals from the DC capitals. But it must be extended following Marx's theory rather than forgetting it. As Marx remarks, 'Capitals invested in foreign trade can yield a higher rate of profit, because, in the first place, there is competition with commodities produced in other countries with inferior production facilities, so that the more advanced country sells its goods above their value even though cheaper than the competing countries.'[25] Tendentially, commodities exchange at international production prices, the prices at which, tendentially, all average OCC capitals in the different sectors in different countries realise the average rate of profit. At these prices, the IC appropriate a share of the surplus value produced in the DC. This is international unequal exchange (UE). Profitability falls in the DC on this account. This unleashes capital's attack on labour and consequent increase in the RSV in the DC. Then exploitation in the DC increases above that of the IC.

A further claim of the super-exploitation thesis is that the greater exploitation in the DC is due to workers in the IC exploiting workers in the DC. However, if workers are more exploited in the DC, the reason is that the agents of exploitation are the capitalists in the DC, not the workers in the IC. The super-exploitation thesis holds that the competition between capital and labour (within both the IC and the DC) has been superseded by that between the workers in the imperialist countries and those in the dominated countries. Supposedly, the former exploit the latter. This borders on the ridiculous. The workers in the imperialist countries lack the means (of production) needed to exploit the workers in the dominated countries. This thesis is not only theoretically wrong; it is also a gift to capital in that it theorises the irreconcilability of interests within international labour. In short, this is a pro-capital reactionary thesis, which deforms Marx's theory beyond recognition.

Lenin had already seen the matter in the proper perspective by focusing on what he called the 'labour aristocracy', namely, that a share of the surplus value appropriated by the IC's capitals from the DC's capitals may be redistributed to sections of labour in the ICs. But this is possible only because workers in the DC have been previously exploited by capital in the DC and a share of the surplus value has then been transferred through unequal exchange from capital in the DC to capital in the IC and not from labour to labour.

The capitalists in the dominated countries do not perceive reality in terms of value and thus are not aware of this loss of value. Rather they see the monetary manifestation of this loss (negative UE), that is, lower prices and profits as a consequence of inferior technologies. As a rule, their technological level remains behind that of the IC. If they cannot compete technologically, they increase the rate of exploitation, that is, slash wages and force longer working hours and speed up the pace of work, often with the help of military dictatorships and other repressive methods. So, higher rates of exploitation in the dominated countries are *objectively determined* by the imperialist countries' vastly more efficient technologies. Higher RSVs are the dominated capitals' weapon against the loss of profitability due to inferior technologies and their labourers are their cannon fodder.

According to widespread opinion, wages in the 'super-exploited' countries follow a downward tendential line. Figure 4.10 shows that wages are much lower in the dominated countries compared to the G7 imperialist countries, but also that the ratio has risen from about 8 per cent in the 1970s to 17 per cent now (with most of the rise since the 1990s), although the rise is slower if China is excluded. In the period from 1992 to 2017, real wages rose an average of 1.7 per cent a year in the IC, while they rose 8.2 per cent a year in the DC, contrary to the super-exploitation thesis.

The super-exploitation thesis should also be taken to task because of the contention that it is imperialist capital alone that exploits labour in the dominated countries. If this were the case, a substantial share of imperialist foreign direct investments (FDI) would have to flow to the dominated countries. The figures tell a different story. In 2017, five host countries – the Netherlands, the UK, Luxembourg, Ireland and Canada – accounted for more than half of the US outward FDI while the UK, Japan, Luxembourg, Canada and the Netherlands accounted for more than half of inward FDI in the US. Thus, more than half of the inward and outward US FDI is accounted for by five imperialist countries. A similar result obtains for the OECD developed economies. The share of FDI inflows into the G7 imperialist countries compared to G7 FDI outflows is

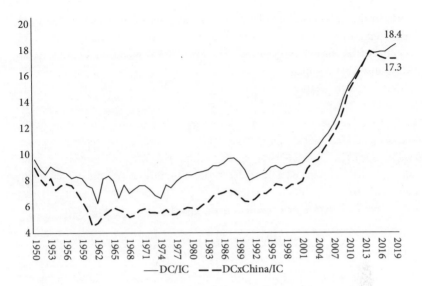

Figure 4.10   Ratio of average wages of dominated bloc to imperialist bloc
Source: Penn World Tables 10.0, authors' calculations.

consistently around 70 per cent and has even increased slightly over the last 50 years. The majority of G7 FDI flows is within the imperialist bloc.[26]

Equally objectionable is the super-exploitation claim that "'Northern" firms do not compete with "Southern" firms [and that] the lead firms' relationship with their suppliers is complementary, not competitive.'[27] This surprising idea is based on a confusion between use values and value and as such marks the definitive departure of the super-exploitation theory from Marx's value theory. Technical complementarity and competition for surplus value are two different and co-existing features. Firms are mutually complementary if they, for example, exchange the *use* values they need (components, spare parts, finished products etc.) as inputs for their production. But at the same time, they compete with their suppliers by reducing as much as possible purchase prices, by seeking the cheapest suppliers etc. often with monopsony power. That 'Northern' firms do not compete with their suppliers in the 'South' flies in the face of evidence.

Lastly, some adherents of the super-exploitation theory define imperialism as the imposition of low wages in the 'periphery' by 'metropolitan' capitalism.[28] But surely it is capital in the dominated countries that imposes hunger wages and horrible exploitation conditions of labour in those countries. Corporations moving from the imperialist to the dominated countries do not impose low wages in the dominated countries. Rather, they apply the low wages imposed by 'peripheral' capital. Imperialist capital profits from local capital's dirty preparatory work. As Sam King says:

[The] value produced by Third World workers must first be appropriated by their employer – the Third World capitalist – via appropriation and ownership of the products produced in Third World factories. Only after the capitalist has appropriated the value … can that same value then be forfeited (in part) on the market.

But we disagree that that value is forfeited 'by selling those commodities below their value to First World capital'.[29] Value is not forfeited to the imperialist countries because the dominated countries' commodities are sold *below their value*. Value is forfeited because tendentially those commodities are sold *at their value*, their international production prices. Any further deviations of actual market prices from production prices will only modify that flow of value.

4.7 MEASURING UNEQUAL EXCHANGE IN TRADE

We can calculate UE in two ways: first, on the basis of bilateral trade (*narrow UE* for short); and second, on the basis of multilateral trade (*broad UE*). In Appendix 1 and 2, we explain in detail our data sources and methods of calculation.

International surplus value flows from the DC to the IC because the former generally have a higher rate of surplus value and lower OCC. This section presents empirical evidence to support this thesis.[30] In Figure 4.11, we base our results on eight economies in the G20 as the imperialist bloc (IC) and eleven economies in the G20 as the dominated bloc (DC).[31] Although this does not

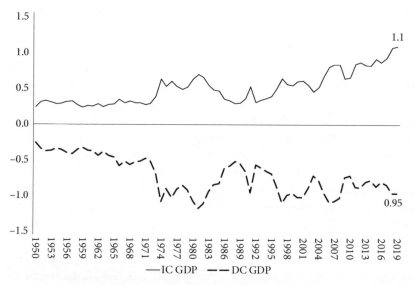

Figure 4.11　Transfer of surplus value for the IC and DC as percentage of GDPs
Source: Penn World Tables 10.0, Appendix 2.

cover all imperialist and dominated economies, it does cover the most important ones and so provides robust support for the trends.

First, we measure UE as transfers of surplus value relative to GDP. We find that the annual transfer of surplus value to the IC bloc averaged about 1 per cent of IC GDP a year while the annual transfer of surplus value from the DC bloc averaged is also about 1 per cent of DC GDP (Figure 4.11).[32] This may seem small, but we are only calculating for eleven DC. No doubt the results would show a larger transfer with more DC included. Moreover, this is an annual transfer and the cumulative transfer over 70 years is thus considerable.

The transfer of surplus value measured against annual profits from exports is much more significant than against GDP. The positive transfer of surplus value to the IC is equivalent to over 40 per cent of annual IC export profits and the negative transfer of surplus value from the DC is equivalent to over 20 per cent of annual DC export profits. The UE transfer is also sizeable when measured against each bloc's bilateral export trade.

We can also measure the contribution of the differential of the OCCs and of the differential of the rates of surplus value between the IC and DC blocs. We find that an average of 60 per cent of the surplus value transfer since 1970 has been due to the OCC differential and 40 per cent due to the rate of surplus value differential.

To sum up, the major cause of UE is the technological superiority of the imperialist countries (high OCC) and the higher rate of surplus value in the dominated countries. Differences in the rates of surplus value between imperialist and dominated countries are significant and this is what matters to labour. But they are a consequence of productivity differentials and play a lesser role in the international transfer of value. Empirically, the question as to which factor contributes more to UE depends upon whether the rate of surplus value is greater or smaller than that of the organic compositions.

In addition to transfers of surplus value through UE, surplus value can be transferred by differences in the market prices in different national currencies compared to the international production price. In conventional economics there are basically three theories of exchange rates. The balance of payments theory states that if a country's balance of payments has a surplus, the greater demand for its currency causes its appreciation, and vice versa for a deficit. Exchange rates tend towards the point at which the balance of payments is in equilibrium. The purchasing power parity theory holds that exchange rates tend towards the level at which the 'purchasing power' between two countries is equalised. This is when the quantities of the countries' currencies can buy the same basket of goods in both countries. At that point, exchange rates have reached their equilibrium level. The monetary theory postulates that the exchange rates are determined through the balancing of the total demand and supply of the national currency in each country. Whatever their differences, these theories share a common matrix: namely, the fundamental, empirically unproven, internally inconsistent and ideologically laden postulate that the capitalist economy tends towards equilibrium, however defined. Yet it is for all to see that the capitalist economy is a non-equilibrium system. It tends not to equilibrium, but to economic and financial crises.[33]

More recently, Shaikh and Antonopoulos (2013) have submitted that 'the sustainable real exchange rate is that which corresponds to the relative competitive position of a nation, as measured by its relative real unit labor costs' (p. 210). The advantage of this approach is that it relates competitivity to the exchange rates (XR). The authors reckon that the DC can improve their profitability (competitive position) by lowering their labour costs while the IC do that by raising their productivity. This is correct. But the point is that the DC lower their wage levels *because* of their lower productivity. So the exchange rates should react to productivity differentials rather than to wage differentials.

We offer a different explanation. As seen above, the IC gain surplus value from the DC through UE in international trade. It follows that if the DC has a lower OCC, *the higher the volume of its exports, the greater the loss of surplus value.* The DC's *profits rise* but the *rate of profit falls.* As a counter-measure, the DC can reduce wages and increase exploitation. But there is an alternative: devaluation. Consider changes in the exchange rate (XR) between the US dollar and the Mexican peso (MXN). In 1991 it was $1= MXN 2.0. By 2021 it was $1= MXN 25.0 (Figure 4.12). In 2021, US-Mexico trade increased to the point that the US became Mexico's major trading partner. Exports to and imports from the US now account for 75 per cent of Mexico's total foreign trade. At the same time, the US appropriated a vast and increasing share of Mexican profits generated in the export sectors.

In the perception of the capitalists, devaluation is meant to increase exports and to correct the deficit in the balance of trade. So it would seem that the XR tends towards the point at which the deficit is corrected. At that point, the movement in the XR would stop (the equilibrium perspective). But in reality, *the XR is determined by a country's productivity.* The higher the TCC in the US relative to Mexico, the greater the devaluation of the peso needed to compensate the export sector. If the DC productivity falls relative to that in the IC, less use values are produced and inasmuch as less are exported relative to the other countries, the demand for that country's currency falls and the exchange rate devalues. The XR follows the reciprocal movement of the TCC, that is, is determined by each country's relative productivity.

Under imperialism, Mexico and other dominated countries can never achieve equality in technical composition with the US. So devaluation of the peso and other currencies against the dollar is a long-term tendency. In the US-China

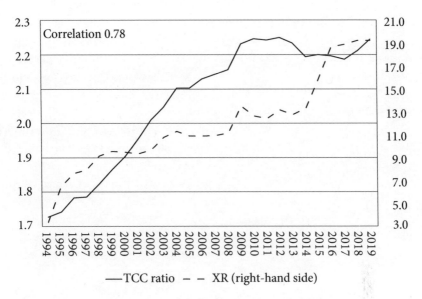

Figure 4.12 US and Mexico TCCs and the exchange rate 1994–2019

case the US-China TCC differential falls as China catches up in technology and so the Chinese renminbi can appreciate against the US dollar.

The greater the differential between the two TCCs, the greater the need by the DC to devalue and the greater the appropriation of surplus value by the IC. But that surplus value is partly produced by the DC and partly appropriated by the IC if it revalues vis-à-vis a third country. So the international flows of value due to the movements in the XR hide the intricacies of reciprocal gains and losses. As an example, consider Taiwan. From 1990 to 2021, the Taiwan dollar appreciated consistently against the Turkish lira. So Taiwan gained surplus value from Turkey. At the same time, the Taiwan dollar depreciated relative to the US dollar. So the US gained surplus value from Taiwan, which in its turn gained surplus value from Turkey. So a share of the surplus value (and thus output) appropriated by the US from Taiwan comes from the Taiwanese workers and another share comes from the Turkish workers.

4.8 IS CHINA IMPERIALIST?

The relation between these two economic giants of the US and China has become increasingly important in the 21st century. A critical question arises: is China an imperialist nation? We find that there is a clear transfer of surplus value from China to the IC bloc, averaging 5–10 per cent of China's GDP since the 1990s. The IC bloc has gained an average of 1 per cent of its GDP from trade with China (Figure 4.13).

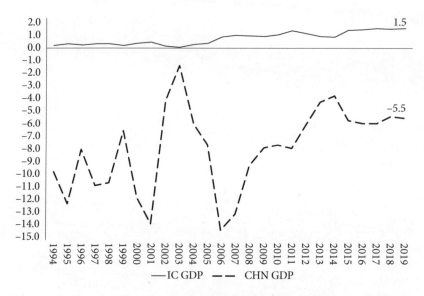

Figure 4.13 Transfer of surplus value between China and the IC bloc as % of GDPs

As China's exports to the imperialist bloc have expanded, the negative transfer of surplus value has risen to reach over 13 per cent of China's export profits. Indeed, China's negative UE transfer to IC averages over 60 per cent of its annual exports to the IC. When we measure the *broad* UE (as defined above), it also shows that the IC bloc gained an average of 5 per cent of its export value in UE in trade with China and the rest of the DC, while China had a net loss on average of around 2 per cent of its exports with the IC and the rest of the DC. The rest of the DC took an average hit to the equivalent of 15 per cent of all its exports to China and the IC. This suggests that China gained little or nothing in surplus value from its trade with the rest of the DC. This confirms that China is not an imperialist country by our definition; on the contrary, it clearly fits into the dominated bloc. If we look at the net value transfer between China and the US alone, up to the 1990s, trade between the US and China was small and thus China's negative UE was limited. But after that, the annual transfer of surplus value from China to the US increased and rose to 6-8 per cent of China's GDP. This is further evidence that China is still part of the group of the dominated countries. If China increases its exports to the US, its balance of trade improves, but its UE worsens because China still has a lower level of productivity. The productivity differential has narrowed over the last 70 years, but China's average productivity level is still less than 25 per cent of that of the US.

For an 'emerging economy' there is no other way to 'development' than by raising productivity through more efficient technologies. But the dominated countries are not catching up fast enough to reduce the transfer of surplus value through trade to the imperialist countries. This general conclusion applies to China as well.

4.9 SUMMARY

In this chapter, we looked at the modern economic aspects of imperialism through the prism of value. We defined imperialist exploitation as a persistent and long-term net appropriation of surplus value by the high-technology imperialist countries from the low-technology dominated countries. We paid particular attention to unequal exchange (UE) of value in international trade by extending Marx's value theory to the international setting. We found that the differentials of the organic composition of capital and the rate of exploitation determine the amount of surplus value transferred by UE in trade among countries, confirming Marx's value theory. And we found that movements in exchange rates between countries are generally determined by the differentials between average productivity of labour in each country. And because imperialism will never allow the gap in productivity levels to be closed, the currencies of the dominated countries will always be weaker than the currencies of the imperialist bloc. This applies in spite of possible changes in the composition of the two blocs. Finally, our analysis shows that China is not an imperialist country in terms of production and appropriation of surplus value.

5

Robots, Knowledge and Value[1]

5.1 ROBOTS AND THE LAW OF VALUE

The 21st century is supposed to herald the arrival of robots and artificial intelligence (AI) to replace human labour and expand the productivity of labour to new heights, and in doing so, save the capitalist mode of production from its internal contradictions (which we have spelt out throughout this book).

Let's consider the implications of the advent of the robotic/AI age through the prism of value. Robots are really just more machines although with the extra dimension of learning for themselves through AI. In that sense, there is nothing new in the rise of the robots. The capitalist mode of production is necessarily 'capital-biased', namely, it aims to replace labour by machines over time. So the current mainstream discussion about the introduction of robots is no more than a Marxist economic insight.

One of the basic Marxist theoretical arguments is that the competitive pressure to make profits and maintain profitability forces capitalist producers to reduce the costs of labour power and to increase the costs of machines, or means of production, per unit of capital invested. It may be possible for newly expanding capitalist economies to use huge supplies of cheap labour to create an increasing mass of surplus value rather than using new technology, which decreases the rate of surplus value (or ideally a combination of both, as in China and East Asia). But in more mature (and ageing) economies the supply of cheap labour has run out and capitalists 'in the West' can only compete in world markets by either exporting their capital into the emerging economies (imperialism or globalisation) or finding new technologies that raise labour productivity exponentially.

'Globalisation' was the story of the period from the late 1970s to early 2000s as the 'solution' to falling profitability in the major capitalist economies. But a new downturn in profitability in the late 1990s and the recessions of 2001 and the Great Recession of 2008–09 has put that solution in jeopardy. Indeed, now it is being argued that it is no longer cheaper to build factories and expand business in emerging economies because wages there are rising fast. According to the International Labour Organization in its *World of Work* report, inflation-adjusted average wages in China more than tripled over the decade from 2000 to 2010. And in Asia as a whole, they have doubled. In Eastern Europe and

Central Asia, average wages almost tripled. Yet, in the developed world, wages are just barely higher than they were in 2000.

This has led some to argue that after its 60-year decline, manufacturing may start to return to the advanced capitalist economies. Then profitability will rise again in the major capitalist economies through a new manufacturing revolution. Much is being made of the likes of Apple opening up factories in the US rather than Asia. Apple says it will invest $100 million in producing some of its Mac computers in the US, beyond the assembly work it already does in the country. Over the last few years, companies across various industries, including electronics, automotive and medical devices, have announced that they are 'reshoring' jobs after decades of shipping them abroad.

But this is really so much wishful thinking in the media. General Electric has hired American workers to build water heaters, refrigerators, dishwashers and high-efficiency top-load washers, but continues to add more jobs overseas as well. Apple's iPad and iPhone products, which amount to nearly 70 per cent of its sales, will continue to be made in low-cost centres of manufacturing like China or Vietnam, mostly on contract with outside companies like Foxconn. American manufacturing has been growing in the last two years, but the sector still has two million fewer jobs than it had when the recession began in December 2007. Worldwide manufacturing is growing much faster, even for many of the American-owned companies that are expanding at home. Wage levels may have risen in emerging economies and stagnated in the advanced economies, but the gap is still huge. Hourly compensation costs in manufacturing in the US are about four times those in Taiwan and 20 times those in the Philippines (see the Chapter 4 on modern imperialism). And while some manufacturing may return to the US, it will not bring jobs with it – on the contrary. A new study by McKinsey, the management consultants, finds that manufacturing now contributes 20 per cent of global economic output and 37 per cent of global productivity growth since 1995. But because investment in manufacturing is 'capital-biased', it does not create jobs and is designed to avoid raising wages. Indeed, according to McKinsey, manufacturing employment fell 24 per cent in the advanced economies between 1995 and 2005. The wider global story is revealed by the rise in the industrial workforce in emerging economies and the fall in advanced economies (Figure 5.1).[2]

In the advanced economies, higher profits can only come from raising the productivity of labour or by a reduction in raw material (energy) costs, rather than lowering or holding wages down through the use of more cheap labour. The shale oil and gas revolution in North America and parts of Europe may help reduce energy costs over the next decade (maybe). But getting overall costs down depends very much on the new technologies. That brings us to the issue

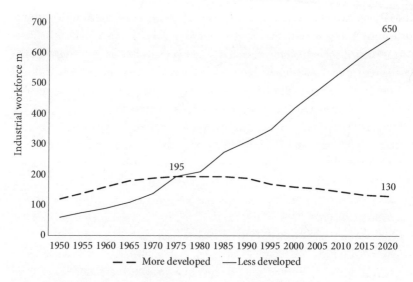

Figure 5.1 Global industrial workforce

of robots, something that is being raised as the imminent way out for advanced capitalist economies to compete in world manufacturing markets.

The International Federation of Robotics (IFR) considers a machine as an industrial robot if it can be programmed to perform physical, production-related tasks without the need of a human controller. Industrial robots dramatically increase the scope for replacing human labour compared to older types of machines, since they reduce the need for human intervention in automated processes. Typical applications of industrial robots include assembling, dispensing, handling, processing (e.g. cutting), and welding – all of which are prevalent in manufacturing industries – as well as harvesting (in agriculture) and inspecting of equipment and structures (common in power plants).

By artificial intelligence is meant machines that do not just carry out pre-programmed instructions but learn more new programmes and instruction by experience and by new situations. AI means in effect robots who learn and increase their intelligence.[3] This could happen to the point where robots can make more robots with increasing intelligence. Indeed, some argue that AI will soon surpass the intelligence of human beings. This is called the 'singularity' – the moment when human beings are no longer the most intelligent things on the planet. Moreover, robots could even develop the senses and form of human beings, thus being 'sentient'.

In some high-profile industries, technology is displacing workers of all, or almost all, kinds. For example, one of the reasons some high-technology manufacturing has lately been moving back to the US is that the most valuable piece of a computer, the motherboard, is basically made by robots, so cheap Asian labour is no longer a reason to produce them abroad. Robots mean that labour costs don't matter so much and capitalists can then locate in advanced countries with large markets and better infrastructure. Even the low wages earned by factory workers in China have not insulated them from being undercut by new machinery. Foxconn plans to purchase one million robots to replace much of the workforce. The robots will take over routine jobs like spraying paint, welding and basic assembly.

Now mainstream economics has noticed that this is not good news for labour and have suggested that 'capital-bias' in technology could explain the falling labour share and growing inequalities. As Krugman put it:

> The effect of technological progress on wages depends on the bias of the progress; if it's capital-biased, workers won't share fully in productivity gains, and if it's strongly enough capital-biased, they can actually be made worse off. So it's wrong to assume, as many people on the right seem to, that gains from technology always trickle down to workers; not necessarily. It's also wrong to assume, as some (but not all) on the left sometimes seem to that rapid productivity growth is necessarily jobs- or wage-destroying. It all depends.[4]

This depends on the class struggle between labour and capital over the appropriation of the value created by labour. And clearly labour has been losing that battle, particularly in recent decades, under the pressure of anti-trade union laws, ending of employment protection and tenure, the reduction of benefits, a growing reserve army of unemployed and underemployed and through the globalisation of manufacturing.

According to an ILO report,[5] in 16 developed economies, labour took a 75 per cent share of national income in the mid-1970s, but this dropped to 65 per cent in the years just before the economic crisis. It rose in 2008 and 2009 – but only because national income itself shrank in those years – before resuming its downward course. Even in China, where wages have tripled over the past decade, workers' share of the national income has gone down (Figure 5.2).

But this is not new in economic theory. Marx explained in detail in *Capital* that this is one of the key features in capitalist accumulation – the capital-bias of technology – something continually ignored by mainstream economics, until now it seems. Marx put it differently to the mainstream. Investment under capitalism takes place for profit only, not to raise output or productivity as such. If profit cannot be sufficiently raised through more labour hours (i.e. more workers and longer hours) or by intensifying efforts (speed and efficiency – time and motion), then the productivity of labour can only be increased by better technology. So, in Marxist terms, the organic composition of capital (the value of machinery and plant relative to the wages of workers) will rise secu-

Figure 5.2 Trends in productivity and wages growth in selected economies

larly. Workers can fight to keep as much of the new value that they have created as part of their 'compensation' but capitalism will only invest for growth if that share does not rise so much that it causes profitability to decline. So capitalist accumulation implies a falling share to labour over time or what Marx would call a rising rate of exploitation (or surplus value).

So could US manufacturing revive under the spread of robotic technologies? Marco Annunziata, chief economist at General Electric company, reckons it could.[6] He claims that a network of 'intelligent machines', software analytics and sensors that he calls the 'industrial internet' can spread through industry, and deliver huge gains in productivity. But the rise in productivity implies decreasing employment and higher rates of exploitation for those retaining their jobs. Harvard's leading economist Ken Rogoff took up the same view:

There are certainly those who believe that the wellsprings of science are running dry, and that, when one looks closely, the latest gadgets and ideas driving global commerce are essentially derivative. But the vast majority of my scientist colleagues at top universities seem awfully excited about their projects in nanotechnology, neuroscience, and energy, among other cutting-edge fields. They think they are changing the world at a pace as rapid as we have ever seen.[7]

If Annunziata and Rogoff are right, does this mean that all is well with capitalism? Will capitalism be saved by robots, while workers will be able to live the happy life of leisure that John Maynard Keynes in the 1930s reckoned would be achieved by capitalism round about now?

Well, clearly, past technology did not do the trick. Those predictions of the 1970s that workers would have to worry more about what to do with their leisure time rather than if they could get enough work to make ends meet have not materialised. But would robots now do the trick?

This first reason for why robotic technology won't save the day is completely ignored or dismissed by mainstream economics because it has no concept of a law of value under capitalism – and for very good ideological reasons. It thinks only in terms of physical things (with money thrown on top) not in value that needs to be appropriated by the owners of capital. The second reason why workers won't get to the leisure society with robots doing the work has been noticed by mainstream economics. It is the falling share of labour in total value. Apart from capital-bias technology, Paul Krugman considers that this may be caused by 'monopoly power', or the rule of 'robber barons'. Krugman puts it this way. Maybe labour's share of income is falling because 'we don't actually have perfect competition' under capitalism, 'increasing business concentration could be an important factor in stagnating demand for labor, as corporations use their growing monopoly power to raise prices without passing the gains on to their employees'.[8]

What Krugman seems to be suggesting is that it is an imperfection in the market economy that creates this inequality and if we root out this imperfection (monopoly) all will correct itself. So Krugman presents the issue in the terms of neoclassical economics. Marxist theory would say it is not monopoly rule, but the rule of capital. Sure, capital accumulates through increased centralisation and concentration of the means of production in the hands of a few. This ensures that the value created by labour is appropriated by capital and that the share going to the 99 per cent is minimised. But this is not monopoly as an imperfection of perfect competition, as Krugman explains it; it is the monopoly of ownership of the means of production by a few. This is the straightforward functioning of capitalism, warts and all.

The falling share going to labour in national income began at just the point when US corporate profitability was at an all-time low in the deep recession of the early 1980s. Capitalism had to restore profitability. It did so partly by raising the rate of surplus value through sacking workers, stopping wage increases and phasing out benefits and pensions. Indeed, it is significant that the collapse in labour's share intensified after 1997 when US profitability again peaked and began to slide again. The counteracting factor under Marx's law of profitability was again applied with a vengeance. According to Emmanuel Saez, the top 1 per cent of US households got 65 per cent of all the growth in the economy since 2002. And the top 0.01 per cent of US households, that is, 14,588 families with income above $11,477,000, saw their share of national income double from 3 per cent to 6 per cent between 1995 and 2007. It's not monopoly power or rising rents going to the 'robber barons' of the monopolies that forced down labour's share, it's just capitalism. Labour's share in the capitalist sector in the US and other major capitalist economies is down because of increased technology and 'capital-bias', from globalisation and cheap labour abroad; from the destruction of trade unions; from the creation of a larger reserve army of labour (unemployed and underemployed); and from ending of work benefits and secured tenure contracts etc. Companies that are not monopolies in their markets probably did more of this than monopolies.

Paul Mason argues that the internet, automation, robots and AI are creating a new economy which cannot be controlled by capitalism.[9] According to Mason, new forces are at work that were replacing the old class struggle between capital and the proletariat, as Marx saw it, with a 'network of communities'. AI technology and the network can lead to a post-capitalist (socialist?) world that cannot be stopped. But are robots and AI set to take over the world of work and thus the economy in the next generation? Will it mean socialist utopia in our time (the end of human toil and a super-abundant harmonious society) or capitalist dystopia (more intense crises and class conflict)?

Industrial robotics has the potential to change manufacturing by increasing precision and productivity without incurring higher costs. 3D printing could generate a new ecosystem of companies providing printable designs on the web, making everyday products endlessly customisable. The so-called 'Internet of Things' offers the possibility to connect machines and equipment to each other and to common networks, allowing for manufacturing facilities to be fully monitored and operated remotely. In health care and life sciences, data-driven decision-making, which allows the collection and analysis of large datasets, is already changing R&D, clinical care, forecasting and marketing. The use of big data in health care has led to highly personalised treatments and medicines. The infrastructure sector, which had no gain in labour productivity in the last 20 years, could be greatly enhanced by, for example: the creation of Intelligent Transportation Systems, which could massively increase asset utilisation; the introduction of smart grids, which could help save on power infrastructure costs and reduce the likelihood of costly outages; and efficient demand management, which could dramatically lower per capita energy use.

Which of these emerging technologies have the greatest potential to drive improvements in productivity? McKinsey Global Institute (MGI) (2013) reckons that 'technologies that matter' are technologies that have the greatest potential to deliver substantial economic impact and disruption in the next decade.[10] Those that make their list are rapidly advancing (e.g. gene-sequencing technology); have a broad reach (e.g. mobile internet); have the potential to create an economic impact (e.g. advanced robotics); and have the potential to change the status quo (e.g. energy storage technology). MGI estimates that the economic impact of these technologies – derived from falls in their prices and their diffusion and improved efficiency – to be between $14 and $33 trillion per year in 2025, led by mobile internet, the automation of knowledge work, the Internet of Things and cloud technology. John Lanchester sums up the picture:

> Computers have got dramatically more powerful and become so cheap that they are effectively ubiquitous. So have the sensors they use to monitor the physical world. The software they run has improved dramatically too. We are on the verge of a new industrial revolution, one which will have as much impact on the world as the first one. Whole categories of work will be transformed by the power of computing and, in particular by the impact of robots.[11]

If robots and AI are fast on their way, will this mean a huge loss of jobs or alternatively new sectors for employment and the need to work fewer hours? In recent work, Graetz and Michaels looked at 14 industries (mainly manufacturing industries, but also agriculture and utilities) in 17 developed countries (including European countries, Australia, South Korea and the US). They found that industrial robots increase labour productivity, total factor productivity and wages. At the same time, while industrial robots had no significant effect on total hours worked, there is some evidence that they reduced the employment of low-skilled workers, and, to a lesser extent, also middle-skilled workers.[12] So in essence, robots did not reduce toil (hours of work) for those who had work, on the contrary. But they did lead to a loss of jobs for the unskilled and even those with some skills. So more toil, not less hours, and more unemployment.

Two Oxford economists, Carl Benedikt Frey and Michael Osborne, looked at the likely impact of technological change on a sweeping range of 702 occupations, from podiatrists to tour guides, animal trainers to personal finance advisers and floor sanders.[13] Their conclusions were frightening:

> According to our estimates, about 47 percent of total US employment is at risk. We further provide evidence that wages and educational attainment exhibit a strong negative relationship with an occupation's probability of computerisation ... Rather than reducing the demand for middle-income occupations, which has been the pattern over the past decades, our model predicts that computerisation will mainly substitute for low-skill and low-wage jobs in the near future. By contrast, high-skill and high-wage occupations are the least susceptible to computer capital.

Lanchester summed up their conclusions: 'So the poor will be hurt, the middle will do slightly better than it has been doing, and the rich – surprise! – will be fine.'

But we should add that, on the other hand, new technologies create new jobs and thus increase employment. All the catastrophic projections ignore this fundamental aspect. Robots do not do away with the contradictions within capitalist accumulation. The essence of capitalist accumulation is that to increase profits and accumulate more capital, capitalists want to introduce machines that can boost the productivity of each employee and reduce costs compared to competitors. This is the great revolutionary role of capitalism in developing the productive forces available to society. But there is a contradiction. In trying to raise the productivity of labour with the introduction of technology, there is a process of labour-shedding. New technology replaces labour. Yes, increased productivity might lead to increased production and open up new sectors for employment to compensate. But over time, a capital-bias or labour-shedding means less new value is created (as labour is the only form of value) relative to the cost of invested capital. There is a tendency for profitability to fall as productivity rises. In turn, that leads eventually to a crisis in production that halts or even reverses the gain in production from the new technology. This is solely because investment and production depend on the profitability of capital in our modern mode of production. So an economy increasingly dominated by the Internet of Things and robots under capitalism will mean more intense crises and greater inequality rather than super-abundance and prosperity.

There are two key assumptions that Marx makes in order to explain the laws of motion under capitalism: (1) that only human labour creates value and (2) over time, investment by capitalists in technology and means of production will outstrip investment in human labour power – to use Marx's terminology, there will be a rise in the organic composition of capital over time. But what does this all mean if we enter the extreme (science fiction?) future where robotic technology and AI leads to robots making robots AND robots extracting raw materials and making everything AND carrying out all personal and public services so that human labour is no longer required for ANY task of production at all?

Let's imagine a totally automated process where no human existed in the production. Surely, value has been added by the conversion of raw materials into goods without humans? Surely, that refutes Marx's claim that only human labour can create value? But this confuses the *dual* nature of value under capitalism: use value and exchange value. There is use value (things and services that people need); and exchange value (the value measured in labour time and appropriated from human labour by the owners of capital and realised by sale on the market). In every commodity under the capitalist mode of production, there is both use value and exchange value. You can't have one without the other under capitalism. But the latter rules the capitalist investment and production process, not the former.

The mainstream economic debate is whether 'technology' will create more jobs than it destroys. After all, the argument goes, new technology may get rid of certain jobs (hand loom weavers in the early 19th century) but provide new ones (textile factories). One thought experiment is that provided by Paul Krugman.[14] In Krugman's celebrated example, imagine there are two goods, sausages and bread rolls, which are then combined one for one to make hot dogs; 120 million workers are divided equally between the two industries: 60 million producing sausages, the other 60 million producing rolls, and both taking two days to produce one unit of output. Now suppose new technology doubles productivity in bakeries. Fewer workers are required to make rolls, but this increased productivity will mean that consumers get 33 per cent more hot dogs. Eventually, the economy has 40 million workers making rolls and 80 million making sausages. In the interim, the transition might lead to unemployment, particularly if skills are very specific to the baking industry. But in the long run, a change in relative productivity reallocates rather than destroys employment.

The story of bank tellers versus the cash machine (ATM) is another example of a technological innovation entirely replacing human labour for a particular task. Did this lead to a massive fall in the number of bank tellers? Between the 1970s (when America's first ATM was installed) and 2010 the number of bank tellers doubled. Reducing the number of tellers per branch made it cheaper to run a branch, so banks expanded their branch networks. And the role gradually evolved away from cash handling and more towards relationship banking. The greater employment in the number of bank tellers is due to the expansion of the number of branches and thus in the number of bank tellers greater than the reduction of bank tellers per branch. In general, technological unemployment can be countered by capital expansion (accumulation). But this is only a counter-tendency and does not contradict the negative effect of new technologies on labour employment.

And even assuming that all jobs lost in one branch are recreated in another, as Marx pointed out with the rise of machines in the 19th century, this is no seamless process of change. As Marx put it:

> The real facts, which are travestied by the optimism of the economists, are these: the workers, when driven out of the workshop by the machinery, are thrown onto the labour-market. Their presence in the labour-market increases the number of labour-powers which are at the disposal of capitalist exploitation … the effect of machinery, which has been represented as a compensation for the working class, is, on the contrary, a most frightful scourge. For the present I will only say this: workers who have been thrown out of work

in a given branch of industry can no doubt look for employment in another branch ... even if they do find employment, what a miserable prospect they face! Crippled as they are by the division of labour, these poor devils are worth so little outside their old trade that they cannot find admission into any industries except a few inferior and therefore over-supplied and under-paid branches. Furthermore, every branch of industry attracts each year a new stream of men, who furnish a contingent from which to fill up vacancies, and to draw a supply for expansion. As soon as machinery has set free a part of the workers employed in a given branch of industry, the reserve men are also diverted into new channels of employment, and become absorbed in other branches; meanwhile the original victims, during the period transition, for the most part starve and perish.[15]

Robots will not be widely applied unless they can deliver more profit for owners and investors in robotic applications. But more robots and relatively less human labour will mean relative less value created per unit of capital invested, because from Marx's law of value, we know that value (as incorporated in the sale of production for profit) is only created by human labour power. And if that declines relatively to means of production employed, then there is a tendency for profitability to fall. So the expansion of robots and AI increases the likelihood and magnitude of profitability crises. So it is very likely that slumps in capitalist production will intensify as machines increasingly replace labour. This is the great contradiction of capitalism: increasing the productivity of labour through more machines reduces the profitability of capital.

Mainstream economics either denies the law of value or ignores it. Back in 1898, neo-Ricardian economist Vladimir Dmitriev, in order to refute Marx's value theory, presented a hypothetical economy where machines (robots) did all and there was no human labour. He argued that as there was still a huge surplus produced without labour, so Marx's value theory was wrong. But Dmitriev's thought experiment is irrelevant because he and other mainstream economists do not understand value in the capitalist mode of production. Value in a commodity for sale is double-sided: there is physical 'use value' in the good or service sold, but there is also 'exchange value' in money and profit that must be realised in the sale. Without the latter, capitalist production does not take place. And only labour power creates such value. Machines create no value (profit). Indeed, Dmitriev's super-abundant robot-only economy would no longer be capitalist because there would be no profit for individual capitalists. As machines replace human labour power, under capitalism, profitability falls even if the productivity of labour rises (more things and services are produced). And falling profitability will periodically disrupt production of individual capitalists because they only employ labour and machines to make profits. So crises are intensified well before we get to Dmitriev's hypothetical robot world.

In our hypothetical all-encompassing robot/AI world, productivity (of use values) would tend to infinity while profitability (surplus value to capital value) would tend to zero. Human labour would no longer be employed and exploited by Capital (owners of the means of production). Instead, robots would do all. This is no longer capitalism. The analogy is more with a slave economy, as in ancient Rome. In ancient Rome, over hundreds of years, the formerly pre-dominantly small-holding peasant economy was replaced by slaves in mining, farming and all sorts of other tasks. This happened because the booty of the successful wars that the Roman republic and empire conducted included a mass supply of slave labour. The cost to the slave owners of these slaves was incredibly cheap (to begin with) compared with employing free labour. The slave owners drove the farmers off their land through a combination of debt demands, requi-sition in wars and sheer violence. The former peasants and their families were forced into slavery themselves or into the cities, where they scraped a living with menial tasks and skills or begged. The class struggle did not end. The struggle was between the slave-owning aristocrats and the slaves and between the aristo-crats and the atomised plebs in the cities.

The question often posed at this point is: who are the owners of the robots and are their products and services going to sell to make a profit? If workers are not working and receiving no income, then surely there is massive overproduction and underconsumption? So, in the last analysis, is it the underconsumption of the masses which brings capitalism down? Again, this is a misunderstanding.[16] Such a robot economy is not capitalist any more; it is more like a slave economy. The owners of the means of production (robots) now have a super-abundant economy of things and services at zero cost (robots making robots making robots). The owners can just consume. They don't need to make 'a profit', just as the aristocrat slave owners in Rome just consumed and did not run businesses to make a profit. This does not deliver an overproduction crisis in the capitalist sense (relative to profit) nor 'underconsumption' (lack of purchasing power or effective demand for goods on a market), except in the physical sense of poverty.

Mainstream economics continues to see the rise of the robots under capital-ism as creating a crisis of underconsumption. As Jeffrey Sachs put it: 'Where I see the problem on a generalised level for society as a whole is if humans are made redundant on an industrial scale (47% quoted in US) then where's the market for the goods?'[17] Or as Martin Ford puts it: 'there is no way to envision how the private sector can solve this problem. There is simply no real alter-native except for the government to provide some type of income mechanism for consumers.'[18] Ford does not propose socialism, but merely a mechanism to redirect lost wages back to 'consumers', but such a scheme would threaten private property and profit. Martin Wolf put it this way:[19]

> The rise of intelligent machines is a moment in history. It will change many things, including our economy. But their potential is clear: they will make it possible for human beings to live far better lives. Whether they end up doing so depends on how the gains are produced and distributed. It is possible that the ultimate result will be a tiny minority of huge winners and a vast number of losers. But such an outcome would be a choice not a destiny. A form of techno-feudalism is unnecessary. Above all, technology itself does not dictate the outcomes. Economic and political institutions do. If the ones we have do not give the results we want, we must change them.

It's a social 'choice' or more accurately, it depends on the outcome of the class struggle under capitalism.

John Lanchester is much more to the point:[20]

> It's also worth noting what isn't being said about this robotified future. The scenario we're given – the one being made to feel inevitable – is of a hyper-capitalist dystopia. There's capital, doing better than ever; the robots, doing all the work; and the great mass of humanity, doing not much, but having fun playing with its gadgets … There is a possible alternative, however, in which ownership and control of robots is disconnected from capital in its current form. The robots liberate most of humanity from work, and everybody benefits from the proceeds: we don't have to work in factories or go down mines or clean toilets or drive long-distance lorries, but we can choreograph and weave and garden and tell stories and invent things and set about creating a new universe of wants. This would be the world of unlimited wants described by economics, but with a distinction between the wants satisfied by humans and the work done by our machines. It seems to me that the only way that world would work is with alternative forms of ownership. The reason, the only reason, for thinking this better world is possible is that the dystopian future of capitalism-plus-robots may prove just too grim to be politically viable. This alternative future would be the kind of world dreamed of by William Morris, full of humans engaged in meaningful and sanely remunerated labour. Except with added robots. It says a lot about the current moment that as we stand facing a future which might resemble either a hyper-capitalist dystopia or a socialist paradise, the second option doesn't get a mention.

But let's come back to the here and now. How likely is it that highly intelligent robots will take over the world of work (and maybe the world) in the near future? It is not going to happen soon, if at all. The level of robotics use has almost doubled in the top capitalist economies in the last decade. Japan and South Korea have the most robots per manufacturing employee, over 300 per 10,000 employees, with Germany following at over 250 per 10,000 employees. The US has less than half the robots per 10,000 employees compared to Japan and the Republic of Korea. The adoption rate of robots increased in this period by 40 per cent in Brazil, by 210 per cent in China, by 11 per cent in Germany, by 57 per cent in the Republic of Korea, and by 41 per cent in the US. This development has been called a 'second wave of automation', one that is centred on artificial cognition, cheap sensors, machine learning and distributed smarts. This deep automation will touch all jobs, from manual labour to knowledge work. And it is reducing employment, just as mechanisation under previous industrial revolutions did.

Just how close are AI robots to doing all human work? The techno-futurists think robots will soon replace humans. But they are running before they can walk – or to be more exact, so far, robots can hardly run and catch compared to humans. This is Moravec's paradox, namely, that 'it is comparatively easy to make computers exhibit adult-level performance on intelligence tests or playing games, and difficult or impossible to give them the skills of a one-year-old when it comes to perception and mobility' (Moravec). So algorithms can vote on whether to invest or not for hedge funds or banks, but a robot cannot even hit a tennis ball, let alone beat a club player. AI researchers have noted that the simplest tasks for humans, such as reaching into a pocket to retrieve a quarter, are the most challenging for machines. For example, iRobot's Roomba robot is autonomous, but the vacuuming task it performs by wandering around rooms is extremely simple. By contrast, the company's Packbot is more expensive, designed for defusing bombs, but must be teleoperated or controlled wirelessly by people.

The Defense Advanced Research Projects Agency, a Pentagon research arm, held a Robotics Challenge competition in Pomona, California. There was $2 million in prize money for the robot that performed best in a series of rescue-oriented tasks in under an hour. In the previous contest in Florida in December 2013, the robots, which were protected from falling by tethers, were glacially slow in accomplishing tasks such as opening doors and entering rooms, clearing debris, climbing ladders and driving through an obstacle course. (The robots had to be placed in the vehicles by human minders.) Reporters who covered the event resorted to such analogies as 'watching paint dry' and 'watching grass grow'. This time, the robots had an hour to complete a set of eight tasks that would probably take a human less than ten minutes. And the robots failed at many. Most of the robots were two-legged, but many had four legs, or wheels, or both. But none were autonomous. Human operators guided the machines via wireless networks and were largely helpless without human supervisors. Little headway has been made in 'cognition', the higher-level human-like processes required for robot planning and true autonomy. As a result, any researchers have begun to think instead of creating ensembles of humans and robots, an approach they describe as co-robots or 'cloud robotics'. Indeed, robot development is heading more towards 'cobots', which act as an extension of the worker, in factories with the heavy work and in hospitals and social care for diagnosis. This does not directly replace the worker.

David Graeber had raised other obstacles to the fast adoption of autonomous AI fully automated robots, namely, the capitalist system itself.[21] Funding for new technology does not go into solving the needs of people and reducing human toil as such, but into what will raise profitability. 'Once upon a time, when people imagined the future, they imagined flying cars, teleportation devices and robots who would free them from the need to work. But strangely, none of these things came to pass.' What happened, instead, was that industrialists poured research funds not into the invention of the robot factories that everyone was anticipating in the 1960s, but into relocating their factories to labour-intensive, low-tech facilities in China or the Global South. And governments shifted funds into military research, to weapons projects, research in communications and surveillance technologies and similar security-related concerns. 'One reason we don't have robot factories yet is because roughly 95 percent of robotics research funding has been channeled through the Pentagon, which is more interested in developing unmanned drones than in automating paper mills.'

William Nordhaus, from Yale University's Department of Economics, has tried to estimate the future economic impact of AI and robots.[22] Nordhaus reckons 'singularity' and its impact is still a long way away. Consumers may love their iPhones, but they cannot eat the electronic output. Similarly, at least with today's technologies, production requires scarce inputs ('stuff') in the form of labour, energy and natural resources, as well as information for most goods and services. Nordhaus says projecting the trends of the last decade or more, it would be in the order of a century before growth variables would reach the level associated with a growth-focused singularity.

Technical advances to meet the needs of people, to help end poverty and create a society of super-abundance without damaging the environment and the ecology of the planet is what we want. If AI/robotic technology can bring us closer to that, all the better. But the obstacle to a harmonious super-abundant society based on robots reducing human toil to a minimum is Capital. While the means of production (and that will include robots) are owned by a few, the benefits of a robot society will accrue to the few. Whoever owns the capital will benefit as robots and AI inevitably replace many jobs. If the rewards of new technologies go largely to the very richest, as has been the trend in recent decades, then dystopian visions could become reality. The new technology of robots and AI is coming. As in all technology under capitalism, it has a 'capital-bias'; it will replace human labour. But under capitalism, that capital-bias is applied to reduce labour and boost profitability, not to meet people's needs.

So robots and AI will intensify the contradiction under capitalism between the drive by capitalists to raise the productivity of labour through 'mechanisation' (robots) and the resulting tendency for the profitability in this investment for the owners of capital to fall. This is Marx's most important law in political economy – and it becomes even more relevant in the world of robots. Indeed, the biggest obstacle to a world of super-abundance is capital itself. A super-abundant society where human toil is reduced to a minimum and poverty is eliminated won't happen unless the ownership of the means of production changes from private control (capitalist oligarchy) to ownership in common (democratic socialism). That's the choice between utopia and dystopia.

5.2 KNOWLEDGE AND VALUE

Artificial intelligence implies that machines can develop their own knowledge without human intervention. But does such knowledge, human or machine-based have any value? In the *Oxford Handbook of Karl Marx*, Thomas Rotta and Rodrigo Teixeira argue that knowledge is 'immaterial labour' and 'knowledge commodities' are increasingly replacing material commodities in modern capitalism.[23]

'Examples of knowledge-commodities are all sorts of commodified data, computer software, chemical formulas, patented information, recorded music, copyrighted compositions and movies, and monopolized scientific knowledge.' According to Rotta and Teixeira, these knowledge commodities do not have any value in Marxist terms because their reproduction tends to be costless. Knowledge can be reproduced infinitely without cost. But Rotta and Teixeira argue that they can 'restore' Marx's law of value as an explanation of knowledge commodities. And their solution is that, although knowledge commodities have no value, the owners of such commodities through patents and copyrights etc. can extract rents from productive capitalist sectors, in the same way, as Marx explained, rents were extracted by landlords (through their monopoly of land) from productive capitalists. They conclude by estimating the increased amount of value being extracted in the form of 'rents' by 'knowledge industries'.

We do not agree with this 'solution'. Rotta and Teixeira, like other authors before them, misunderstand Marx's value theory on this question. Just because knowledge is intangible, it does not make it immaterial. Knowledge is material. Both tangible objects and mental thoughts are material. Both require the expenditure of human energy, which is material, as shown by human metabolism. This theme will be expanded upon in Section 5.3 below. Here suffice it to mention that there is no 'immaterial' labour, despite the claims of all the 'knowledge Marxists', including it seems Rotta and Teixeira. The dichotomy is not between material and mental labour, but between objective and mental labour and thus whether the output is tangible or not.

The second mistake that Rotta and Teixeira make is that because they consider knowledge is 'immaterial', it is unproductive labour that produces no value. But productive labour is labour expended under the capitalist production relation. Productive labour is not just what produces physical goods. Productive labour also includes what mainstream economists call services. As Marx explained: if a capitalist has a servant, that is unproductive labour. But if he goes to a hotel and uses a valet to take his luggage to the room, that valet delivers productive labour because s/he is working for the capitalist owner of the hotel for a wage. Rotta and Teixeira give us the example of a live concert performance.

> Hence, what we call a concert is in act a bundle of several commodities, among them knowledge-commodities such as musical compositions. The live performance is a combination of the productive labor of musicians and technical staff, plus the unproductive labor of those who composed the songs in the first place.

But what is unproductive about the composer? He/she can sell that piece of music as copyright and performance royalties on the market. Royalties must be paid if the music is used in the concert. Surplus value is created and realised. For Marx, a composer who does not work for a wage is an independent producer. If s/he is paid to do so by capital, s/he is productive. S/he is unproductive because s/he is not in the service of capital and not because s/he produces something 'immaterial'.

Then there is the example of a smartphone.

> When you buy a smartphone, part of the phone price covers the production costs of the physical components. But another part of the price remunerates the patented design and the copyrighted software stored in the memory. The copyrighted parts of the phone are therefore knowledge-commodities, and the revenues associated with these specific components are knowledge-rents.

But why are the revenues from copyright and patents considered only rents? The idea, the design and operating system have all been produced by mental labour employed by capitalist companies. The companies exploit that labour and appropriate surplus value by selling or leasing the software. This is pro-ductive labour and it produces value. It is no different from a pharma company employing scientists to come up with a formula for a new drug which they can sell on the market with a patent held for years.

More generally, the production of knowledge (mental labour) can be productive of value and surplus value if it is mental labour performed for capital. In this case, the quantity of *new* value generated during the mental labour process is given by the length and intensity of the abstract mental labour performed, given the value of the labour power of the mental labourers. Surplus value, then, is the new value generated by the mental labourers minus the value of their labour power; and the rate of exploitation is that surplus value divided by the value of their labour power. The computer programmer or website maker is in principle just as productive as the worker making the computer if both work for the computer company. Thus, knowledge *production* implies production of value and surplus value (exploitation) and not rent. Once produced, the capitalist owners of mental products (knowledge) can then extract profit, not rent, from the mental labour. The capitalist, in order to appropriate that surplus value, must apply intellectual property rights. But there is production of value first. The difference between production and appropriation is fundamental.

In sum, knowledge is material (if intangible) and if knowledge commodities are produced under conditions of capitalist production, that is, using mental labour and selling the idea, the formula, the program, the music etc. on the market, then value can be created by mental labour. Value then comes from exploitation of productive labour, as per Marx's law of value. There is no need to invoke the concept of rent extraction to explain the profits of pharma companies or Google.

5.3 HOW IS KNOWLEDGE PRODUCED?

The previous section on the value of knowledge as a commodity must now be dealt with more accurately. Here we meet Marxism's theoretical backwardness, to say nothing of non-Marxist epistemology. With the increasingly generalised use of the computer and digitalised production and their colonisation of all spheres of technologically developed societies, the need for a modern theory of knowledge has taken centre stage. Concepts such as information society, cognitive capitalism and digital capitalism attempt to make sense of this changing reality. While highlighting some significant aspects, they displace from their central role or ignore altogether the basic pillars of Marxist value theory.

We must start from the notion of transformation. There are two types of transformations: objective and mental. The former transform reality outside us. The latter transform our perception of the objective processes. Both objective and mental transformations are material. In fact, both require the expenditure of human energy, which is material, as shown by human metabolism.

The view that knowledge is material runs counter to the commonly accepted belief among Marxist scholars: knowledge would be determined by material reality, but itself is not material. Lenin advanced the twin thesis that the sole property of matter is its objectivity, its existence outside and independently of our mind. We agree with it. But we disagree that knowledge is a *reflection* of objective reality in our mind. The mastery of nature manifested in human practice is a result of an objectively correct reflection within the human head of the phenomena and processes of nature and is proof of the fact that this reflection (within the limits of what is revealed by practice) is objective, absolute and eternal truth (Lenin, 1972, pp. 153–4). The use of terms such as reflection and elsewhere in the same work of copies, photographs, images (p. 192) suggest a passive and mechanistic view (Sayers, 1983, p. 20). It can be argued that knowledge is a reflection, but not a passive one because it interacts and changes objective reality. This is indeed the case. But then knowledge, if it is not a reflection, must be the outcome of a process that generates it. The reflection theory taken literally is an obstacle to the inquiry into this process, and thus obstructs the development of a truly materialistic Marxist epistemology. Lenin's view can be taken as a first step towards a Marxist theory of knowledge. But it is insufficient.

Lenin's view in its literal rendition became the official doctrine in the Soviet Union. According to the *Handbook of Philosophy* (Rosenthal and Yudin, 1949), 'ideas, are a reflection of reality in the human consciousness ... [and] are influenced in their formation by the character of the social structure' (p. 56). The qualification of the influence of the social structure, on the one hand, calls for an analysis of how the social structure exerts its influence in the shaping of not only individual but also of collective knowledge; and on the other, does not avoid the central question: if knowledge is a reflection of matter, is it itself matter? If not, what is it?

The official Soviet theory of knowledge has never been able to solve this problem. The *Great Soviet Encyclopedia* speaks of the 'interrelationship of material and spiritual phenomena' (so that spiritual phenomena are not material) while, on the other hand, holding that 'consciousness constitutes a special property of highly organized matter' (so that consciousness, by being a property of matter, is material).[24] But the problem is not solved by distinguishing between the material base and the essence of knowledge. As Kol'banovsky holds, 'the material basis of thought and knowledge are the nervous processes of the human brain [but] the essence of thinking and knowledge is an ideal reflection of the objective world' (quoted in Lobkowicz, 1961, p. 183). Then the ideal reflection is not objective. Kol'banovsky argues that if knowledge were material, the distinction, and thus the struggle between materialism and idealism would be meaningless (Lobkowicz, 1961, p. 182). But first, this is a justification rather than a theoretical argument; and second, it is only by granting materiality to knowledge that idealism is delivered a decisive blow because it becomes clear that the world of ideas is a material world, that nothing exists outside matter. The only coherent materialist position substitutes the notion of reflection with that of the materiality of mental transformations and processes. This point is crucial: it is only by accepting that knowledge is material that it is possible to theorise that the production of knowledge can also be production of value and surplus value.

The rejection of the immateriality of knowledge counters the argument that Marxist theory deals only with material reality and that therefore it becomes increasingly irrelevant in the modern world where the production of knowledge becomes increasingly significant. This work shows that there is in Marx an original epistemology which, if properly developed, can account for why, how and under which conditions the production of knowledge is also production of value. Alternative theories not only fail to tackle this problem, as a rule they are not even aware of it.

The above begs the question: what is knowledge? Knowledge is not a reflection, but the outcome of a mental process. The conceptualisation of a mental process rests on Marx's analysis of the production process in *Capital* Vol. I, as the unity of the labour process and of the surplus value producing process, exploitation. This section deals with the labour process.

A labour process is a transformative process, that is, a sequence of transformations of use values into new use values. Marx does not distinguish systematically between objective transformations and mental transformations. However, in dealing with the production of knowledge this distinction is necessary. *Objective transformations* transform objective reality, reality existing independently of our perception of it, even if we need to perceive it in order to transform it. In objective transformations labour power transforms the *means* of objective transformations (e.g. a hammer) and the *objects* of objective transformations (e.g. wood) into a new objective output (a table).

In *mental transformations*, labour power transforms its own knowledge as well as the knowledge contained in objective means (computers) and object (books) of mental transformation into new knowledge. If knowledge is material, so must be the transformations that generate it. Like objective transformations, mental transformations are the expenditure of human energy, which is material, as shown by human metabolism. Mental transformations cause a change in the nervous system, in the interconnections between the neurons of the brain. They are called *synapses*. It is these changes that make possible a different perception of the world. To deny this means to ignore the results of neuroscience. There is no 'immaterial' labour, *pace* the workerist authors.[25] Second, while synapses make possible (changed) perceptions of the world, what is perceived is eminently social; it is the myriad of social relations and processes constituting a society. *Knowledge* is always *both material and socially determined.* So the form taken by new knowledge is always indeterminate.

Transformations are transformations of *use* values. Objective transformations transform objective use values. Mental transformations transform *mental use values*, that is, the use to which a form of knowledge lends itself. The distinction between the two types of transformations is only analytical because, in reality, objective transformations require mental transformations and vice versa. However, this distinction is necessary to conceptualise the labour process. A labour process is the transformation of use values, both objective and mental. But it is either objective or mental according to which type of transformations is determinant. The relation of determination should be clarified (see Carchedi, 2011b). The objective labour process is the determination of the mental transformation by the objective transformations and whose output is a new objective use value. Similarly, in the mental labour process the mental transformations are determinant, so that the outcome is new knowledge. It is thus mistaken to think of objective labour, sometimes erroneously called physical or manual or material labour, as separated from mental activities (transformations).[26] While all humans engage in mental transformations, not all of them are mental labourers.

It also follows that given a certain mental labour process, the knowledge entering it as an input is not the same knowledge exiting it as its output even if input and output might have the same form. There is a succession of mental labour processes in which the knowledge-output of one process is the knowledge-input of the following one. This is contrary to the view that 'Information is circular, in the sense that it is both input and output … therefore it becomes very difficult to distinguish production, distribution and consumption of information' (Kostakis, 2012, p. 2). The misunderstanding arises because information is seen as both the input and the output of the *same* mental labour process, a common mistake reminiscent of a similar one made by both Marxist and non-Marxist writers alike when dealing with the transformation of values into (production) prices.

How do we know which type of transformation has been determinant in a given labour process? This can be seen only at the moment of realisation. If the mental transformations have been determinant, the commodity is bought because of its knowledge content. Vice versa, if the objective transformations have been determinant, the commodity is bought because of its objective features. But this does not mean that realisation (sale) determines production. For example, a book is sold because of its knowledge content. Its physical features (it must be easily readable, the graphics must be appealing, typographical mistakes must be kept at a minimum etc.) are necessary but subordinate to its mental, or knowledge content. Both transformations are necessary for the production of that book so that both transformations are a realised feature of that product. But only one type of transformations is determinant, its knowledge content. This is what that book is bought for. Notice that it is the general use that reveals which of the two types of transformation has been determinant. Anomalous use can diverge from the generalised use, but this does not change *a posteriori* the nature of the labour process. A book is the outcome of a mental labour process. If it is bought as an ornament, this individual, anomalous use does not reverse the direction of determination.

It is often argued that in a materialist position objective (wrongly called material) labour processes determine the mental labour process. The above shows that this is incorrect. An objective labour process can determine a mental labour process if the mental transformations inherent in the former detach themselves to become an independent, mental labour process. And the opposite also holds. So the societal labour process is an articulation of both types of labour processes in which both types can be determinant.

5.4 MACHINE 'THINKING'

That's human thinking. What about machine thinking? Basically, if we assume that machines and especially computers think, knowledge – which is the product of something material, a computer – must be material too. However, the crux of the matter is another one: whether machines do indeed think and whether they think as humans do. This is especially relevant since the arrival of the computers. This question has been answered in a number of ways. Some hold that computers think because they can be made to learn. For some others, computers do think but cannot think anything new. Then there are those who argue that computers simply imitate human thinking. And finally, those who deny that computers think because human cognition is affected also by social relations, process and interests. Each of these positions makes some valid points. However, they do not get to the heart of the matter: *machines behave according only to the rules of formal logic. So contrary to humans, machines are structurally unable to behave according to the rules of dialectical thinking. Only humans do that.*

Formal logic can explain quantitative changes, not qualitative ones. Consider an analogy from the natural world. Formal logic can explain why water turns into ice at a given temperature. Dialectical logic adds that ice is a potential inherent in water. When ice turns again into water it becomes again a potential inherent in water. At a given temperature (an external factor), the outcome is *determinate*. Not so in knowledge. Formal logic cannot explain why a particular form of knowledge emerges from previous forms of knowledge. For it, previous knowledge is a formless, unquantifiable potential so that new knowledge is unquantifiable and thus *indeterminate*. Simply put, formal logic cannot explain where new ideas come from. Disregard of the potential is where formal logic meets its limits. 'Since basic logic is finite and since first-order logic is countable, neither is adequate to axiomatize theories whose universes of discourse are uncountable' (Corcoran, 2001, p. 72). The existence of potential reality and thus of an alternative, dialectical logic is a prerequisite for a theory of knowledge and of society.

Formal logic rests on three basic laws.[27] The *law of identity* states that something is equal to itself, that is, A = A. This is a truism. As such, it cannot generate any knowledge about A and thus about its change. The *law of the excluded middle* states that A = A is either true or not true, that is, either A = A or A ≠ A. There is no third possibility. The *law of non-contradiction* states that two contradictory propositions cannot both be true. A proposition, A = A, and its denial, A ≠ A, cannot both be true.

Dialectical logic too, at least as submitted here, is based on three basic principles.[28] First principle: *social phenomena are always both realised and potential.* For example, a commodity is only potentially such, as long as it is not offered for sale, that is, as long as it does not realise its potential use value and value.[29]

This holds also for knowledge. In the analysis of both the objective labour process and the mental labour process the inputs have been considered as realised entities. But they are also potentials inherent in the output of which they are inputs. This would seem to be a contradiction, since inputs are seen as both realised and potentials. But what is a contradiction in a timeless dimension disappears as soon as time is introduced. The inputs are realised entities before entering the labour process (they are outputs of the previous labour process), but potential elements of the output of the present labour process.

Second principle: *realised social phenomena are always both determinant and determined.* If these two principles are combined, given two phenomena, A and B, a relation is said to be dialectical if A in its realised form contains B as a formless potential so that A is the realised condition of existence of B; and B, upon its realisation, becomes the realised condition of reproduction or supersession of A. A is determinant and B is determined.

The third principle follows logically from the first two: *social phenomena are subject to constant movement and change.* The picture of social reality that emerges from dialectical thinking is a temporal flow of realised (both determining and determined) contradictory phenomena continuously emerging from and continuously going back to a potential state. This dynamic and thus temporal and contradictory movement escapes formal logic. Formal logic pertains only to the realm of the realised. Dialectical logic pertains also to the realm of the potential. Moreover, dialectical logic too deals with the realised, but at any given time realised phenomena can be either determinant or determined. At another moment the order of determination can be reversed.[30]

It follows that human thinking is much more than formal logic thinking. But this is all computers can do. Computers can only mimic one aspect of human's thinking (computation) in the sense that any algorithm that can be carried out by a human can be carried out by a computer. But computers are constitutionally barred from dialectical thinking. Human thinking is always and at the same time computational (in terms of formal logic) and dialectical. Traditional computer software is an example of propositional formal logic. It is based on Boolean logic, or algebra, which in spite of its specific features, exclude the possibility for statements to be both true and false, to be both O and 1.[31] Computers cannot think in terms of potentialities and thus in terms of dialectical contradictions. If they could perceive them, they would see them as logical mistakes.

However, quantum logic seems to include the notion of potentiality.[32] If this were the case, quantum computers could work in a manner closer to the human mind. But they don't. Potentiality in quantum logic (QL) is not the same as in dialectical logic; it is not the potentiality that is the humus for the production of *new* knowledge. This aspect is necessary to decide if quantum computers do think in human-like fashion.

Consider first a game of heads or tails. This is a macro phenomenon and as such it is not relevant to the sub-atomic world. Yet it is an intuitive illustration of the QL. In formal logic, the result is either heads or tails. A classical computer functions on the basis of this binary logic. But QL is different. The central notion is the quantum bit, which has an amorphous existence because it can be *both* heads and tails. This shapelessness collapses at the moment of measurement. At that point, the outcome is either heads or tails. But before that, the Copenhagen interpretation holds that shapelessness exists as a superposition of heads and tails, of zero and one, with some probability of being zero and some probability of being one. As long as the coin spins in the air, the actual outcome is unknown or undecided. QL concludes that heads and tails are two superimposed states that exist in a timeless dimension. But at any given moment the coin is *not both* heads and tails but *either* heads *or* tails: when it is heads it is not tails and vice versa. This does not exclude intermediate states, the probability of being either heads or tails. If at the time the coin starts its revolution it is heads, it has 100 per cent probability (the certainty) of being heads and no probability of being tails. As the revolution starts, its probability of becoming tails increases until when at t_1 it becomes tails. The time to t_1 is the first half of the complete revolution at the end of which heads has become tails. As the spinning proceeds, the coin's probability of becoming heads again increases (and that of becoming tails decreases) until the revolution is completed and at t_2 it becomes heads. So given the initial state (heads), if the spinning stops at t_1 it is tails, if it stops at t2 it is heads. We don't know the final result, not because it cannot be known but because we disregard an essential element, time. The result depends on the time at which the spinning is stopped, at t1 or t2. But suppose the coin stops between t0 and t1. At each point, it has more (even if decreasing) probabilities of being heads. It is *potentially* heads. It becomes realised heads if the movement is stopped at any moment within that sub-period. Similarly, between t1 and t2 it is potentially tails. It becomes realised tails if the movement is stopped at any moment during the second half of the complete revolution.

This example highlights the difference between simple causation, as cause and effect, as held by QL, and dialectical determination, as the realisation of a potentiality. Dialectical determination explains also a specific case. At t1 as the end of the first half revolution and *at the same time* the beginning of the second half, the coin is potentially *neither* heads *nor* tails. Therefore, it falls on the edge dividing heads from tails, not horizontally, but vertically. Thus, in throwing the coin, there are not two, but three alternative outcomes. The third is usually disregarded, but nevertheless it can occur. It could be held that at t1 the coin is potentially *both* heads *and* tails, rather than neither one nor the other. The choice would seem to be inconsequential, but it is not. Both heads and tails would become realised at the same time. This is what the popularised version of superposition in QL implies. But there is no reason to hold onto this view, except a faulty epistemology. In the realm of realisations, something cannot become realised as something and *contemporaneously* as something else. This not only eliminates time, also it is untenable and unnecessary, given the alternative dialectical view submitted above. Moreover, timelessness in its turn implies motionlessness. But this is contrary to the experiments on which QL rests. Far from explaining the behaviour of sub-atomic reality, superposition exposes QL to internal inconsistency. At t1 (and t2) the coin does not fall on both sides at the same time. Rather it falls either on one side, or on the other, or on neither (the edge), but never on both sides at the same time.

Consider next a more pertinent example in the sub-atomic world. This is the oft-cited double-slit experiment (for a more detailed account within the context of the discussion between Bohr and Einstein, see Bohr, 1958, pp. 42ff.). Electrons are fired at a screen. The screen has two slits. A detector behind the screen records the impact (intensity, I) of the electrons. If slit 1 is closed, the electrons go through slit 2. Their intensity (I_2) is measured. The same procedure is repeated with slit 2 closed. Then I_1 is measured. If both slits are open, classical physics predicts an intensity equal to $I_1 + I_2$. But for quantum theory, the combined intensity has a different outcome, which is different from $I_1 + I_2$. This is explained by the superposition of the two (superposed) states at the same time. As de Ronde and Massri (2019, p. 7) recount, in the orthodox Copenhagen interpretation superposed states 'might, or might not become actualized in a future instant of time and thus, cannot be considered as elements of physical reality'. They become actualised at the moment of observation, at which time they collapse into a single value.

It is not hard to see that this is an *ad hoc* hypothesis, a metaphysical one. The superposed states cannot be known and thus cannot be proved to exist. Only its actualisation at the moment of observation and thus of their collapse can they be known. But 'sophisticated experiments have clearly demonstrated that in interaction processes on the sub-microscopic, microscopic and mesoscopic scales collapses are never encountered' (de Ronde and Massri (2019, p. 7), or 'the experimental research seems to confirm there is nothing like a "real collapse process" suddenly happening when measurement takes place' (p. 8), or 'collapses have no empirical ground nor play any role within the operational application of the theory' (p. 8). As argued by Einstein, 'quantum theory nowhere makes explicit use of this requirement' (p. 8). The superposition hypothesis and thus metaphysics are not indispensable for quantum mechanics formalism.

Other interpretations are possible. We submit the following, realistic one. Bohr holds that 'The lack of causality ... manifests itself in the fact that with the same experimental arrangements one obtains different results'.[33] But when we open slit 1 we observe a certain situation, I1. This is experiment 1. When we open slit 2, we observe another situation, I2. This is another experiment, experiment 2. And when we open both slits, we observe yet another situation, I3, the outcome of experiment 3. These are not the same experiment; they are three different experiments with three different actual, realised outcomes. These outcomes are a temporal succession of different experiments producing different realised states. I1, I2 and I3 are three different windows open on the same, objective reality. They are what we see if we change the portion of reality we observe. This holds for all sciences, both natural and social.

This view excludes (instantaneous) superposition. If superposition is excluded, time and causality can be reintroduced. Within the range of all possible interpretations, ours seems to us to be a reasonable alternative recovering causality, a necessary step to support Marx's notion of potentiality and of its role in the production of knowledge. As Daniel put it: 'The study of the foundations of quantum mechanics which has been performed during the last twenty years by the "school of Geneva" has shown that ... the usual formalism of quantum mechanics can be recovered, but with a consistently realistic interpretation' (1989, p. 255).

From the standpoint of dialectical logic, the weak point of the QL's interpretation of the double-slit experiment is that the intensity of the electrons when both slits are open is not an unknown. It can be measured and as such it is a realised state. If it can be measured, it is not amorphous and cannot be a potential state from which something qualitatively different can arise. The same applies when either of the two slits is open. I1 and I2 as well are realised, not potential. But for QL the intensity of the electrons with both slits open is a potential state. According to Werner Heisenberg, the concept of the probability wave 'was a quantitative version of the old concept of "potentia" in Aristotelian philosophy' (Quantum Logic, in the Internet Encyclopedia of Philosophy). 'The probability wave function ... meant a tendency for something' (Heisenberg, 1958). We have seen that I3 is not a potential state, but a realised state that becomes visible under specific circumstances. No qualitatively new knowledge can come from it, only a quantitatively different one.

We come now to the crux of the matter. Potentiality as the possibility to come into actual existence is common to both QL and dialectical logic. The difference is that potentiality in QL is the possibility to come into existence as something *quantitatively* different, but qualitatively the same. For dialectical logic, potentiality is also the possibility to come into existence as something *qualitatively* different. It is this that explains the generation of new knowledge, rather than the transformation of old quantitative knowledge into new, but equally quantitative knowledge, as in computations by computers.[34] Computers, both traditional and quantum, cannot think. There is also a second reason why computers do not and will never think as humans. In the above, the dichotomy is between humans and machines. But 'humans' is the general name for different social groups and classes with different interests and world views (see sections below). Machines (computers) not only cannot think like humans, *they cannot think like class determined humans* with different conceptions of what is true and false.[35]

The question of the interpretation of quantum theory is politically relevant. This method of computation is a gigantic leap forward in the productive forces. Quantum computers can perform computations that classical computers cannot do in any feasible time, from modelling nature to searching large amounts of data, to more secure anti-hacking systems. It is too early to envisage how these new developments will shape capitalist societies in the future. But it is possible to glimpse some tendencies without falling into science fiction. The impact of capitalism entering a new phase based on the generalised use of quantum theory and quantum computers might be even more radical than that following the introduction and spreading of the – by now classical – computers in the second half of the previous century. But whether this is the case or not, there is a basic difference which seems to have escaped the participants in the quantum theory debate. The practical success of *classical* computers has been used to propagate the anti-labour myth of the neutrality of knowledge (see Section 5.7 below). The epistemological distortion surrounding *quantum* computers goes a step further.

Their practical success has been and is being used to support not an objective and deterministic (in the sense of dialectical) view of the physical world. Rather, the predominant (Copenhagen) interpretation is based on an alleged

ROBOTS, KNOWLEDGE AND VALUE

timeless dimension at the sub-atomic level, that is, on unrealism and irration-alism (Einstein opposed this view of the quantum theory).[36] If the universe expands and if expansion is movement in time, then either this applies to the whole of the universe and in this case QL fails – or it does not apply to the sub-atomic level, and in this case QL should explain why this is so. But so far it has done neither. The practical success of a technology (quantum computers) has been embedded within and lends credibility to an irrational epistemology as if this epistemology were the only one compatible with QL's formalism. And irra-tional thinking inasmuch as it contaminates other spheres of knowledge is a powerful ideological weapon in the hands of capital.

5.5 INDIVIDUAL AND SOCIAL KNOWLEDGE

Marx indicates in a well-known passage in the *Grundrisse* how individual knowl-edge arises. This is a sequence of two fundamental labour processes: induction and deduction. Marx considers the example of population. In the analysis of 'the foundation ... of production' it seems correct to start from the population, 'the real and the concrete'. However, population presupposes classes, which in their turn presuppose wage labour and capital. Thus, population is a chaotic conception [Hostelling] of the whole. Through a process of induction, we reach the ultimately determinant factor, the production relations. One ascends from the lower to the higher levels of abstraction and finally to the highest one. At this point, induction terminates and deduction begins. 'From there the journey would have to be retraced until I had finally arrived at the population again, but this time not as the chaotic conception of a whole, but as a rich totality of many determinations and relations.' This is what Marx calls the 'concrete in thought'. Both induction and deduction are mental labour process, unity in determina-tion of mental and objective transformations. It goes without saying that an initial knowledge is untheorised only relative to a previous stage of knowledge. The empiricist search for observations not influenced by previous theoretical frameworks and theoretical outcomes is senseless.

Marx provides also some elements of a theory of social knowledge: 'when I am engaged in activity which I can seldom perform in direct community with others – then I am social, because the material of my activity [is] given to me as a social product'.[37] So, individuals generate social knowledge, knowledge with a social content even when they do not interact because the knowledge contained in their labour power has been previously charged with a specific social content. Individuals generate social knowledge even in this extreme example.

It is commonly assumed that social knowledge is the outcome of the sum-mation of individual forms of knowledge. This is impossible. If individuals are by definition unique and thus different, it is impossible for them to combine their unique views of reality. If they aggregate, they must share some feature that cannot be their specific features. How then can individual forms of knowledge be uniquely different and at the same time the same? The answer depends on the distinction between *concrete* and *abstract* individuals. The former are individuals in their specificity and uniqueness. The latter are individuals as carriers of the same social relations and thus sharing some common interests and aims. Then the condition for concrete individuals to aggregate into social groups – thus becoming (also) abstract individuals – is that they share some common views, interests and aims. These are the glue forming social groups. At the highest level of abstraction, the two fundamental social groups are the working class and the capitalist class. It follows those different concrete individuals by being also abstract individuals who represent in their own and often contradictory way opposing class interests. Different representations of common interest can be combined because they represent, in spite of their uniqueness, something common. This is why individual forms of knowledge have a class content in spite of their incomparability: they are different, concrete forms of the same interests, views and aims.

The relation between individual and social knowledge can be understood only dialectically, on the basis of the distinction between potential and realised elements of reality. Individual knowledge is potential social knowledge that can become realised social knowledge; and realised social knowledge can go back to its potential state and become again individual knowledge. Concrete individuals internalise realised forms of social knowledge. Through these individual internalisations, social knowledge is reduced to individual knowledge. This is again transformed into social knowledge through the aggregation of individual form of knowledge sharing the same view, interests and aims. This is a continuous process in which realised individual knowledge becomes a potential social knowledge and the latter becomes again individual knowledge through the individuals' internalisation.[38]

5.6 CLASS KNOWLEDGE[39]

That said above about social knowledge applies to all groups constituting a society. This and the following sections restrict the focus of analysis to the two fundamental classes, capital and labour as producers of alternative forms of knowledge. Let us begin with an analogy. Under capitalism, labour is the only producer of value. But a part of it, surplus value, is appropriated by capital. Similarly, labour is the only producer of knowledge. Capital forces mental labourers to work for a time longer than that needed for their reproduction. But knowledge has a specific feature. Knowledge is not something objective that can be taken away. Capital owns not only the objective means of mental production (computers) and the mental objects of mental production (data); it also owns the mental means of mental production. This is the knowledge contained in the workers' labour power. This transforms the knowledge outside itself and its own knowledge. Thus, the workers' knowledge is both the mental means of mental production and the mental objects of mental production.

In the words of Tanner Mirrlees,

> Private corporations like these, not the public, own the labs where digital hardware and software is researched and developed (R&D), the networks of factories and offices where digital goods and services are assembled, the retail nodes where these goods are circulated, and the databases where digital information about users is stored. Capital, not the commons, controls the patents to digital innovations, as well as the copyrights to digital designs.[40]

Under capitalism the mental labour process, just as the objective one, is carried out by mental labourers at the service of and for capital. Their labour power must transform the knowledge contained in the objective means (computers) and in the mental objects (data) of mental transformations. In the process they transform their own knowledge. So the knowledge contained in their labour power is the mental means of mental production. At the same time, it is also the mental object of mental production. Capital, by owning labour's labour power, owns the means of mental production (labour's knowledge) and thus it can decide *which knowledge should be produced, how it should be produced, and for whom (pro-capital forms of knowledge).* Under these conditions, the knowledge produced by mental labour within the capitalist production relations must be informed by capital's rationality, not by labour's rationality. They are specular opposites. The former is based on exploitation, competition and inequality; the latter is based on egalitarianism, cooperation and self-management. The former must be functional for increasing exploitation and profitability. The latter for the satisfaction of labour's needs as defined by labour itself in its struggles for a socialist society. Capital's rationality leads to crises, wars, abysmal differences in levels of living, the destruction of nature etc. Labour's rationality leads to the satisfaction of human needs as defined by the producers themselves, in harmony with themselves and with nature.

This cognitive antagonism spreads to and imbues the immense variety of individual forms of knowledge. Each individual internalises the conflicting rationalities in his/her own way, thus giving rise to a kaleidoscope of forms of individual knowledge. Given that they have an antagonistic class character, the knowledge individuals internalise is usually *internally contradictory*. Both rationalities co-exist in conflicting ways and in different balances within each individual's knowledge. But only one of these two rationalities is usually

175

dominant. There is no cognitive neutral space. Individual knowledge has always a class content, whether individuals are conscious of it or not. As a rule, capital's rationality predominates over labour's rationality because that knowledge has been produced by the collective intellect with capital's means of mental production. Labour can use it to resist capital's rule but that resistance *stays within the contours* of capital's rule. For example, the rhythm of the assembly line can only be slowed down, but its pernicious effects remain as long as it is used (Lenin's use of Tayloristic techniques). Or take the knowledge needed for cooperation within a team of workers under capitalism. Solidarity as viewed by labour is transformed by capital into a weapon of capitalist domination. Within that team, the rules are not those that maximise the free development of the workers' potentialities. Rather, they are meant to increment productivity and thus profitability by pitting the team workers against each other. Labour can restrict capital domination by modifying it, but these modifications do not change their class nature. Pharmaceutical firms produce medicines that ameliorate human health but only those that maximise profits. But the domination by capital's rationality is not absolute. As argued below, there are ways for labour to generate pro-labour forms of knowledge (see Section 5.8 below). *The production of knowledge is thus a cognitive class struggle.*

Typically, capitalists do not have the competence needed for the generation of pro-capital forms of knowledge. So they delegate this task to the *collective intellect*, the structure of the mental labourers at their service. At the top there is what Gramsci called the *organic intellectuals*, the mental labourers who have the qualities needed to plan, direct and formulate the tasks for the rest of the collective intellect. To this end, the organic intellectuals must have internalised the aims of capital and must have made them their own. This structure is fragmented in such a way that the rest of the collective intellect cannot reconstruct the overall view of the labour process. The fragmented structure of the production of knowledge is thus an instrument of labour's domination by capital.[41] The knowledge of the organic intellectuals becomes their personal interpretation of a collective knowledge; they become the specific forms of a generality. The relation between the knowledge of the organic intellectuals and that of the mental labourers they represent is fluid and changing. Each social group and not only labour has its organic intellectual. The organic intellectual is the very opposite of the mythical lone genius.

Another feature specific to the production of knowledge under the rule of capital is that in objective production capital appropriates the surplus product and thus the surplus value contained in it: nothing remains to labour. In mental production knowledge is appropriated by capital, but a fraction of it is also retained by the individual mental labourers. Capital cannot erase it from labour's subjectivity. Each labourer retains the knowledge s/he has generated.

Capital appropriates the copy, as it were, but the original stays with labour. Then, subject to a number of conditions, the collective intellect can use that original for its own purposes, and thus also to resist the rule of capital. Within a group there can emerge more than one organic intellectual. Each has a different interpretation of that group's interests and each vies to become the dominant organic intellectual (leader). Also, within a group there might be sub-groups. Each can be represented by one or more organic intellectuals who operate at a lower level of aggregating capacity. Thus, the collective intellect of a group is the result of the interaction among the collective intellects of the several sub-groups. This process can entail the change of the class nature of that collective intellect. This implies the continuous struggle between the two rationalities to become dominant, that is, it implies the cognitive class struggle, the production of knowledge as class struggle.

5.7 THE MYTH OF THE NON-NEUTRALITY OF KNOWLEDGE

The thesis of the class content, or of the non-neutrality of knowledge is commonly rejected even by most Marxists, certainly if it comes to natural sciences and more specifically to mathematics. It is held that knowledge is class neutral and that it is its use that is socially determined. The extension of the analysis in the previous sections shows that this is not the case. A fundamental difference between objective and mental production is that the former is produced while the latter is reproduced. A hammer is produced only once. If it is used several times its use value depletes and the value contained in it decreases accordingly (in the capitalist production process its value is transferred to the product). A statue made of marble, once made, is consumed by the action of time, even if only very slowly. But this is not the same for the production of knowledge.

It would seem that a form of knowledge (a mathematical formula) remains the same every time it is used. But actually, a form of knowledge, after it has been conceived the first time, is *recreated every time it is used*. Even if that formula is formally the same, the inputs necessary for its use, labour power (the mental means of mental transformation) and the objective means of mental transformation, are different from those in its previous use. They are the product of new mental labour processes replicating the same formula. If that formula is recreated each time it is used, it is new knowledge with the same form. So how can that formula be new while retaining its form? The reason is that the mental labour process is each time a *new process* while the output has the *same form*. In the production of knowledge, replication is reproduction, it is the reproduction of the same mental use value. An analogy is the production of a hammer. Exactly the same hammer can be made each time, but each time what would seem to be the 'same' hammer is a replica of the original one and not the original one.

So a replica is different from the original. But *how* is it different? Recall that knowledge is both material and socially determined. Then when a form of knowledge is replicated, it is replicated within a new social context. This social context determines the social content of knowledge and thus of that form of knowledge. The replicas acquire different social contents during their reproduction. This is why a form of knowledge can be used by different classes and in different epochs. This explains the trans-class and trans-epochal elements of knowledge. Let us provide two examples.

For the ancient Greeks, the world was a well-ordered arrangement of concrete things. The order of numbers was a succession of discrete entities. It was then natural to conceive of numbers as numbers of some things, as discrete, concrete numbers that could be ordered and counted. Given their discrete nature, numbers could be represented as dots and thus ordered in triangular, square or other shapes. Accordingly, the Greeks developed the notion of shaped numbers (e.g. triangular). Numbers had visible and tangible bodies. Moreover, since numbers could be ordered, their position revealed their being and nature, things had arithmetical properties, and these properties concerned the being of things. The classification of numbers was then a means to grasp the meaning of life. An abstract idea of numbers was incompatible with the ancient Greeks' ontology (see Carchedi, 1983, pp. 16–18).

With the development of industrial capitalism 'numbers came to perform a new function by indicating the properties of moving, active processes of change. For example, number and measurement become central to an intellectual grasp of ballistic, navigation and the use of machinery' (Carchedi, 1983, pp. 16–18). These were of central importance to the birth and development of industrial capitalism. These new functions required that numbers had to become abstract numbers, separated from the things they measure and related by general relations. Numbers became likened to a continuous straight line of homogeneous entities, rather than to a succession of discontinuous and heterogeneous dots (pp. 16–18).

Let us further consider the critics' favourite argument, that is, that $2 + 2$ is always equal to 4. The argument is that $2 + 2 = 4$ is immutable and thus cannot have a social content. But first, $2 + 2 = 4$ is not always equal to 4. It all depends on the time frame within which $2 + 2 = 4$ is placed. For example, our system of recording the time of the day goes from 0 to 24. At 24, the first day ends and at the same time the second day begins. Then, if the time frame is one day, $24 = 0$ and $24 + 2$ is $0 + 2 = 2$. But if the time frame is two consecutive days (i.e. 48 hours), then $24 + 2 = 26$. Similarly, within a time frame going from 0 to 4, $2 + 2$ is 4. But if the time frame is 0 to 2, $2 + 2 = 0$. It is the time period that determines the quantitative result and the choice of the time period is socially determined. When $2 + 2 = 4$ is reproduced within a wider theoretical and social context, it acquires the social content of that wider system not because it is neutral but because it is (re)produced within that different context.[42]

The thesis of the non-neutrality of knowledge applies also to logic. It is not by chance that both formal logic and dialectical logic arise in the mid-19th century. This is the age of the upcoming industrial capitalism, whose fundamental feature is the antagonism between capital and labour. Marx is the representative of the logic of labour, or dialectical logic, which is the logic of movement and change. Formal logic, on the other hand, hides this basic antagonism. For it, propositions are true or false independently from the class appurtenance of those who use them. Dialectical logic explains movement, formal logic negates it by hiding it. But formal logic can be used by labour if immersed within the context of dialectical logic.

Just as (the same) form of knowledge can be used by different social classes, the same social class can give rise to alternative forms of knowledge with the same purpose. The choice is then made on the basis of which form is most suitable for the interests of that class. David Noble provides a classic example: the choice of numerically controlled machines instead of the record-playback technique. There were several reasons for this choice. The most significant was that the record-playback machine repeated the same motion of the machinist that were recorded on a magnetic tape. The machinist retained some control over the machine. The numerically controlled machine, on the other hand, transferred the knowledge needed to operate the machine from the shop floor to production engineers and managers by a mathematical description of the path of the cutting tool. This type of knowledge was out of the reach of the machinist. Clearly, this was more suitable for capital's interests.[43]

Up to here, knowledge has been dealt with as if independent of the objective shell in which it is incorporated. However, the knowledge which has been used to make a machine is frozen into that machine. So, the social relations within which that machine has been made are frozen into it as well. A machine born as an instrument of exploitation or oppression can be used by labour and immersed in different, socialist production relations, *provided* it has been cleansed of its original class content and adapted to the new social circumstances. But sometimes this is impossible. Then the objective shell should be destroyed and not reproduced. The same applies to forms of organisation of work devised to oppress labour. This point is vital for a society in transition from capitalism to socialism. The a-critical adoption of the means of production (which include also forms of organisation of labour) born from capitalism and bearing the stamp of its relations is one measure and indication that that process of transition is slowing down or has come to a halt. Vice versa, efforts to change those means of production to make them consonant to radically different production relations denote that that process is moving forward.

5.8 VALUE AND THE INTERNET

Up to here, this work has considered the labour process, the production of use values by labour. But the capitalist production process is also a surplus value production process. Use values are made by labour for capital as a means for capital to realise surplus value. Then the question is whether the labour theory of value, the generation of value and surplus value, applies to the generation of knowledge. This section focuses on the internet as a specific case study of a site where value and surplus value is generated and reviews three debated questions. As a preliminary step, a distinction should be drawn among

(a) Labourers in the service of capital. They are *mental labourers*.
(b) The self-employed. Since they are not employed by capital, they do not produce value and surplus value. This category will not be dealt with here.
(c) The users of the internet in their own free time for recreation, education, research etc. They are called *mental agents*.

The quantity of new value generated during a mental labour process, that is, the value of a form of knowledge, is given by the number, length and intensity of its mental and objective transformations. This is the individual value of a form of knowledge. Given that under capitalism the mental labour process (like the objective one) is divided into a number of different positions (jobs), the individual value of a form of knowledge is given by the value created by all the mental and material labourers interconnected in that process. The individual values of the different mental processes are equalised into an average value to which participate not only all the mental labour processes but also the objective ones. The value of the mental labourer's labour power is determined by the quantity of the mental and objective commodities needed to produce it. The same holds for the objective labourers needed for the mental labour process. Surplus value can be computed, given the value of the labour power of the mental and objective labourers and the value of the mental and objective means of production. Upon the sale of the different forms of knowledge, the socially necessary labour time is found after the equalisation of the profit rates.

Mental production on the internet has its own specificities, namely, specific labour processes, positions and forms of exploitation. But these specificities do not cancel their capitalist nature. Let us take the example of a new labour process studied by Legault (2013, p. 84): the production of videogames. Each videogame is a unique piece, the technologies change rapidly, and the personnel are highly qualified. The development of each videogame is a 'project'. For a section of the labourers, the function of capital as brute external coercion, as in the Tayloristic assembly line, is ill suited for the control of a labour process based on the relatively free creativity of those labourers. New ways to control labour are necessary. The capitalists see to it that the labourers complete their tasks within the time allocated to them. Project managers monitor the developers' progress and pay them when the project has reached some important points (milestones). But within these limits, labourers are free to take their own decisions. Labourers have internalised the function of capital. Therefore, control has changed semblance. But this neither cancels exploitation nor frees labour from capital.

The greater autonomy of these mental labourers is far from being absolute. Flexible and intellectually and emotionally rewarding labour hides long working hours, long and frequent hours of unpaid overtime work (Legault, 2013, p. 79) and the maximisation of labour intensity (Pitts, 2013, p. 102). It is not only, as Pitts aptly puts it, disciplined autonomy (Pitts, 2013, p. 101). It is also creativity moulded by capital. Capital pays labourers to be creative, but this creativity must be consonant with capital's aims and not with the labourers' full and all-round development. New divisions of tasks emerge. For example, some of the labourers working on search engines analyse blogs, both quantitatively in terms of the number of visitors, and qualitatively in terms of the comments left by the visitors and thus in terms of their ideas, preferences etc. Other labourers navigate the web looking for ideas helpful for advertising campaigns, for example, by analysing chat lines. Still others transform this material in knowledge as commodity to be sold to advertising agencies. Capital creates a hierarchy that includes more as well as less qualified tasks.

Some commentators have emphasised another aspect: the blurring of the frontier between working time and private life. For example, labourers solve 'creative problems' arising from their jobs in their free time (Pitts, 2013, p. 95). Or labourers can answer emails or keep their correspondence with bloggers at home, also in their free time. This is exploitation. It makes no difference whether labour works for capital in an office or at home, whether it works according to a prefixed schedule or when s/he decides to do so, provided s/he meets some requirements set by capital. What is described as blurring the line between free time and labour time is in fact an erosion of free time and a corresponding enlargement of working time.

Some critics hold that the productivity of mental production cannot be measured because knowledge is supposedly 'immaterial' and therefore 'resists quantification' (Terranova, 2000, p. 43). This is a faulty deduction. Knowledge does resist quantification and yet its productivity can be measured. Productivity is measured by output divided by variable capital. The output is in terms of use values, which are by definition different. Thus, productivities can be measured only for the same output (the same use value). Then it would seem that the productivity of different forms of knowledge cannot be measured and compared.

However, while the forms of knowledge are different, productivities can be measured if the shells containing them are similar or the same.

Take a videogame. It is incorporated into DVDs. The DVDs can be counted. It can also be downloaded from one computer into another. The number of downloads can also be counted. A competitor producing a different videogame will have to be more competitive and thus more productive. S/he will have to produce and sell more DVDs per unit of variable capital invested. Whether s/he sells more DVDs or that DVD is downloaded more than another depends on the specific, concrete features of the form of knowledge (mental use values) incorporated in it. Different forms of knowledge cannot be quantitatively compared, but the shells containing them can. Or consider a patent. The piece of paper on which it is written cannot be used to measure productivity. The patent shows its productivity only after it is incorporated in a labour process as one of its inputs and leads to a change in the products per unit of labour. If it is not applied, it is of no use to capital and the question of productivity is void.

Another related myth is that the unit value of the copies of an original form of knowledge tends to zero. Take again a videogame. After the prototype has been made, the unit value of the replicas is the constant and variable capital invested to produce them plus the surplus value generated during the life cycle of the production of the replicas, divided by the number of replicas. Consider first fixed constant capital (computers, premises, facilities, chips foundries, assembly plants etc.). Given a certain quantity of capital invested, the unit value of the replicas decreases as output increases. Theoretically, it tends to zero. This assumes that the demand for those replicas is unchanged or increases. This is totally unrealistic. Due to intense competition, demand for the replicas falls to the point at which it is not profitable any longer to produce them. In the videogame sector, this causes a 'high rate of business failures' (Dyer-Witheford and de Peute, 2009, p. 64). But let us disregard this point for the sake of argument. The constant fixed capital used to produce one replica might tend to zero, but the constant circulating capital (raw materials) does not. Rather, it is a constant share. The same applies to variable capital. Even if the production of the replicas were completely automated and variable capital would be zero, constant circulating capital would increase, rather than decreasing with the greater production of the replicas. The same holds for the labour of technical coordination and maintenance of the means of production, advertising etc.

The labour theory of value works, contrary to the critics. In spite of this, critics submit alternative theories. For Jodi Dean (2010), 'Just as industrial capitalism relied on the exploitation of labor, so does communicative capitalism rely on the exploitation of communication.' But who produces knowledge and communicates it if not labour? For Arvidsson and Colleoni (2012), value is the affective attachment to a commodity, to a brand. Presumably, the greater the number of customers attached to a brand (and thus buying that product), the greater its value. This is the view of the capitalists who aim at maximising their share of the market by manipulating the subjectivity and consciousness of the consumers, that is, by influencing the redistribution of value. To be credible, this view should explain the basic features of capitalism, like crises, unemployment, inflation, imperialism, income differentials and poverty, just to mention a few. Nothing of the sort has been submitted, and presumably will never be submitted.

Consider an unproductive objective labour process, for example, commerce. It deals with objective commodities without transforming them. Objective commodities are dealt with, but not changed. If the objective commodities are not changed, there are no objective transformations. There are mental transformations, but they are unproductive because they are determined by unproductive objective activities. So whether mental transformations within an objective labour process are the substratum for the production of value depends on the nature of that process. This holds also when the mental transformations detach themselves from the original objective labour process and become a separate branch of the economy, a separate mental labour process (e.g. advertising).

It follows that not all mental labour processes are productive of value. There are four cases in which they are not. (1) The labour employed in *commerce*. It deals with objective use values without changing them. So, the mental transformations in this sector are unproductive. (2) The labour employed in *finance and speculation*. It does not deal at all with objective use values and thus it is unproductive. (3) What Marx calls *non-labor*, the performance of the work of control and surveillance of labour, which is the function of capital. They cannot transform use values because one cannot transform use values if one forces others to perform that transformation.[44] (4) Labour destroying value. The mental labour needed for this process cannot transform mental use values for obvious reasons. The question is not whether the generation of knowledge *tout court* is productive or not. The question is when it is and when it is not by applying Marx's criteria to the generation of knowledge.

As mentioned above, on the internet operate also the *mental agents*. Consider 'social buttons' in Facebook. The mental agents who press social buttons, or who discuss a variety of issues on blogs, or who develop technological innovations through their interaction, transform mental use values. They do not produce value because they are not employed by capital. But they provide knowledge to whoever is interested in it and thus also to capital. This knowledge is for free, not because it costs nothing (think of the wear and tear of the computer, of the energy consumed etc.) but because anybody can appropriate it free of charge. An example is the mental agents using a search engine. They provide the output of their mental labour process as the raw material for the mental labourers using those data for capital. These latter transform the knowledge they collect into quantifiable data on tastes, desires, interests etc. This is productive knowledge because it is collected and transformed for capital. Then these data can be sold to companies that use them to plan advertising campaigns and investments, to evaluate the creditworthiness of clients etc. While the use of those data is productive labour, their sale, that is, the sale of the knowledge contained in them, is unproductive.

Or consider the mental agents contributing voluntarily to open source (OS) projects through the internet. If they are not employed by capital they are unproductive. They enjoy great freedom to apply their creativity. However, the individual contributions require coordination and thus a more or less formal organisation. This coordination is the task of the project initiator or of those programmers with particular skills and commitment to the project. They decide which contributions to accept and give form and direction to the project (Riehle, 2007, p. 30; Ross, 2013, p. 214). Wikipedia and Linux are two examples (Kostakis, 2010).

The coordinators are often employed by IT firms. These coordinators are unproductive, unless they are in the service of capital. This apparent paradox is explained by a series of advantages accruing to the firms 'lending' labourers to this common project. First, that firm can accept only those contributions that fit its techniques and interests. Second, it pays only a fraction of the total costs (West and Gallagher, 2006, p. 329) while appropriating the whole technology. Third, it reckons that its advantages from such technologies are greater than those accruing to its competitors. Fourth, by observing through its mental labourers how the mental agents can be controlled and managed, that firm can draw useful indications as to how to control and manage its own labourers.

Some authors (Fuchs, 2010) deny that the mental agents are unproductive and, following in the footsteps of Negri, extend the notion of exploitation beyond wage labour and into the whole society. Supposedly, surplus value is increasingly created in the sphere of recreation and consumption. All labour, then, becomes the source of surplus value. Fuchs has criticised this view. Additionally, if all labour is the source of surplus value, why should capital try to increase the time that labourers work for it and reduce the labourers' free time? Fuchs holds also that mental agents produce value but are not paid for it. It would follow that the value of their labour power is nil. Thus, all the value they produce is surplus value that goes to capital. The rate of surplus value is infinite (Fuchs, 2010). But then, how can something that has no value (labour power) produce value and surplus value? Also, if all value were surplus value, the mental agents would have to live on air.

Some authors have introduced a new figure, the so-called prosumer. This term refers to a mental agent whose production of knowledge co-determines the characteristics of an objective commodity produced by a capitalist. Subsequently, the prosumer commissions that commodity through the internet to the capitalist and purchases and consumes it. Supposedly, the distinction between production and consumption has disappeared. But this is not the case. The knowledge produced (possibly on request) by the so-called prosumers is a mental use value that enters into and shapes a future capitalist production process. They do not participate in the production of value and surplus value because they are not employed and paid by capital. But they participate in the creation of a mental use value, which will be incorporated for free into future production. When the prosumers purchase the commodity they have ordered, they become consumers. They are *present* producers of mental use values (but not of value) and *future* consumers. The prosumption thesis cancels time and collapses production into consumption. As such, it is worthless.

Of course, mental agents can be the source of innovations in many fields (Banks and Deuze, 2009; Lakhani and Wolf, 2005; Prahalad and Ramaswamy, 2000). But behind the hype, the truth is that mental agents are a new source of 'competence' for the corporations (Prahalad and Ramaswamy, 2000), a new form of appropriation of knowledge for free. An example is modding, the modifications of videogames by the consumers (mental agents) using the tools provided by the games' manufacturers. They are 'an increasingly important source of value for the games industry' (Küklich, 2005). The character behind the Janus face of the prosumer is not the empowered consumer but capital with its new techniques to increase efficiency, sales and profitability at no cost. In sum, the internet has generated new forms of production of value and surplus value and thus new forms of work of control and surveillance. To analyse them, one need not discard Marx's value theory. It is sufficient to know it and apply it.

5.9 CONCLUSION

The increasing saturation of all facets of contemporary capitalism, including human labour by the computer and digital technologies (Lohmann, 2021, p. 56), has given rise to a number of apologetic views, varyingly termed information society, cognitive capitalism and digital capitalism. These are ideological concepts.

'Information' glosses over the class content of knowledge. The myth of the class neutrality of knowledge is thus fostered and reproduced. 'Cognitive society' reflects, as Henninger (2007, p. 173) rightly remarks, the way 'certain relatively privileged sectors of the world's working population' perceive contemporary capitalism. Even if, for the sake of argument, all objective labour processes were to disappear worldwide and only mental labourers were left, the old and debilitating features of capitalism would re-emerge, even if in new guise.

As for 'Computerized capitalism', the discussion above shows that some mental labourers, for example, some programmers in IT firms, may use their creativity to solve conceptual problems. This can be a psychologically rewarding activity, often well paid. However, far from being a prefiguration of the working class of the future, they could be considered to be a new form of labour aristocracy. As such, in spite of their privileges, they are subjected to the rule of capital. They must apply their creativity (highly skilled labour) also in their (possibly unpaid) free time. The skills they are under pressure to develop are those that can be used by capital, that is, their conceptions are informed by capital's rationality. Their employment is subjected to the ebb-flow of the economic cycle. Highly skilled positions are under constant threat of dequalification.

Contemporary sociological literature has generated a host of examples of how the mental agents' interaction through the internet and the forms of knowledge springing from this interaction provide glimpses of a social structure based on labour's rationality as well as specific forms of resistance against capital's rule. But it would be a dangerous illusion to think that a simple multiplication of these attempts can lead to a radical societal change if the capitalist production relation is not done away with. The internet does not cancel the divide between capital and labour and thus does not change the law of value. The internet only provides a specific global arena for the production and appropriation of knowledge and reshapes the multitude of the cognitive forms of manifestation of the capital/labour contradiction.

If history is the history of class struggle, there is no capitalist rule without resistance against it, and thus without the production of pro-labour knowledge as a weapon against that rule. The difference is the extensive and intensive use of the internet and thus the new and specific contradictory forms of knowledge. The generation of knowledge on the internet is at the same time a battle for knowledge. It is part of the wider cognitive class struggle between capital's and labour's rationality in its multifarious and ever-changing forms of manifestation.

6

Socialism

6.1 VALUE AND SOCIALISM

Does value exist under socialism? This has been debated by Marxists for years. The answer depends on the definition of socialism as well as value. Marx and Engels were clear that the fundamental definition of capitalism was commodity production by labour for the private owners of the means of production (the capitalists), or in short, production for profit. Value, then, is the labour which goes into the production of commodities. But this is not the value realised by the individual capitalists. They realise that value through their sale in such a way that all capitalists realise not the value contained in the commodities (i.e. the value with which they enter the production process) but the average rate of profit. *Realisation is redistribution.* So socialism would be a society without commodity production, that is, production for profit.

Value is two-fold in commodity production: use value (what people need or think they need) and exchange value (the value in money of these use values in the market). Socialism would be a mode of production without exchange value, that is, without those who produce value (the labour class) and those who appropriate a share of that value (the capitalist class). Capitalism is a system of exploitation of the labour class for surplus value by the capitalist class (private owners of the means of production). Socialism would mean a society without classes and without the exploitation of wage labour. Under socialism, the means of production would be commonly owned and production would not be for the market but direct to the consumer without any process of exchange for money. Production would be by the free association of producers in common, distributed by society through democratic decisions.

Both Marx and Engels defined communism simply as 'dissolution of the mode of production and form of society based on exchange value. Real positing of individual labour as social and vice versa' (Marx, 1973, p. 264). The most basic feature of communism in Marx's projection is its overcoming of capitalism's social separation of the producers from necessary conditions of production. This new social union entails a complete decommodification of labour power plus a new set of communal property rights. Communist or 'associated' production is planned and carried out by the producers and communities themselves, without the class-based intermediaries of wage labour, market and state.

So, communism is the 'historical reversal' of 'the separation of labour and the worker from the conditions of labour, which confront him (or her) as independent forces' (Marx, 1971, pp. 271–2). This new union of the producers and the conditions of production 'will', as Engels phrases it, 'emancipate human labour power from its position as a *commodity*' (1939, p. 221; emphasis in original). Naturally, such an emancipation, in which the labourers undertake production as 'united workers' 'is only possible where the workers are the owners of their means of production' (p. 525).

Accordingly, Marx describes communism as 'replacing capitalist production with cooperative production and capitalist property with a *higher form* of the archaic type of property, that is, communist property' (1989b, p. 362; emphasis in original). One reason why communist property in the conditions of production cannot be individual private property is that the latter form 'excludes co-operation, division of labour within each separate process of production, the control over, and the productive application of the forces of Nature by society, and the free development of the social productive powers' (Marx, 1967, I, p. 762).

As stated in *The German Ideology*, 'the appropriation by the proletarians' is such that 'a mass of instruments of production must be made subject to each individual and property to all. Modern universal intercourse cannot be controlled by individuals, unless it is controlled by all. ... With the appropriation of the total productive forces by the united individuals, private property comes to an end' (Marx and Engels, 1976, p. 97). Marx's vision thus involves a 'reconversion of capital into the property of producers, although no longer as the private property of the individual producers, but rather as the property of associated producers, as outright social property' (Marx, 1967, III, p. 437). Communist property is collective precisely in so far as 'the material conditions of production are the co-operative property of the workers' as a whole, not of particular individuals or sub-groups of individuals (Marx, 1966, p. 11).

With associated production,

> it is possible to assure each person 'the full proceeds of his labour' ... only if [this phrase] is extended to purport not that each individual worker becomes the possessor of 'the full proceeds of his labour,' but that the whole of society, consisting entirely of workers, becomes the possessor of the total product of their labour, which product it partly distributes among its members for consumption, partly uses for replacing and increasing its means of production, and partly stores up as a reserve fund for production and consumption. (Engels, 1979, p. 28)

The latter two 'deductions from the ... proceeds of labour are an economic necessity'; they represent 'forms of surplus labour and surplus product ... which are common to all social modes of production' (Marx, 1966, p. 7; 1967, III, p. 876). Further deductions are required for 'general costs of administration', for 'the communal satisfaction of needs, such as schools, health services, etc', and for 'funds for those unable to work'. Only then 'do we come to ... that part of the means of consumption which is divided among the individual producers of the co-operative society' (Marx, 1966, pp. 7–8). Only in this way can communism replace 'the old bourgeois society, with its classes and class antagonisms', with 'an association, in which the free development of each is a condition for the free development of all' (Marx and Engels, 1968, p. 53).

The Communist Manifesto is unambiguous on this point: 'Communism deprives no man of the power to appropriate the products of society; all that it does is to deprive him of the power to subjugate the labour of others by means of such appropriation' (Marx and Engels, 1968, p. 49). In this sense, 'social ownership extends to the land and the other means of production, and private ownership to the products, that is, the articles of production' (Engels, 1939, p. 144). In Volume I of *Capital*, Marx says that: 'The total product of our community is a social product. One portion serves as fresh means of production and remains social. But another portion is consumed by the members of society as means of subsistence' (Marx, 1967, I, p. 78). So Marx envisaged 'the mode of this distribution will vary with the productive organisation of the community and the degree of historical development attained by the producers'.

In the *Critique of Gotha Program*, Marx outlines two stages of communism in order to show the difference with the capitalist mode of production of commodities. The lower stage is also called socialism. Any distribution whatever of the means of consumption is only a consequence of the distribution of the conditions of production themselves. The latter distribution, however, is a feature of the mode of production itself. The capitalist mode of production, for example, rests on the fact that the material conditions of production are in the hands of non-workers in the form of property in capital and land, while the masses are only owners of the personal condition of production, of labour power. If the elements of production are so distributed, then the present-day distribution of the means of consumption results automatically. If the material conditions of production are the cooperative property of the workers themselves, then there likewise results a distribution of the means of consumption different from the present one.

What we have to deal with here is a communist society, not as it has developed on its own foundations, but, on the contrary, just as it emerges from capitalist society; which is thus in every respect, economically, morally, and intellectually, still stamped with the birthmarks of the old society from whose womb it emerges. Accordingly, the individual producer receives back from society

189

– after the deductions have been made – exactly what he gives to it. What he has given to it is his individual quantum of labour. For example, the social working day consists of the sum of the individual hours of work; the individual labour time of the individual producer is the part of the social working day contributed by him, his share in it. He receives a certificate from society that he has furnished such-and-such an amount of labour (after deducting his labour for the common funds); and with this certificate, he draws from the social stock of means of consumption as much as the same amount of labour cost. The same amount of labour which he has given to society in one form, he receives back in another.

Since labour is always, together with nature, a fundamental 'substance of wealth', labour time is an important 'measure of the cost of [wealth's] production ... *even if exchange value is eliminated*' (Marx, 1971, p. 257; emphasis in original).
And then in

a higher phase of communist society, after the enslaving subordination of the individual to the division of labour, and therewith also the antithesis between mental and physical labour, has vanished; after labour has become not only a means of life but life's prime want; after the productive forces have also increased with the all-around development of the individual, and all the springs of co-operative wealth flow more abundantly – only then can the narrow horizon of bourgeois right be crossed in its entirety and society inscribe on its banners: From each according to his ability, to each according to his needs!

It is in this higher phase that communism's 'mode of distribution ... *allows all members of society to develop, maintain and exert their capacities in all possible directions*' (Engels, 1939, p. 221; emphasis in original). Here, 'the individual consumption of the labourer' becomes that which 'the full development of the individuality requires' (Marx, 1967, III, p. 876).

Even in communism's lower phase, the means of individual development assured by communal property are not limited to individuals' private consumption claims. Human development will also benefit from the expanded social services (education, health services, utilities and old age pensions) that are financed by deductions from the total product prior to its distribution among individuals. Hence 'what the producer is deprived of in his capacity as a private individual benefits him directly or indirectly in his capacity as a member of society' (Marx, 1966, p. 8). Such social consumption will, in Marx's view, be 'considerably increased in comparison with present-day society and it increases in proportion as the new society develops' (p. 7). The basic idea

190

here is that 'the fact of the collective working group being composed of individuals of both sexes and ages, must necessarily, under suitable conditions, become a source of human development' (1967, I, p. 490). Another related function of theoretical and practical education 'in the Republic of Labour' will be to 'convert science from an instrument of class rule into a popular force', and thereby 'convert the men of science themselves from panderers to class prejudice, place hunting state parasites, and allies of capital into free agents of thought' (Marx, 1985, p. 162).

Along with expanded social consumption, communism's 'shortening of the working day' will facilitate human development by giving individuals more free time in which to enjoy the 'material and social advantages ... of social development' (Marx, 1967, III, pp. 819–20). Free time is 'time ... for the free development, intellectual and social, of the individual' (1967, I, p. 530). As such, 'free time, disposable time, *is wealth itself,* partly for the enjoyment of the product, partly for free activity which unlike labour is not dominated by the pressure of an extraneous purpose which must be fulfilled, and the fulfilment of which is regarded as a natural necessity or a social duty' (Marx, 1971, p. 257; emphasis in original). Accordingly, with communism 'the measure of wealth is ... not any longer, in any way, labour time, but rather disposable time' (Marx, 1973, p. 708). Economy of time, along with the planned distribution of labour time among the various branches of production, remains the first economic law on the basis of communal production. It becomes law, there, to an even higher degree (Marx, 1973, pp. 172–3). Communism's economy of labour time serves use value, especially the expansion of free time, whereas capitalism's economy of time is geared towards increasing the surplus labour time expended by the producers (Marx, 1967, III, p. 264, 1973, p. 708).

Under capitalism and other class societies, 'a particular class' has 'the power to shift the natural burden of labour from its own shoulders to those of another layer of society' (Marx, 1967, I, p. 530); under communism, 'with labour emancipated, every man becomes a working man, and productive labour ceases to be a class attribute' (Marx, 1985, p. 75). Hence, 'the workers assert in their communist propaganda that the vocation, designation, task of every person is to achieve all-round development of his abilities, including, for example, the ability to think' (Marx and Engels, 1976, p. 309). Communism can represent a real union of all the producers with the conditions of production only if it ensures each individual's right to participate to the fullest of her or his ability in the cooperative utilisation and development of these conditions. It must enhance 'the development of human productive forces' capable of grasping and controlling social production at the human level in line with 'the development of the richness of human nature as an end in itself' (Marx, 1968, I, pp. 117–18).

191

A system run by freely associated producers and their communities, socially unified with necessary conditions of production, by definition, excludes commodity exchange and money as forms of social reproduction. Along with the decommodification of labour power comes an explicitly 'socialised production', in which 'society' – not capitalists and wage-labourers responding to market signals – 'distributes labour–power and means of production to the different branches of production'. As a result, 'the money-capital' (including the payment of wages) 'is eliminated' (Marx, 1967, II, p. 358). During the new association's lower phase, 'the producers may ... receive paper vouchers entitling them to withdraw from the social supplies of consumer goods a quantity corresponding to their labour–time'; but 'these vouchers are not money. They do not circulate' (p. 358). In other words, 'the future distribution of the necessaries of life' cannot be treated 'as a kind of more exalted wages' (Engels, 1939, p. 221). Within the cooperative society based on common ownership of the means of production, the producers do not exchange their products; just as little does the labour employed on the products appear here as the value of these products, as a material quality possessed by them, since now, in contrast to capitalist society, *individual labour no longer exists in an indirect fashion but directly as a component part of the total labour* (Marx, 1966, p. 8; emphasis in original). The communal character of production would make the product into a communal, general product from the outset. The exchange which takes place in production – which would not be of exchange values but of activities determined by the communal needs and communal purposes – would from the outset include the participation of the individual in the communal world of products.

Hence, the reason communism is 'a society organised for cooperative working on a planned basis' is not in order to pursue productive efficiency for its own sake, but rather 'to ensure all members of society the means of existence and the full development of their capacities' (Engels, 1939, p. 167). This human developmental dimension also helps explain why communism's 'cooperative labour ... developed to national dimensions' is not, in Marx's projection, governed by any centralised state power; rather, 'the system starts with the self-government of the communities' (Marx, 1974, p. 80, 1989a). In this sense, communism can be defined as 'the people acting for itself by itself', or 'the reabsorption of the state power by society as its own living forces instead of as forces controlling and subduing it' (Marx, 1985, pp. 130, 153). So the state, as defined as bodies of armed men and connected state officialdom separated from people and controlled by capitalist class, must wither away and disappear under communism. As Engels put it, 'State interference in social relations becomes, in one domain after another, superfluous and then dies down of itself. The government of persons is replaced by the administration of things and by the conduct of processes of production. The state is not "abolished". It withers away.'

6.2 THE TRANSITIONAL ECONOMY

So the law of value would *not* operate under socialism and the gradual transition to socialism from capitalism requires the reduction of the dominance of the law of value in society towards zero. Commodity production became sufficiently generalised to dominate within capitalist economies over a long period. Engels argued that commodity production was 'the result of a past historical development, the product ... of the extinction of a whole series of older forms of social production.' Only when it was dominant could we talk about a capitalist mode of production. In the same way, socialism will not emerge from the overthrow of capitalism overnight, but only gradually. This is not the result of a spontaneous, peaceful or automatic growth, but rather the outcome of the struggle between capital and labour as capital will not relinquish power without strenuous and violent opposition. So class subjectivity and struggle plays a pivotal role and this is why socialism is not assured.

The question then arises: what transformation will the state undergo in communist society? In other words, what social functions will remain in existence there that are analogous to present state functions? This question can only be answered scientifically, and one does not get a flea-hop nearer to the problem by a thousand-fold combination of the word 'people' with the word 'state'. 'Between capitalist and communist society there lies the period of the revolutionary transformation of the one into the other. Corresponding to this is also a political transition period in which the state can be nothing but the revolutionary dictatorship of the proletariat.'

The term, the dictatorship of the proletariat seems alien to 'democracy' as used now, but for Marx and Engels it was simply a description of the takeover of the state and economy by the working class. Capitalism may have the trappings of 'democracy' with its somewhat blunted universal suffrage and elected leaders. In reality, this democracy is the dictatorship of capital: the rule of finance capital and big oligopolies controlling the 'democratic' institutions. The dictatorship of the proletariat would mean the democratic rule of the majority of working people 'dictating' to capital, not vice versa.

The term, dictatorship of the proletariat comes the communist journalist Joseph Weydemeyer who in 1852 published an article entitled 'Dictatorship of the Proletariat' in the German language newspaper *Turn-Zeitung*. In that year, Marx wrote to him, stating:

Long before me, bourgeois historians had described the historical development of this struggle between the classes, as had bourgeois economists their economic anatomy. My own contribution was (1) to show that the existence of classes is merely bound up with certain historical phases in the development of production; (2) that the class struggle necessarily leads to the dictatorship of the proletariat; [and] (3) that this dictatorship, itself, constitutes no more than a transition to the abolition of all classes and to a classless society.

When asked to give an example of the dictatorship of the proletariat, both Marx and Engels replied: the Paris Commune. In the 1891 postscript to *The Civil War in France* (1872) pamphlet, Engels stated: 'Well and good, gentlemen, do you want to know what this dictatorship looks like? Look at the Paris Commune. That was the Dictatorship of the Proletariat.' To avoid bourgeois political corruption, Engels recommended that

the Commune made use of two infallible expedients. In this first place, it filled all posts administrative, judicial, and educational by election on the basis of universal suffrage of all concerned, with the right of the same electors to recall their delegate at any time. And, in the second place, all officials, high or low, were paid only the wages received by other workers. The highest salary paid by the Commune to anyone was 6,000 francs. In this way an effective barrier to place-hunting and careerism was set up, even apart from the binding mandates to delegates [and] to representative bodies, which were also added in profusion.

Lenin wrote that the use of the term dictatorship 'does not refer to the Classical Roman concept of the *dictatura* (the governance of a state by a small group with no democratic process), but instead to the Marxist concept of dictatorship (that an entire societal class holds political and economic control within a democratic system)'.

Can the proletarian revolution be achieved without force? Marx was asked in 1872 when in Amsterdam. He replied:

You know that the institutions, mores, and traditions of various countries must be taken into consideration, and we do not deny that there are countries – such as America, England, and if I were more familiar with your institutions, I would perhaps also add Holland – where the workers can attain their goal by peaceful means. This being the case, we must also recognise the fact that in most countries on the Continent the lever of our revolution must be force; it is force to which we must some day appeal to erect the rule of labour. (La Liberté Speech delivered by Karl Marx on 8 September 1872)

The dictatorship of the proletariat may begin in individual nation states, but such states cannot progress towards socialism, that is, the withering of such state machines towards the 'administration of things' unless the dictatorship spreads internationally into the major economies and eventually globally, just as the capitalist mode of production has. Communist production is not simply inherited from capitalism, needing only to be signed into law by a newly elected socialist government. It requires 'long struggles, through a series of historic processes, transforming circumstances and men' (Marx, 1985, p. 76). Among these transformed circumstances will be 'not only a change of distribution, but a new organisation of production, or rather the delivery (setting free) of the social forms of production ... of their present class character, and their *harmonious national and international coordination*' (our emphasis, p. 157). That means the ending of imperialism and its replacement by an association of nations based on democratic planning and common ownership.

Russian economist Preobrazhensky studied the contradictory laws which govern the transitional economy, namely, the law of primitive socialist accumulation and the law of value. Capitalist accumulation within feudalism engaged in primitive accumulation *before* becoming the dominant form of production; so for Preobrazhensky socialism needs to engage in primitive accumulation *before* it can demonstrate the peculiar advantage of the socialist mode of production. Primitive socialist accumulation is particularly complicated in countries where capitalist production is underdeveloped. According to Marx, primitive capitalist accumulation had depended upon the expropriation of the peasant and the creation of 'free' labour: 'free' in the sense of being turned away from the soil and transformed into an exploitable commodity on the labour market. Only then could merchant capital grow and emerge as industrial capital. Reasoning analogically, Preobrazhensky saw the nationalised Soviet enterprises in a position roughly comparable to Marx's merchant capitalist. The merchant had been surrounded by feudal elements, just as the nationalised enterprises had been cut adrift in a sea of capitalist relations. The merchant had accumulated the social surplus, transforming it into industrial capital and universalising the new mode of production to the extent permitted by the inherent contradictions of the capitalist system. In like manner, socialist enterprises would accumulate the social surplus by means of monopoly control – only with the critical difference that the socialist mode of production would achieve true universality by overcoming the contradiction between town and country (Day, 1975, p. 218).

Preobrazhensky (1965, pp. 79, 81) made it clear that socialist accumulation is based on the nationalisation of large-scale industry and the system of ownership for socialist reconstruction; this presupposes the overthrow of the old system, that is, it can only begin after a social revolution. This is different to primitive capitalist accumulation, which begins under feudalism. Preobrazhensky showed that socialised planned production in the Soviet Union required resources not only from expropriating the internal bourgeoisie or surplus extraction from the proletariat. The Soviet state needed to obtain surplus through petty production, trade and inward foreign investment. The state would then use surpluses to realise its plan and expand the planned sector. So capitalists should be allowed to operate in the economy or will form joint enterprises with the state sector that extract surplus value from workers. However, they operate within the overall plan and are constrained by the control of credit as the banks are owned and controlled by the state. The capitalists play a subordinate role in the economy and are forced to support state planning objectives. The contending tendencies of the two laws of socialist accumulation and the law of value are not only demonstrated in the competition between the state sector and the private sector, but also in the control and ownership of surplus in the production process.

The driving force of capitalist production is the striving for profit, its regulator the law of value. Capitalism satisfies the consumer needs of society by way of this mechanism. In particular, the worker receives his share from the fund of means of consumption through selling his labour-power. In what way is state economy different from capitalism on this point? On the one hand, it has *already* ceased to be production for profit, for surplus value. On the other, it is not *yet* production for the sake of consumption by the workers of the state economy and still less by all the people in private economy ... it [the state economy] can be overthrown in its mobile equilibrium if the necessary proportion of expanded reproduction dictated by the whole economic situation is not guaranteed by an adequately and steadily growing rate of accumulation of surplus product in material form and this always means restriction of individual demand. The contradiction between these two tendencies within state economy does not take the form of antagonism between classes, but it exists nevertheless. (Preobrazhensky, 1965, pp. 72–7)

We can thus categorise a transitional economy between capitalism towards socialism. It must involve:

1. The loss of state power by capital and its 'armed bodies of men'.
2. Capitalist state power is replaced by workers' democracy based on Engels' two principles of democratic right of recall and the wages of officials at the same level as average workers' wages.
3. The common ownership of the bulk of the means of production and credit.
4. The planning of investment and production rather than being left to market forces.
5. A high and rising level of technology and productivity of labour to reduce working hours and gradually end scarcity in social needs.
6. The gradual replacement of commodity production with direct production for use.

7. The gradual ending of wage labour and money, both as a means of exchange and as a store of value.
8. The progressive 'withering away' of state power (armies, police, officialdom).

The second point is vital in categorising any transition to socialism or communism. It must involve two principles. First, all posts must be filled through elections, which may be a combination of direct choice and delegation, but with the vital condition that the elected are subject to recall, if needed. But this is not enough. The fundamental question is the class nature of the positions to be filled through elections. In this connection, Marx makes the essential distinction between those performing the function of capital (control and surveillance) and those who perform the function of labour (coordination and unity of the labour process). Bourgeois sociology obliterates this distinction. Marx makes an analogy with an orchestra, where the music director coordinates the musicians. Those performing the work of coordination and unity of the labour process are not managers in the usual meaning. They do not oversee and police, they are not agents of capital who exploit the labourers on behalf of capital. Rather, they are members of the collective labourer. Those performing the work of coordination and unity of the labour process are the opposite of managers in capitalist production relations.

Engels' second principle is that the elected should not earn more than the electors. This is not only a potent anti-corruption element; it also means that the principle that skilled workers should earn more than unskilled workers is a residue of archaic capitalist production relations. Workers are skilled either because of their inherent qualities (and there is no reason to reward them for this) or because they have benefited from the educational system. In either case, there is no reason to reward them for this. Garbage refuse collectors are just as important to society as economics professors, if not more.

These two principles are the key indicators of a workers' democracy required for the transition to socialism. Their expansion or withering away indicates whether a society is moving towards or away from socialism. The other features of a transitional economy should be considered in the light of whether they are an expression of these two principles. For example, production in a transitional economy should be increasing the production of use values, that is, the goods workers themselves decide to produce in order to satisfy their needs as expressed by themselves, for example, environmental investments over arms. This requires planning and thus a democratic decision process. It also requires the common ownership of the means of production, democratic decision-making in investments and in the choice of the techniques in the various labour processes that are most suited for a full development of every worker's potential. The extent to which and the speed at which a society is moving towards socialism is given by the extent and speed at which these categories of a transitional economy replace capitalist social relations and institutions.

6.3 CASE STUDY: THE SOVIET UNION

In trying to answer this question, we shall start by drawing upon the experience of Russia, the first attempt to install a socialist regime, which has shaped the vicissitudes not only of socialism but of the world at large. We restrict our focus on Russia, although we shall refer to other economies following the Soviet Union model. Let us then begin by considering Russia's transition.

In November 1917 there was an insurrection in St. Petersburg, Russia, that led to the Bolshevik wing of the Russian Social Democrats gaining control of the major organs of state power and establishing the rule of workers' Soviets (Councils). In hindsight, that the Russian people decided to end the 370-year rule of the Ivanov monarchy in 1917 was no surprise. The world was changing: capitalism was becoming dominant and, with it, industrialisation. An absolute monarchy sitting on a peasant country that was industrialising in the cities was an anachronism. What was unique was that the Russian people went on to establish a republic and eventually a state where capitalism and imperialism had no control within just a few months.

The objective conditions for change were ripe. Russia was a poor country. It had great natural and human resources, but these were 'locked in' by the vast size of the country and the extreme climate. Even in 1914, 85 per cent of the population were still peasants. Peasants had to practise subsistence farming. Rural peasants had been emancipated from serfdom in 1861, but the land was still owned by a few: 1.5 per cent of the population owned 25 per cent of it. Workers too had good reasons for discontent: overcrowded housing, long hours at work: usually as much as ten hours a day, six days a week, very poor safety and sanitary conditions, harsh disciplines and maybe worst of all, inadequate wages with concurrently rising inflation; a recipe for economic turmoil. In one 1904 survey, it was found that an average of 16 people shared each apartment in St. Petersburg, with as many as six people in each room.

But from the 1890s, under a succession of Tsarist ministers, railways were built, foreign investment attracted and landholdings partially reformed. Economic growth rates averaged 9 per cent from 1894 to 1900. These were huge rates of change, even though most industrial investment was wasted on armaments because Tsar Nicholas II wanted to protect Russia's position as a great power in competition with Japan in the East and Germany in the West. The Witte years of economic reform from 1890 to 1905 brought some certain modernisation and industrialisation with them, but this expansion was uneven and depended on foreign capital, mainly French bank loans. Then there were five consecutive years of bad harvests from 1901 to 1905. And the defeat by Japan in a war was the straw that broke the camel's back and sparked the 1905 revolution – the dress rehearsal for 1917. From 1905 to 1914, the economy grew at an annual rate of growth of 6 per cent. Between 1890 and 1910, the population of St. Petersburg doubled from just over a million and Moscow experienced similar growth. This created a new proletariat, a much more dangerous threat to Tsarism than the peasantry had been. From 1911 to 1914, political discontent grew.

World War I only added to the chaos; the vast demand for war supplies and workers caused more strikes, at the same time as conscription stripped skilled workers from the cities, who had to be replaced by unskilled peasants. The war brought famine due to the poor infrastructure of the railways and the need for supplying soldiers at the front. Ultimately, the soldiers themselves turned against the Tsar, bringing him down and with the formation of a republic, eventually under the Bolsheviks, the war was ended through an agreement on harsh terms with the Germans. In the two years following the Revolution, there was an economic catastrophe. By 1919, average incomes in Soviet Russia fell by half that of 1913, a fall that had not been seen in Eastern Europe since the 17th century (Maddison, 2001).

Worse was to come. After another run of disastrous harvests, famine conditions began to appear in the summer of 1920. An average worker's daily intake fell to 1,600 calories, about half the level before the war. Spreading hunger coincided with a wave of deaths from typhus, typhoid, dysentry and cholera. In 1921, the grain harvest collapsed further, particularly in the southern and eastern grain-farming regions. More than five million people may have died prematurely from hunger and disease. Russia suffered 13 million premature deaths from conflict and famine. This was one in ten of the population living within the future Soviet borders in 1913. And all this while a savage civil war raged as invading foreign armies and reactionary domestic forces tried to displace Soviet rule. It was during this period of so-called 'war communism' that the expropriation of landlords and capitalists was completed. Eventually, after the victory of the Soviet government in the civil war and the stabilisation of the regime, economic performance began to pick up, particularly after the New Economic Policy reforms from 1924 which allowed the development of markets in agriculture (Figure 6.1).

The introduction of five-year plans for investment and industrialisation also led to rapid expansion.[1] And then during the period up to 1945, there was a dramatic rise in GDP per capita through further industrialisation, where nearly all means of production were in state ownership and subject to the dictats of planning officials (GosPlan). That accelerated after 1945 and up to the 1970s. Indeed, from 1928 to 1970, the USSR was the fastest growing economy except for Japan (Figure 6.2)!

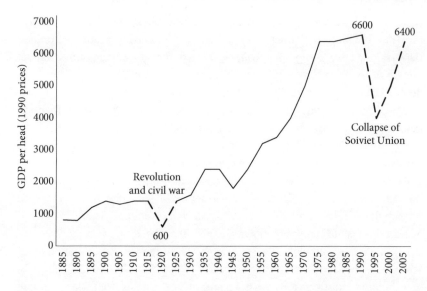

Figure 6.1   Soviet Union: Real GDP per head, 1990 prices in dollars, 1880–2005

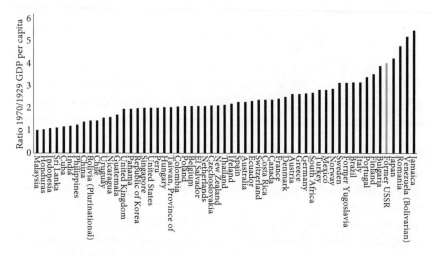

Figure 6.2   Economic growth, 1928–70

Note: Turkey is classified as a non-OECD country.
Source: Maddison (1995a).

And compared to the rest of the Third World, its performance was remarkable. In 1952, the Soviet Union was only behind Ireland and Western Europe as a whole. By 1975, the USSR had a higher GDP per capita than Mexico, Latin America, Colombia, South Korea and Taiwan (Figure 6.3).

The success of the Soviet planning model in the 1950s and 1960s was undeniable. But a phase of economic stagnation began in the 1970s. The attempt

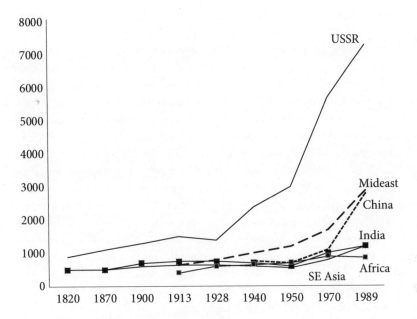

Figure 6.3   USSR versus rest of world, GDP per capita
Source: Maddison (1995b, table 1.1).

to move from a regime of intensive accumulation of fixed assets to one based on high productivity growth failed. The reasons are manifold: bureaucratisation inherent in a planning system not based on socialist decision-making; the alienation of the workers from socialist principles as expressed in the Soviet bureaucratic system; the monopoly of advanced technologies by imperialism (except for space and arms); imperialism's threat that forced the Soviet Union to derail vast resources to the arms race. The militarisation of the economy because of the 'cold war' used up valuable productive investment potential. The Russian elite tried to alter the economic model to one relying on the export of natural resources, rather than further develop industry and technology.

The attempt of Perestroika to build 'market socialism' and dismantle the plan was the final straw. Gorbachev's reforms disrupted the system of planning and distribution and provoked chronic excess domestic demand and the need for foreign imports. With the collapse of the Soviet state, the wealth acquired by Soviet state managers during the Perestroika allowed them to take advantage of the 'shock therapy' reforms in the 1990s, turning themselves into what we now call the Russian oligarchs. In the early and mid-1990s Russian President Boris Yeltsin launched an ambitious privatisation programme. In what was the largest sell-off of state-owned property in history, enterprises were sold at a rate of about 800 a month and by the time it was complete, 77 per cent of Russia's large and mid-size enterprises and 82 per cent of the small ones were private.

The 15,000 privatised factories accounted for two-thirds of industrial output and 60 per cent of the industrial workforce. The 85,000 privatised shops, restaurants, small business and service establishments represented 70 per cent of the national total. Everything from sawmills to rolls of barbed wire was auctioned off. Tyres were sold at a price that was equal to a month's wage for a Russian worker and MiG-29 jet fighters went for $23 million.[2]

The privatisation programme was at the core of economic restructuring and was a critical consideration for foreign loans and investment in Russia's economy. On the surface, the privatisation of Russian industry seemed to go fairly smoothly, but the reality was a different story. Many state-owned companies involved with natural resources were raped by gangsters and corrupt officials. Jeffrey Sachs, a Harvard economist who advised the Russian government in the 1990s, wrote in the *New York Times*: 'Russia's resources provided unparalleled opportunities for theft by officials. Oil, gas, diamonds and metal ore deposits were nominally owned by the state and thus by nobody. They were ripe for stealing ... the system was often skirted or compromised by ad hoc decrees and hidden arrangements.'[3] This 'shock therapy' introduction of capitalism led to the worst peacetime collapse in a major economy since the industrial revolution. By 1998, Russia's GDP was 39 per cent below its 1991 level (Figure 6.4).

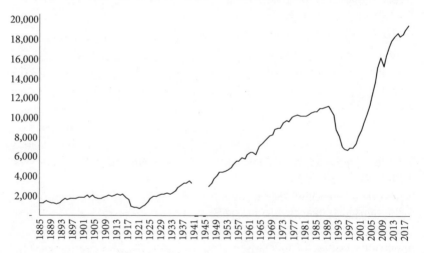

Figure 6.4   Soviet Union: Real GDP per head, 1990 prices, 1885–2010

If we review the progress of transition achieved by the Soviet Union, we can tick off the following:

1. The loss of state power by capital and its 'armed bodies of men'. The loss of state power by capital was a feature at the beginning of the Russian transition. But then the process was reversed.

2. Capitalist state power is replaced by workers' democracy based on Engels' two principles of democratic right of recall and the wages of officials at the same level as average workers' wages. That was not implemented.
3. The legal common ownership of the bulk of the means of production and credit.
4. The planning of investment and production rather than being left to market forces.
5. A high and rising level of technology and productivity of labour to reduce working hours and gradually end scarcity in social needs. For some decades but eventually no.
6. The gradual replacement of commodity production with direct production for use. This stopped.
7. The gradual ending of wage labour and money, both as a means of exchange and as a store of value. This never progressed.
8. The progressive 'withering away' of state power (armies, police, officialdom). On the contrary.

Within a few years of 1917, the principles of workers' democracy in the Soviet Union were gradually removed. And in 1989–90 even the criteria 1, 3 and 4 of a transitional economy were dismembered and reversed. In every sense, based on the above criteria, Russia is now a capitalist state with an economy based on commodity production for the profit of the private owners of means of production. The loss of workers' democracy and control of the state (criterion 2) in Russia blocked any further transition towards socialism and eventually led to the capitalist restoration of state power (criterion 1) and the shock therapy privatisation of the economy (criterion 3).

Janos Kornai was a prominent analyst of the Russian case. Having started out as a supporter of 'socialist' regimes like the Soviet Union and Hungary, Kornai became deeply disillusioned. Based on his view that economies in transition to socialism could only exist as bureaucratic 'command' economies, he eventually concluded that 'democracy can only exist under capitalism'. Socialism is restricted to dictatorial and autocratic forms because 'democratic socialism is impossible' (Kornai, 2016). But Kornai's view of what he calls 'classical socialism' is not Marx's. Kornai finds three elements of 'classical socialism': rule by Communist Party guided by the ideology of 'Marxism-Leninism'; the dominance of public ownership within the economy; and preponderance of bureaucratic coordination. But as we argue above, these are not the elements of a country in the transition to socialism. Kornai's criteria inevitably leads him to the conclusion that 'democratic socialism is impossible'.[4]

One key lesson that we can draw from the Russian transition is that it could not succeed indefinitely in the face of world capital. Marx and Engels remarkably anticipated the eventual failure of the Russian Revolution. Marx thought that a successful communist revolution presupposed the existence of an integrated world economy.

> The proper task of bourgeois society is the creation of the world market … the colonisation of California and Australia and the opening up of China and Japan would seem to have completed this process. For us, the difficult question is this: on the Continent revolution is imminent and will, moreover, instantly assume a socialist character. Will it not necessarily be crushed in this little corner of the earth, since the movement of bourgeois society is still in the ascendant over a far greater area?

And yet Marx also saw that the socialist transformation would not have to wait for each national capitalist economy to 'mature'. As he wrote, 'If the Russian Revolution becomes the signal for a proletarian revolution in the West, so that the two complement each other, the present common ownership of land may serve as the starting point for communist development.' Unfortunately, the revolution in the West did not materialise. While the planned economy succeeded in transforming the lives of millions, Russia was isolated, surrounded and very quickly the regime itself degenerated into a totalitarian dictatorship and finally into a corrupt capitalist autocracy far from the aims of the Revolution of 1917.

The Soviet model of centralised planning based on a predominant state sector with limited development of a capitalist sector was replicated in Cuba, North Korea and the Eastern European bloc. The Eastern European transitional states were the result of the occupation by Soviet armed forces after World War II, with the possible exception of Yugoslavia, where a guerrilla force liberated the Balkans from Nazi rule. North Korea was also the result of Soviet occupation and follows the Soviet model too, and not only in an economic sense; but also politically with no workers' democracy; instead with the most extreme totalitarian leadership based on one family.

On the other hand, Cuba had an indigenous revolution first based on the countryside that eventually moved to nationalise the economy and bring industrial enterprises, small businesses and the plantation farms into a centralised plan. The revolution seized power from the Batista dictatorship in January 1959, but it was not until 1960 that all financial institutions, 83.6 per cent of industry, including all sugar mills and 42.5 per cent of land, were nationalised. The imposition of the US blockade in 1960 forced Cuba to be firmly incorporated into the trading system of the socialist countries. The Cuban leaders were firm supporters of central planning and opposed to so-called 'market socialism'. As Guevara put it: 'the law of value and planning are two terms linked by a contradiction and its resolution. We can therefore state that centralised planning is characteristic of the socialist society, its definition' (Yaffe, 2012, p. 25). Guevara argued that the use of capitalist mechanisms in the production process in socialist Cuba risked reproducing capitalist social relations and a capitalist consciousness, despite state planning and state ownership of the means of production. Guevara believed that moral incentives should be developed to undermine the law of value as early as possible during the transition process.

Between 1970 and 1985, Cuba experienced high-sustained rates of growth. But after 1985, the economy entered a phase of economic stagnation. Following the fall of the Soviet Union, Cuba's GDP declined by 33 per cent between 1990 and 1993, partially due to the loss of Soviet subsidies and a crash in sugar prices in the early 1990s. It rebounded in the early 2000s due to a combination of some liberalisation of the economy and heavy subsidies from the friendly government of Venezuela, which provided Cuba with low-cost oil and other subsidies worth up to 12 per cent of Cuban GDP annually (Figure 6.5). In 2011, some economic reforms were introduced, allowing the formation of small capitalist businesses. Despite the harsh US blockade of trade and investment; despite the continual attacks of the émigré community based in Florida, the Cuban economy has actually done better than the rest of the Caribbean and retains high levels of health care and education. In 2019, Cuba ranked 70th out of 189 countries, with a Human Development Index of 0.783, placed in the high human development category.

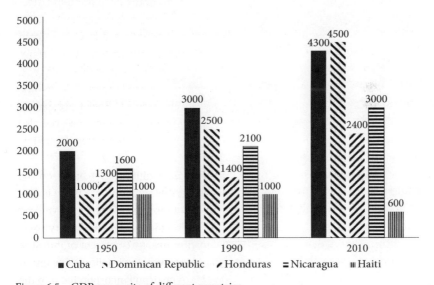

Figure 6.5   GDP per capita of different countries

6.4 CASE STUDY: CHINA'S TRANSITION

In our chapter on imperialism, we argued that China is not imperialist or even 'sub-imperialist'. On the contrary, the imperialist powers extract value and surplus value out of China through trade and investment in the same way as Brazil or Nigeria or Mexico or India or South Africa. But is China capitalist? Is the mode of production that is dominant in China that of commodity production for the profit of private owners of the means of production? And what is the class character of the Chinese state? Are Chinese capitalists as a class in control of the state machine including the armed forces and directing policy in the interests of Chinese capital? We can answer these questions by considering China against our criteria of a transitional economy.

The Marxist explanation of China's economic development must start from the law of value. China has a large state sector that is supposed to follow a plan set by the Chinese Communist Party (CPC) leaders. But this does not necessarily change the class nature of that state sector as being exploitative, that is, based on capitalist production relations. Wage labour still operates and the CPC, the state enterprises and the capitalist sector bosses dictate the form and direction of that labour, whether for the production of use values, or for profit. The contradiction in China is between the capitalist production (state and non-state) for profit and the production of schools, medical services etc. which is state planned production of use values (for social needs) rather than value. The state sector itself is not 'socialist' because the production of use values is not directed by labour; so the production *relations* in this sector are still essentially capitalist. But the higher production of use values by the state sector is a feature of China's transitional economy. Even if this production of use value is still on the basis of capitalist production relations, the CPC backs the state sector for its own political survival.

Of our eight criteria for a transitional economy (see Section 6.1), only 1, 3 and 4 are in operation in China, while no. 5 depends on the balance of economic forces between the state sector, the capitalist sector and imperialism. The second feature and the last three components of the transition to socialism are far away from being achieved. So China is not moving 'towards socialism'. It is a transitional economy that cannot move towards socialism because it lacks the key features of a workers' democracy; and is surrounded by imperialism. It is in a 'trapped transition'. And it is in a 'trapped transition' which could eventually be reversed, as proved for the Soviet Union.[5] To avoid that and to move towards socialism, workers' democracy must first be achieved and then China must raise its productivity levels to that of the imperialist core to reduce working hours and scarcity in social needs and then end wage labour and monetary exchange. And China needs working-class revolutions in the imperialist core that can establish transitional economies there and then allow the democratic planning of production and distribution globally for social need not profit.

In the case of China, the qualitative change that ended capitalism came as the result of a devastating civil war pitting the Soviet-aligned CPC against Chiang's imperialist-backed forces, the latter containing all the politically or militarily organised supporters of the Chinese capitalist class. With North Korea, the move came amid imperialist aggression on the Korean Peninsula during the Korean War. With North Vietnam (later extended to encompass all of Vietnam), the issue was the imperialist attempt to partition the country in 1954 as a wedge to prevent the spread of socialised economies. And with Cuba, the precipitating factor was the nationalisation of large US holdings on the island, followed by the Bay of Pigs invasion. None of the parties and their armies that led these revolutions had a revolutionary socialist programme. In the case of China, the Communist Party had a policy of a 'bloc of four classes', that is, an alliance with the 'progressive national capitalist class'. Rather, the decisive factor was the pressure brought to bear by imperialism that compelled these parties and armies to go along the Soviet route. Despite the lack of workers' democracy, replaced by autocratic and even totalitarian control by a bureaucratic state machine, these 'transitional' states are based on a mode of production where the public ownership of the means of production is dominant. In China, despite the rise of a large capitalist sector (unlike the Soviet model), state ownership and the planned economy is still decisive.

The CPC took power in 1949 after a long period of war against occupying Japanese armies and then after a civil war with war lord armies and the comprador nationalist government of Chiang Kai Shek. The communists under Mao supposedly looked to the Soviet model of 'socialism' and in the struggle against the Japanese, they adopted the two-stage theory of Russian leadership: of first, an alliance in government with Chiang and only after 'democracy' had been achieved, to strike out for socialism. But after the crushing of the communist workers in the cities by Chiang's armies, Mao Tse Tung was forced to lead the remnants of his forces into a 'long march' across China and build a peasant-based army.

From hereon, this was not going to be a workers' revolution in the cities as in Russia, but a peasant army occupying the cities. From the beginning, the Chinese revolution excluded and indeed repressed any forms of workers' councils as emerged in the Paris Commune or early Soviet Russia. And indeed, for several years after taking state power, there was no move by the Chinese government to expropriate capitalist enterprises or nationalise the land. However, most capitalists had fled with Chiang's defeated army to the island of Formosa, where they set up a new statelet of Taiwan. And what finally drove the CPC to expropriation was the invasion of Korea by the Americans which if the Americans had won would have meant the revival of capitalist forces alongside and inside China. So the CPC nationalised what industrial enterprises there were, nationalised the land and distributed it to the peasantry. And they launched a massive industrialisation programme based on state planning of the economy.

At this point, we could say that some of the components of a transition from capitalism to socialism had been introduced in China.

But this was no state with organs of workers' democracy. The Chinese state was entirely controlled by the People's Army and the Communist Party officials. There was mass support for the revolution, especially in the countryside. Without that, the excesses and disasters of economic policy directed by Mao and his fellow leaders would have brought China down. The Great Leap Forward of 1958–61 aimed at industrialising the economy in basic industries but it was done with intense hardship for millions, particularly in the countryside. Then Mao's 'Cultural Revolution' of 1966–70 destroyed and disrupted economic development, apart from imposing grotesque repression on millions of skilled workers, students and officials. In both these adventures and zig zags in policy, the Chinese economy took steps back. Nevertheless, the economic power of state investment and planning, supported by massive human labour inputs, enabled the Chinese economy to sprint forward from abject poverty.

Contrary to current views, economic growth in China before 1978, before the so-called major economic reforms, was strong. Official Chinese figures reckoned that from 1949 to 1978, the total 'social output value' increased at an average annual increase of 9 per cent and the annual growth rate of industrial production was 11.4 per cent. In 27 years, the population increased by 400 million. Life expectancy rose from 35 years in 1949 to 63.8 years in 1975. These official growth figures are disputed by Western analyses. The most pessimistic is that provided in the Penn World Tables, using Conference Board sources, where China's growth is recorded at just 2.4 per cent a year, putting the pre-Deng period of growth at about that of the G7 growth, higher than India but lower than Japan, East Asia and Brazil.[6]

However, other sources put the average real GDP growth rate at 6.7 per cent a year, close to the East Asian Tigers (Hong Kong, Singapore, South Korea and Taiwan) (Figure 6.6).[7] The zig zags of policy under Mao are exposed in the graph in Figure 6.6, with the shocking collapse in GDP during the Great Leap Forward and the slump in the Cultural Revolution. Also, China's industrial expansion was beginning to be exhausted prior to the change in policy under Deng in 1978.

This forced the Chinese leadership under Deng to consider a different path from the Soviet Union to achieve faster economic growth and industrialisation. China opened up the economy to domestic capitalist production and foreign investment – but within limits. Indeed, it has been argued that Deng wanted to go the whole hog and privatise the economy but was persuaded to opt for a gradual approach.[8] China began to get the investment necessary to expand the economy over and above available agricultural surpluses and domestic household savings. In effect, this was a New Economic Policy (NEP) as in 1924 in

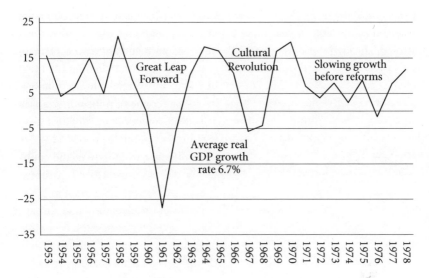

Figure 6.6   China: real GDP growth rate 1952–78 (%)

Soviet Russia but going much further and longer[9] into what some have called a new socio-economic formation within the transitional economy.[10]

However, a key World Bank report in 2003 concluded that the capitalist mode of production still did not dominate in China – indeed that was the problem according to the World Bank. Commodity production for profit, based on spontaneous market relations, governs capitalism. The rate of profit determines its investment cycles and generates periodic economic crises. This does not apply in China. The regular and recurring crises of investment and production experienced in the major capitalist economies since 1949 have not been mirrored in China; the only impact being any reductions in trade as the G7 economies suffer slumps. Unlike the major capitalist economies, China has not experienced a slump in national output in any year since 1973. Only South Korea can compare with that record, while other so-called emerging economies have been hit by sharp slowdowns in growth and even outright contractions (Table 6.1).

Table 6.1   Real GDP growth in various economies during global recessions

	China	G7	G20xChina	Japan	Korea	Brazil	India
1974–75	6.8	−0.1	0.6	3.1	7.8	2.6	9.1
1980–81	9.2	−0.1	−0.5	3.3	8.3	−2.2	3.5
1990–91	4.8	1.2	1.4	3.4	10.8	0.4	1.1
2000–01	7.8	1.3	1.6	0.4	4.9	4.0	4.8
2007–09	17.2	−3.8	−1.1	−6.5	3.8	4.0	11.2

The World Bank grudgingly recognised that China's incredible economic success over the last 30 years was based on an economy where growth was achieved through bureaucratic state planning and government control of investment. Its rate of economic growth may have been matched by emerging capitalist economies for a while back in the 19th century when they were 'taking off'. But no country has ever grown so fast for so long and been so large (with 22 per cent of the world's population). This is an achievement without precedent, even if China's growth slows down over the medium-term future. Over the period since 1978, China has had an average growth rate double that of India. Indeed, India has been left behind (Figure 6.7).

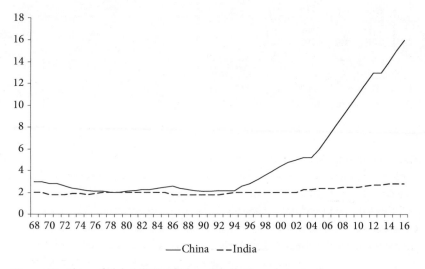

Figure 6.7   Share of global GDP: China and India ($ market prices)

China has raised 850 million people out of internationally defined poverty, while the majority of Indians remains deep in poverty (Figure 6.8).

So far China's state-owned sector has not been dominated by the market, or by investment decisions based on profitability alone; or by capitalist companies and bosses; or by foreign investors. Are these elements of socialist relations? We think that they are *possible* conditions for the re-emergence of those relations if embedded in the expansion of the socialist production relations. For example, the rolling back or even the abolition of poverty is vital for labour, but in and of itself it is not an indicator of a socialist direction. The reduction of poverty is necessary for the CPC's legitimisation as holder of power and to increase the internal market. But also, the reduction of poverty has been an element of the CPC's policies and can reacquire their original socialist substance.

Although the state sector controls the 'commanding heights' of the Chinese economy, capitalist accumulation competes with 'socialist accumulation', pro-

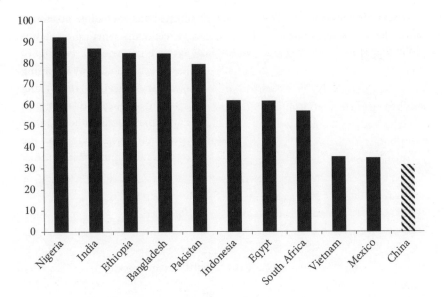

Figure 6.8   Share of population living at below $5 a day

ducing a zig-zag development. In the first half of the reform era to the early 1990s, there was an explosive growth of the mechanical and electronics industry and rises in wages. However, financial liberalisation, large-scale privatisation and the downsizing of state-owned and collective enterprises started to tip the balance away from state-led accumulation, leading to rising debts and surging unemployment. But the 1997–98 Asian financial crisis forced the Chinese leadership to make a fundamental policy reversal from the liberalisation tack with the launch of several state-led packages to expand investment; the reversal of stagnant consumption through a range of welfare policies; the revitalisation of state enterprises and banks; and putting the liberalisation of the country's capital account on hold.

6.5 PRODUCTIVITY VERSUS PROFITABILITY

For Marxist theory, it is the productivity of labour that is key. In so far as there is a capitalist sector in a developing economy and world markets, then profitability is the other key indicator. The Marxist model is that the level of productivity will decide economic growth because it reduces the cost of production in labour time and enables a developing nation to compete in world markets. But in the capitalist mode of production, there is a contradiction.

There is also the law of profitability. There is a long-term inverse relationship between productivity and profitability (as workers can only be squeezed so much before they can no longer work), given that the introduction of technology to replace or reduce labour becomes subject to the law of the tendency of the rate of profit to fall. It is this diminishing factor (surplus value relative to the capital invested) that Marx highlighted as one of the ultimate contradictions of capitalism. This results in regular occurrences of crises in production. In the Marxist model of capitalist development, productivity growth must be weighed against the contradiction of the tendency of the rate of profit to fall as capital is accumulated. In so far as China's private capitalist sector expands its contribution to the overall economy and the public sector is reduced, then the profitability of that sector becomes relatively more important and the contradiction between productivity growth and profitability intensifies. In so far as it does, profitability becomes more relevant to investment and growth.

There have been various attempts to estimate the rate of profit in China.[11] Data on profitability before 1978 are dubious, given that the capitalist sector was very small before then. After 1978 there have been two cycles of profitability (Figure 6.9). Between 1978 and 1997, there was an upswing in profitability as capitalist production expanded through the Deng reforms and the opening up of foreign trade. But from 1997 onwards, there has been a decline as investment gathered pace and the capitalist economy globally also suffered a decline in profitability. The falling rate of profit then was accompanied by a slowing in the rate of GDP growth. There was a limited recovery after China entered the World Trade Organization in 2000, which also saw a significant rise in the rate of economic growth (as the world too expanded at a credit-fuelled pace). After 2007, the slump in world capitalism drove down Chinese profitability. Rising

Figure 6.9 China internal rate of return (%)

wages were not matched by increased sales abroad, so the rate of surplus value slumped, while investment in fixed capital remained high. Profitability fell. This also had a deleterious effect on GDP growth in the recent period.

Does this mean that China is heading for major slump along classic capitalist lines some time in this decade? Marquetti et al. seem to suggest that:

> The larger profit rate explained the robust mechanization in the early stages of the process. Fast capital accumulation diminishes capital productivity and the profit rate. Then the success in catching up must hinge on raising the saving and investment rates. It may further reduce capital productivity and the profit rate, putting the process at risk, which seems to be the case in China and India.[12]

And they quote Minqi Li that 'if China were to follow essentially the same economic laws as in other capitalist countries (such as the United States and Japan), a decline in the profit rate would be followed by a deceleration of capital accumulation, culminating in a major economic crisis'.[13] But the question is whether the Chinese economy is dominated by those same economic laws – yet. The evidence of its economic success to date is that it is not. Its economy is not yet dominated by the market, by investment decisions based on profitability; or by capitalist companies and bosses; or by foreign investors.

There has been minimal positive correlation between the profitability of Chinese capital stock and real GDP growth for most of the period since the formation of the People's Republic of China (Figure 6.10). This suggests that China has directed its investments towards the more productivity-enhancing sectors even if they were not its more profitable ones. The profitability of capital did not decide the level of investment in productive assets and economic growth during the Chinese growth miracle before 1978. After Deng's reforms in the 1980s, the correlation did turn positive, although still less positively correlated than in the rest of the G20 economies or the G7. However, after China privatised sections of its state sector in the 1990s and joined the World Trade Organization in 2000, there was a significant increase in the positive correlation between the profitability of Chinese capital and real GDP growth. This suggests that the Chinese economy has become increasingly vulnerable to a crisis in its capitalist sector and to developments in international capital and their profitability.[14]

In the end, in a capitalist economy lower profitability comes into conflict with productivity growth. In so far as China's private capitalist sector expands its contribution to the overall economy and the public sector is reduced, then the profitability of the private sector becomes relatively more important and the contradiction between productivity growth and profitability intensifies. In so far as it does, profitability becomes relevant to investment and growth.

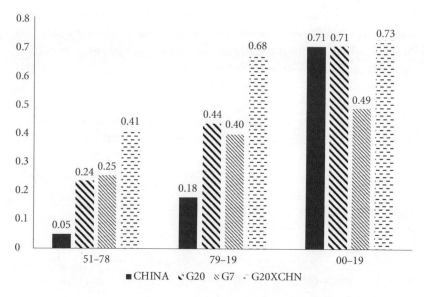

Figure 6.10 Correlation between rate of profit and real GDP growth
Source: Penn World Tables 10.0; IRR series for profitability; real GDP growth calculations.

The effects of foreign investment have a double content. On the one hand, in the absence of foreign investment, China would have had a structural trade deficit and foreign debt – or an import level restricted to the level supportable by a reduced export sector. So foreign investment was an agency of modernisation from the outside. However, the risk is that large-scale domestic industry would become dominated by foreign capital, side by side with backward industries in which local capital predominates. This might help the trade balance but would accelerate the devastation of local (capitalist and non-capitalist) production and act as a powerful blocking mechanism against the development of the indigenous forces of production. The destruction of native industry would displace more workers than can be newly employed in the relatively new hi-tech industries. This was the story of many new capitalist economies in the late 19th century onwards as imposed by imperialist economies. It remains the story of most of Africa, much of Latin America and parts of Asia with some exceptions.

China remains the glaring exception. Because the law of value operating in markets and foreign investment was at first totally blocked and later curbed and controlled by a large state-owned sector, central planning and state policy, as well as by restricting foreign ownership of new industries and imposing controls on the flow of capital in and out of the country. As leading Chinese economist Yu Yongding put it: 'China has to maintain its capital controls in the foreseeable future. If China were to lose control over its cross-border capital flows, it could lead to panic and so capital outflows would turn into an avalanche and eventually bring down the whole financial system.'[15] It was these very restrictions that enabled China to expand investment and technology, employ swathes of labour and generally avoid control of its destiny by multinational combines, up to now.

The law of value operates in the Chinese economy. But the impact is distorted, curbed and blocked by bureaucratic interference from the state and the party structure to the point that capitalists cannot yet fully dominate and direct the trajectory of the Chinese economy. China's 'socialism with Chinese characteristics' is a weird beast. It is not socialism by any Marxist definition or by the benchmark of workers' democracy in a transitional economy as defined above. And there has been a significant expansion of privately owned companies, both foreign and domestic over the last 30 years, with the establishment of a stock market and other financial institutions. But the vast majority of employment and investment is still undertaken by publicly owned companies or by institutions that are under the direction and control of the Communist Party. The biggest part of China's world-beating industry is not foreign-owned multinationals, but Chinese state-owned enterprises (SOEs). The major banks are state-owned and their lending and deposit policies are directed by the government. There is no free flow of foreign capital into and out of China. Capital controls are imposed and enforced and the currency's value is manipulated to set economic targets (much to the annoyance of the US Congress).

In 2018 (latest data available), total assets of Chinese SOEs stood at 194 per cent of GDP – higher than in the early 2000s, and several orders of magnitude larger than in any other country (IMF Fiscal Monitor). Every other major capitalist economy has public assets equivalent to less than 50 per cent of national GDP (Figure 6.11). Every year, China's public investment to GDP is around 16 per cent compared to 3–4 per cent in the US and the UK. And there is nearly three times as much stock of public productive assets to private capitalist sector assets in China. In the US and the UK, public assets are less than 50 per cent of private assets. Even in 'mixed economy' India or Japan, the ratio of public to private assets is no more than 75 per cent. This shows that in China public ownership in the means of production is dominant – unlike any other major economy.

A report by the US-China Economic and Security Review Commission found that

The state-owned and controlled portion of the Chinese economy is large. Based on reasonable assumptions, it appears that the visible state sector – SOEs and entities directly controlled by SOEs, accounted for more than 40% of China's non-agricultural GDP. If the contributions of indirectly controlled entities, urban collectives and public TVEs [Township and Village Enter-

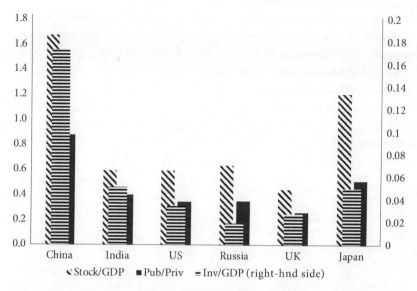

Figure 6.11 China's public sector dominates: public investment and stock to GDP/ public to private stock (ratios)

prises] are considered, the share of GDP owned and controlled by the state is approximately 50%.[16]

At the same time, the Communist Party/state machine infiltrates all levels of industry and activity in China. According to a report by Joseph Fang and others, there are party organisations within every corporation that employs more than three Communist Party members. Each party organisation elects a party secretary. It is the party secretary who is the lynchpin of the alternative management system of each enterprise. This extends party control beyond the SOEs, partly privatised corporations and village or local government-owned enterprises into the private sector or 'new economic organisations' as these are called. In 1999, only 3 per cent of these had party cells. Now the figure is nearly 13 per cent. The reality is that almost all Chinese companies employing more than 100 people have an internal party cell-based control system. This is no relic of the Maoist era. It is the current structure set up specifically to maintain party control of the economy.

China's Communist Party is now writing itself into the articles of association of many of the country's biggest companies, describing the party as playing a core role in 'an organised, institutionalised and concrete way' and 'providing direction [and] managing the overall situation'. There are 102 key state enterprises with assets of 50 trillion yuan that include state oil companies, telecom operators, power generators and weapons manufacturers. These 102 big conglomerates contributed 60 per cent of China's outbound investments by the end of 2016. Communist Party committees have been installed at many tech firms, reviewing everything from operations to compliance with national goals. Regulators have been discussing taking a 1 per cent stake in some giants, including Alibaba and Tencent, along with a board seat. Tech companies have been widely encouraged to invest in state-owned firms, in the hopes of making them more productive. The common denominator of all these efforts is that the government wants more control. One recent report found that 60 per cent of Chinese start-up companies have either direct or indirect investment from the state. China's venture-capital sector is dominated not by traditional tech dealmakers but by the state: there are more than 1,000 government-owned venture-capital firms in China, controlling more than $750 billion.

SOEs have assimilated Western technologies – sometimes with cooperation and sometimes not – and are now engaged in projects in Argentina, Kenya, Pakistan and the UK. And the great 'one belt, one road' project for central Asia is not aimed to make profit. It is to expand China's economic influence globally and extract natural and other technological resources for the domestic economy. China is not investing abroad through its state companies because of 'excess capital' or even because the rate of profit in state and capitalist enterprises has been falling.

Similarly, the great expansion of infrastructure investment after 2008 to counteract the impact of collapsing world trade from the global financial crisis and the Great Recession hitting the major capitalist economies was no Keynesian-style government spending/borrowing, as mainstream and (some) Marxist economists argue. It was a state-directed and planned programme of investments by state corporations and funded by state-owned banks. This was proper 'socialised investment' as mooted by Keynes, but never implemented in capitalist economies during the Great Depression, because to do so would have been to replace capitalism.

6.6 STATE CAPITALISM OR A TRANSITIONAL ECONOMY?

There are some analyses of the transitional economy which argue that there was no transition at all from capitalism to socialism in the Soviet Union, China and other states like Cuba, Vietnam or North Korea. These states remained capitalist or are 'state capitalist'. Let us consider the latter formulation in relation to the law of value. One leading proponent of 'state capitalism' argues that 'state capitalism and a workers state are two stages in the transitional period from capitalism to socialism'.[17] This flies in the face of Marx and Engels' components for the transitional economy. Now we have a new stage in the transition, 'state capitalism' which is also apparently 'diametrically opposed' to socialism. According to this version of state capitalism, the Soviet Union or China cannot be transitional economies because wage labour exists in both and that should disappear under socialism. But what Marx and Engels argue is that, after the takeover of power by the proletariat and the establishment of the 'dictatorship', the law of value does not disappear, indeed it is still present in the transitional economy, particularly in the market for labour power. This would only disappear under socialism. A transitional economy is precisely where the law of value is in competition with the planning mechanism and collective production – the economy is in transition. There is no need to create a new stage called state capitalism.

In the early years of the Soviet Union, Lenin did apply the term 'state capitalism' but not to the Soviet economy as a whole, only to a certain section of it: the foreign concessions, the mixed industrial and commercial companies and, in part, the peasant and largely kulak (rich peasant) cooperatives under state control. All these are indubitable elements of capitalism, but since they are controlled by the state and even function as mixed companies through its direct participation, Lenin conditionally, or, according to his own expression, 'in quotes', called these economic forms 'state capitalism'. The conditioning of this term depended upon the fact that a proletarian, not a bourgeois, state was involved; so the quotation marks were intended to stress just this difference of no little importance. However, in so far as the proletarian state allowed private capital and permitted it within definite restrictions to exploit the workers, it shielded value relations under one of its wings. In this strictly limited sense, one could speak of 'state capitalism'.[18]

Moreover, the view that the likes of China or Vietnam are a new form of capitalism, 'state capitalism', suggests that world capitalism is now today stronger than it ever was before in history. Alongside the decline of the imperialist powers, state capitalism has apparently ushered in a new and sensational phase of the development of the productive forces, in a backward country like China, and thus much more impressive even than anything Marx described for 19th century capitalism.

In the case of one particular proponent of 'state capitalism' there is further confusion because the author suggests that the Soviet Union did not operate under the law of value from 1917 until 1928, but only did so thereafter when five-year plans were introduced and when the Soviet government entered the arms race with the imperialist powers.[19] It is strange to argue that the law of value did not operate in the Soviet economy when for nearly a year after the November revolution, the Bolsheviks did not expropriate capitalist enterprises; or that it did not operate during the period of the New Economic Policy when the peasantry were allowed to sell their produce in farming markets, but somehow it did operate after the government introduced a planning mechanism and targets in 1927 – presumably because the state played a bigger role in directing investment and production than before! And it is absurd to assume that capitalist production was somehow reintroduced because of 'competition on the capitalist world market' (i.e. that the tail of 1 per cent of output imported from and exported to advanced capitalist countries was wagging the dog of the Russian economy).

What is wrong with the theory of state capitalism is that it is based on formal logic not on a dialectical analysis. Formally, there is capitalism and socialism. With formal logic, if the features of socialism in an economy do not exist ie collective production by producers in association for direct consumption without markets or monetary exchange, then an economy must be capitalist. An economy is either black or it is white. But this is not a dialectical analysis. Everything is in motion and in transition from one thing to another; and from one mode of production to another. In a transitional economy, there are elements of the old mode of production and there are elements of a potentially new mode of production – side by side. Just as the duck-billed platypus has elements of mammalia (it suckles its young), it also has elements of reptilia (it lays eggs). The transition from capitalism to socialism does not happen overnight; black and white are thus both present.

However, a dialectical approach in this context also means recognising when a qualitative change has taken place, opening up the potential for a new economy. The duck-billed platypus has made a qualitative transition to mammalia (because it suckles its young and is warm-blooded). A transitional economy from capitalism to socialism is defined from its start by the revolutionary overthrow of the capitalist state machine and its replacement by a proletarian state and that state can only survive if the means of production and resources are expropriated from the capitalist class, atomising that class as a ruling class. With state planning as the next step, the laws of motion of the transitional economy are qualitatively different from a capitalist economy. This is not socialism, but no longer is it capitalism. There is no need to invent another stage in the transition called 'state capitalism'.

For Marx, 'capital' could only exist in the form of different capitals; otherwise, there was no more compulsion to accumulate. Consequently, capital could only exist in the form of 'different capitalists', that is, a social class constituted so that each part of it was, by compelling economic interest, tied to the survival of 'its' own unit of production or circulation. Consequently, the 'thirst for profit' of each part of that class and the 'drive to capital accumulation' are identical, the second one being only realisable through the first (the attempt at profit maximisation of each unit or firm). If there is no competition, and the allocation of resources are not left to the decisions of individual capitals and the 'invisible hand of the market', then there is no capitalism. Capitalism cannot exist as one capital, the state.[20]

The empirical proof that transitional economies are qualitatively different from capitalist economies is in the success of planned economies, where the law of value is controlled, curbed and regulated so it does not dominate. In neither the Soviet Union before 1990 nor in China since 1949 have there been regular and recurring slumps in investment and production caused by a collapse in the profitability and profits of the capitalist sector.[21] The capitalist sector and the capitalists as a class do not control the economy or the state power. History has shown this does not mean that transitional economies must have democratic workers control of the state or they must be categorised as capitalist or state capitalist. Workers' democracy did not exist for long in Russia, after the early beginnings of the Soviets; and it was never the case in China, Cuba, Vietnam, North Korea or in the states of Eastern Europe under Soviet control.

It is true that the inequality of wealth and income under China's 'socialism with Chinese characteristics' is very high. There are growing numbers of billionaires (many of whom are related to the communist leaders). China's gini coefficient, an index of income inequality, has risen from 0.30 in 1978 when the Communist Party began to open the economy to market forces to a peak of 0.49 just before the global recession. Indeed, China's gini coefficient has risen more than any other Asian economy in the last two decades. China has a high level of inequality of incomes by international standards (although it is still lower than many other 'emerging' economies like Brazil, Mexico or South Africa) – but the gini inequality ratio peaked just before the Great Recession and has been falling since (Figure 6.12). This rise was partly the result of the urbanisation of the economy as rural peasants move to the cities. Urban wages in the sweatshops

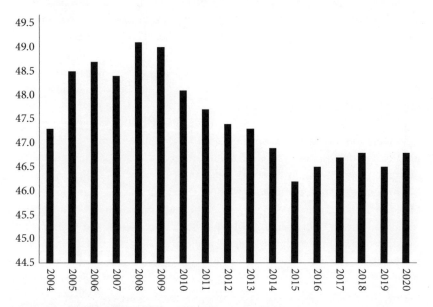

Figure 6.12   China: gini coefficient of income inequality

Source: National Bureau of Statistics.

and factories are increasingly leaving peasant incomes behind (not that those urban wages are anything to write home about when workers assembling Apple i-pads are paid under $2 an hour).

But it is also partly the result of the elite controlling the levers of power and making themselves fat, while allowing some Chinese billionaires to flourish. Urbanisation has slowed since the Great Recession and so has economic growth – along with that, the gini inequality index has fallen back a little. The main reason for the high inequality ratio is the disparity of incomes between urban and rural workers and between the wages in coastal and inland cities, as well as educational qualifications. Much is made of the number of billionaires in China, but given the size of the population and GDP, the per capita ratio compared to the US and other major economies is relatively low. Despite the large expansion in the number of millionaires, millionaires in China remain relatively rare. Millionaires account for 3 per cent of adults in Italy and Spain; about 4 per cent in France, Austria and Germany, around 6 per cent in social democratic Scandinavia, above 8 per cent in the US and Australia, and highest of all in Switzerland (15 per cent).[22] And the inequality of wealth in China is centred on property, not financial assets (so far), unlike the main capitalist economies of the G7. And that is because finance has not been fully opened up to the capitalist sector (Figure 6.13).

And when it comes to inequality of personal wealth, China is not so unequal as many of its economic peers. The gini inequality of wealth ratio is much higher

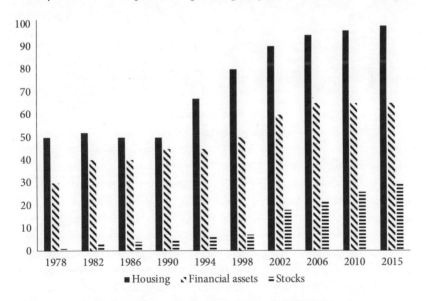

Figure 6.13   China: share of private property in national wealth (%)

Source: Piketty et al., https://blogs.lse.ac.uk/businessreview/2019/04/01/income-inequality-is-growing-fast-in-china-and-making-it-look-more-like-the-us/

in Brazil, Russia and India, and higher in the US and Germany. According to the latest estimates, the top 1 per cent of wealth holders in China take 31 per cent of all personal wealth compared to 58 per cent in Russia, 50 per cent in Brazil, 41 per cent in India and 35 per cent in the US. This is a good measure of the economic power of the top elite and oligarchs in these countries.

But the threat of the 'capitalist road' remains. Indeed, the IMF data show that, while public sector assets in China are still nearly twice the size of capitalist sector assets, the gap is closing (Figure 6.14).

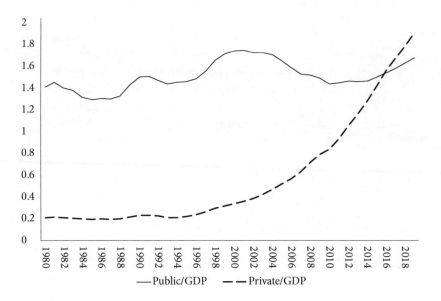

Figure 6.14 China: public and private sector investment stock to GDP – ratio

Many 'experts' on China claim that it is imperialist in the same way as the Western advanced capitalist economies. In our chapter on imperialism, we find that this is not the case, in so far as imperialist economies suck surplus value out of the rest of 'emerging' world. On that definition, China is also 'dominated' by imperialism. China has been expanding its investments abroad (although the size of foreign direct investment is still small), particularly the Belt and Road Initiative (BRI). Again, many authors claim that these investments and loans to poorer countries are exploitive and designed to put weaker countries into a 'debt trap'. Yet the evidence of the most detailed studies shows no such thing and that the terms of China's loan and investment deals are not iniquitous and are not draconian as they often are with loans from the imperialist bloc.[23]

The contradictions of China's state-controlled economy alongside a large and growing capitalist sector intensified during the COVID pandemic. And that was expressed by the factions in the Chinese leadership. Officials in the financial and banking sector want to open up the economy to foreign capital and allow the renminbi to become an international currency. They argue that the economy is too biased towards investment and exports over consumption. Chinese economists trained in America and Europe, backed by resident foreign economists in Chinese universities and the World Bank, press continually for a 'switch from investment to consumption'. Ironically, in the G7 capitalist economies consumption has failed to drive economic growth and wages have stagnated in real terms over the last ten years, while real wages in China have shot up (Figure 6.15).

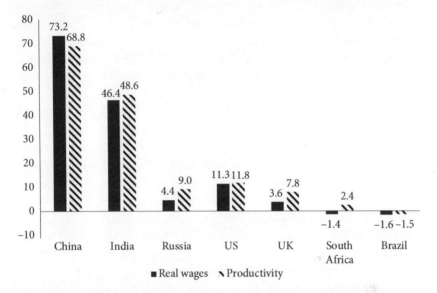

Figure 6.15 Percentage change in productivity and real wages since end of Great Recession (2010–19)

Source: Penn World Tables 10.0, authors' calculations.

Indeed, consumption is rising much faster in China than in the G7 because investment is higher. One follows the other; it is not a zero-sum game. And not all consumption has to be 'personal'; more important is 'social consumption', that is, public services like health, education, transport, communicationsm housing; not just motor cars and gadgets. Increased personal consumption of basic social services is what is necessary. And it is here that China needs to act.

Much is also made of China's rising debt levels. Mainstream economists have been forecasting for decades that China is heading for a debt crash of mega proportions. It's true that according to the Institute of International Finance (IFF), China's total debt hit 317 per cent of gross domestic product in the first quarter of 2020. But most of the domestic debt is owed by one state entity to another:

from local government to state banks, from state banks to central government. When that is all netted off, the debt owed by households (54 per cent of GDP) and corporations is not so high, while central government debt is low by global standards. Moreover, external dollar debt to GDP is very low (15 per cent) and indeed the rest of the world owes China way more: 6 per cent of global debt. China is a huge creditor to the world and has massive dollar and euro reserves, 50 per cent larger than its dollar debt.

A financial crisis is ruled out as long as the state controls the banking system, so that credit support and state bailouts are easily organised, backed by state funding and reserves. But there are dangers because of the recent attempts to loosen it up for private and foreign institutions to enter the arena (e.g. there are a growing number of bankruptcies in speculative financial entities). Chinese leaders want to curb the debt level. Controlling the debt level can come in two ways; through high growth from productive sector investment to keep the debt ratio under control and/or by reducing credit binges in unproductive areas like speculative property. Japan's secular stagnation was the result of the lack of applying these two factors in its capitalist economy. But given the power of state control over the levers of investment, China can avoid the Japanese outcome.

Nevertheless, the growing size and influence of the capitalist sector in China is weakening the performance of the economy and widening the inequalities exposed during the pandemic. Indeed, it has been the state sector that has helped the Chinese economy climb out of the pandemic slump, not its capitalist sector. The debate within the leadership will continue about which way to take China: towards a full market economy open to the winds of global capital flows or to stay as they are. So far, there has been no change in the general philosophy of 'socialism with Chinese characteristics' and thus the maintenance of the dominance of the state sector. But there is no move towards 'democracy' either; or allowing control of even local legal systems and decisions by the people. On the contrary, the leadership is setting up even more repressive state security services to monitor and control the population and curb any dissidence.

The size of the state sector is not decisive in characterising the class nature of the Chinese state, but it is an indicator of the process of transition. In the state sector, workers generate surplus labour. And a bureaucratic elite control that surplus. In this sense, the state sector is capitalist in character. Workers are exploited and the law of value operates here. But the state sector produces goods and services primarily according to planning targets and not for individual profits. So in this sense they are not capitalist as state enterprises are in the capitalist countries. The bureaucracy and the CCP want to pursue policies to strengthen their grip on power, but in so doing they must defend the 'socialist' aspects of the transition. In this sense, to invoke the 'socialist nature' of the Chinese economy is an ideological move.

The class struggle remains in China. Since the late 1970s, millions of peasants have entered the cities in pursuit of waged employment. Migrant workers, particularly in the capitalist sector, who make up a third of China's total workforce, are brutally exploited:

> One study conducted by the Communist Party Youth League in six cities in Guangdong polled 1,800 migrant workers in December 2001. It found that 80 percent worked more than ten hours per day. Most worked twelve to fourteen hours per day, and 47.2 percent said they rarely had any holidays or rest on weekends.[24]

The CCP often faces reaction from an increasingly self-confident working class. The China Labor Bureau recorded more than 10,000 strikes between 2015 and 2020, including more than a thousand in Guangdong province where private companies are centred.

The current Xi leadership has launched not only yet another drive against 'corruption', but also revived the earlier CCP concept of 'common prosperity' that aims to reduce inequalities and increase the value of public services over private consumption. Xi wants to avoid another Tiananmen Square protest in 1989 after a huge rise in inequality and inflation under Deng's 'social market' reforms.[25] Workers' democracy is crucial to the transition from capitalism to socialism. The seizure of political power makes possible the emergence of workers' democracy. The transition cannot be completed without it. In transitional economies some elements of capitalism prevail. The question is: which ones prevail? That depends on the class struggle not only between capital (both private and public) and labour but also between the state sector and the private sector. China's great achievements in the reduction of poverty and in the provision of social facilities (like education) and its vastly superior economic performance in terms of GDP do not indicate that China is socialist. But they do indicate that possible conditions for socialism are present. However, without workers' democracy, China will remain in a 'trapped transition'; as will other transitional economies like Vietnam and Laos, which have followed the Chinese model.

6.7 SOCIALIST PLANNING VERSUS THE LAW OF VALUE

Capitalism is the only form of class society in which commodity production becomes generalised, in which all elements of production (land, labour power, fixed assets etc.) become commodities. For Marx, production relations are those relations between producers which are indispensable for the 'production of their material life' at a given level of development of productivity of human labour. This means that they encompass not only the relations inside economic units, but also those between them. Under capitalism, the law of value governs these shifts. All producer goods are commodities. All producing units react to increases or decreases of sales of their commodities on the market, to increases or decreases of profits. The law of value through commodity production allocates and reallocates resources 'behind the backs' of the producers in a society in which social labour is fragmented into private labour as a result of the private property of the means of production. The law of value is the 'invisible leviathan'. In short, under capitalism, the means of production are owned by the capitalists. Once these means of production are collectively owned, however, they are no more commodities. They are not sold and bought on the market. The law of value ceases to govern their allocation and reallocation between different producing units. Competition between 'commodities' or 'capitals' ceases to be the basic force to regulate investment. And then the only other means to assert the social nature of human labour is planning.

Indeed, Marx describes 'freely associated' production as 'consciously regulated ... in accordance with a settled plan' (Marx, 1967, I, p. 80). With 'the means of production in common, ... the labour power of all the different individuals is consciously applied as the combined labour power of the community ... in accordance with a definite social plan [which] maintains the proper proportion between the different kinds of work to be done and the various wants of the community' (pp. 78–9). Under communism, in short, 'united cooperative societies are to regulate national production upon a common plan, thus taking it under their own control, and putting an end to the constant anarchy and periodic convulsions which are the fatality of capitalist production' (Marx, 1985, p. 76).

Planning is not equivalent to the 'perfect' allocation of resources, nor 'scientific' allocation, nor even 'more humane' allocation. It simply means 'direct' allocation, *ex ante*. As such, it is the opposite of market allocation, which is *ex post*. You can have 'despotic' planning and 'democratic' planning. But, whatever their forms, all of these involve direct prior allocation of resources (including labour) through the deliberate choice of some social body. At the opposite pole is resource allocation through objective market laws that counteract or correct previously fragmented decisions taken by private bodies, separately or autonomously from each other.

What has been the basic historical trend of capitalist development, from the industrial revolution onwards? A growing objective socialisation of labour. Engels formulated that contradiction strikingly in a famous passage in the *Anti-Dühring*:

The greater the mastery obtained by the new mode of production over all decisive fields of production and in all economically decisive countries, the more it reduced individual production to an insignificant residuum, the more clearly was brought out the incompatibility of socialized production with capitalistic appIriation ... The contradiction between socialized production and capitalistic appropriation now presents itself as an antagonism between the organization of production in the individual workshop and the anarchy of production in society generally.

Already today, in the most advanced capitalist countries, the bulk of both consumer and producer goods are not produced in any way in response to 'market signals' shifting violently from year to year, let alone month to month. The bulk of current production corresponds to established consumption patterns and predetermined production techniques that are largely if not completely independent of the market. How has this come about? It is precisely a result of the growing objective socialisation of labour: workforces must cooperate to produce; firms must expand economies of scale.

With the advance of social wealth, the growth of productive forces and the emergence of post-capitalist institutions, the number of goods and services characterised by such inelasticity of demand, and thereby capable of being distributed, can progressively increase. When – let us say – up to 60–75 per cent of all consumer goods and services are so allocated, this cumulative increase will have altered the overall 'human condition' dramatically. As Mandel puts it: the socialist prospect is one of a gradual satisfaction of more and more needs, not of a restriction to basic requirements alone.[26]

Marx was never an advocate of asceticism or austerity. On the contrary, the concept of the fully developed personality that is at the very heart of his vision of communism implies a great variety of human needs and their satisfaction, not a narrowing down of our wants to elementary food and shelter. The withering away of market and money relations envisaged by Marx would involve the gradual extension of the principle of *ex ante* resource allocation for the satisfaction of these needs to a greater and greater number of goods and services, in a wider and not lesser variety than exists under capitalism today.

There is a hierarchy of need that can be satisfied in stages. The first category is basic food and drink, clothing, shelter and standard comforts linked to it (heating, electricity, running water, sanitation, furniture); education and health provision; guaranteed transport to and from the workplace; and the minimum of recreation and leisure indispensable to the reconstitution of labour power at a given level of work pace and stress. These are the needs which for Marx must be satisfied if an average wage-earner is to continue working at a given level of effort. They can be subdivided into a physiological minimum and a historical-moral supplement. In the second category of goods and services, there are more sophisticated foods, drinks, clothes and household appliances (excepting the fanciest ones), the more elaborate 'cultural' and 'leisure' goods and services and private motor vehicles (as distinct from public transport). As the first category is increasingly met through direct allocation, free at the point of use, this will reduce the role of money in the economy as a whole, as non-priced goods and services become more numerous than goods and services bought. This would provide the objective basis for the withering away of commodity production and monetary exchange.

Through the rationalisation of technology and labour organisation a democratic plan could reduce the working week and open up the opportunity for all to participate in the plan for society. The absence of market competition in no way necessitates a lack of product innovation. Throughout history, indeed, most key discoveries and inventions have been made wholly outside any commercial nexus.

Starting from these choices, a coherent general plan would then be drawn up, utilising input-output tables and material balances, indicating the resources available for each separate branch of production (industrial sectors, transportation, agriculture and distribution) and social life (education, health, communications, defence if that remains necessary etc.). The national or international congress would not go beyond these general instructions and would not lay out specifications for each branch or producing unit or region. Self-managing bodies – for example, congresses of workers' councils in the shoe, food, electronic equipment, steel or energy industries – would then divide up the workload flowing from the general plan among the existing producer units and/ or project the creation of additional producing units for the next period, if the implementation of output goals made that necessary under the given workload. They would work out the technological average (gradually leading up to the technical optimum on the basis of existing knowledge), the average productivity of labour, or average 'production costs' of the goods to be produced.

In 1920, with the Bolsheviks victorious in the Russian civil war and the spectre of communism once more haunting Europe, Austrian school economist, Ludwig von Mises produced his classic article on 'Economic Calculation in the Socialist Commonwealth'. He argued that planning in a collectively owned economy without markets was impossible because there are just too many calculations for planning to deliver a proper allocation of resources to meet consumer needs.[27] Ironically, von Mises accepted that 'socialist production', that is, planning, was rationally realisable if it provided an objectively recognisable unit of value, which would permit of economic calculation in an economy where neither money nor exchange were present. And only labour can conceivably be considered as such (Ludwig von Mises, 1935, p. 116). But although rational calculation (using a labour time measure) was logically possible under socialism, there was 'no practical way of realizing it'.[28] The abolition of market relations would destroy the only adequate basis for economic calculation, namely, market prices. However well meaning the socialist planners might be, they would simply lack any basis for taking sensible economic decisions: socialism was nothing other than the 'abolition of rational economy'.

Later von Mises (1949, pp. 701–2) noted that Marxists seemed to accept this conclusion because they looked for ways to incorporate market pricing into planning: so-called 'market socialism'. Mises stated that on the traditional definition, socialism necessarily involves 'the entire elimination of the market and competition'. The presumed superiority of socialism rested on the 'unification and centralization' inherent in the notion of planning. 'It is therefore nothing short of a full acknowledgment of the correctness and irrefutability of the economists' analysis and devastating critique of the socialists' plans that the intellectual leaders of socialism are now busy designing schemes … in which the market, market prices for the factors of production, and catallactic competition are to be preserved.'

Oscar Lange was the leading exponent of this market socialism. However, even he by 1967 began to recognise that with electronic computers the equations necessary for planning resource allocation could be achieved. Lange: 'The market process with its cumbersome tatonnements appears old-fashioned. Indeed, it may be considered as a computing device of the pre-electronic age' (1967, p. 158).

Alec Nove (1977) attacked the idea of planning by arguing that the planners could not have the means to calculate the required output of intermediate goods in full detail, in order to support any given targets for final outputs. As a result, the plan would always be ill-formulated: instructions to enterprises would be excessively aggregated, specific supplies and demands would fail to match, and so a good deal of 'informal barter' and 'fixing' would be required to achieve even a rough approximation to balance. For Nove, socialism without commodity production was impossible to achieve, because there were just too many decisions to make for the planning process, however democratically organised: 'In no society can an elected assembly decide by 115 votes to 73 where to allocate ten tonnes of leather, or whether to produce another 100 tonnes of sulphuric acid.'[29]

But democratic self-management does not mean that everybody decides about everything. If one was to assume that, the conclusion would be obvious: socialism is not possible. Seven billion human beings could not find sufficient life-span to settle even the tiniest fraction of each other's affairs, in that sense. But it is not necessary. Certain decisions can be best taken at workshop level, others at factory level, others again at neighbourhood, local, regional, national, continental and finally at world level.

But let us consider the calculation problem more closely in the light of the huge advances made in computers, particularly with the latest quantum computers. Haerdin points out that in real economies, firms only depend on a finite set of other firms much smaller than the economy as a whole. Indeed, the average number of firms any one firm depends on is bounded by some constant regardless of the size of the economy. An economy has a small set of core industries and a larger 'long tail' of less crucial industries and these core industries have lots of industries that depend on them, whereas the rest do not. Because of these features of a modern economy, Haerdin reckons that a single computer with just 8 GiB of RAM can deal with a linear program corresponding to an economy with one million industries. It therefore does not seem unreasonable that the entirety of the world economy, a system with billions of industries, could be planned using a relatively modest computer cluster.[30] Similarly, Robin Hahnel and Mitchell Szczepanczyk through iterative computer simulations of the planning process from local to central level and back, using a new computer coding technique, found that it would not take long at all to reach a feasible and practical annual plan to meet social needs with available resources which involved the participation and democratic decisions of people.[31]

Can planning be rational, efficient and democratic? Legault and Tremblay-Pepin (2021) reviewed three models of democratic economic planning, called respectively negotiated coordination, participatory economics and computerised central planning.[32] Adaman and Devine (1996) offer 'negotiated coordination' which allows for participation in the plan at various levels of society. Devine keeps the idea of a representative government elected by the people and law-making within a Representative Assembly, but with genuinely participatory political parties and a much more democratic electoral system (Devine, 1988, pp. 189–90, 212–13). The equivalent of enterprises, what he calls production units, are owned collectively. Representatives from four sectors sit on the decision-making body of each production unit: the general interest (national, regional and local Planning Commissions and Negotiated Coordination Bodies); these representatives then agree on the most appropriate use of productive capacities through negotiation, considering each other's interests. These governing bodies decide on the general administrative orientation of the production unit, while workers organise the day-to-day operations through self-management. Although production units are self-managed, their decisional power is limited to the capacity of their existing infrastructures. They cannot choose to invest in new assets or close facilities by themselves. In negotiated coordination, it is not the capitalist who makes investment decisions through an atomistic, *ex post* coordinated process that aims for profit maximisation.

Instead, it is the social owners (all the affected parties) that take investment decisions through an *ex ante* negotiated coordination process aiming to fulfil collectively decided social objectives. In the plan allocation process, the Negotiated Coordination Body will review and approve them in light of what other production units are doing. Everyone affected by the sector sends a representative to the Negotiated Coordination Body: production units of the sector, but also suppliers, consumers, government and interest groups from civil society.

Michael Albert and economist Robin Hahnel take a different tack.[33] Their planning model is called participatory economics. In participatory economics, all workplaces are managed by Workers' Councils. Contrary to what negotiated coordination proposes, only workers have the right to vote in these councils, but all do so directly at the local level, not through representatives. Iteration Facilitation Boards (IFB) would support the councils' work. These boards are workplaces in charge of producing economic analyses and indicative prices based on workers' and consumers' desires, previous years' results, and the enormous amount of data shared during the planning process. After receiving prices and information from the IFB, each council writes a proposal for consumption or production. Each actor modifies its proposal through iterations before they all reach a final proposal without any goods or services in excess demand or supply. Once every proposal is approved, the Facilitation Boards adjust indicative prices according to what goods and services are now in excess supply and excess demand. A new round starts with these new data: the councils can then develop new plans to consider these new prices. The iteration continues until no good or service in the economy is in excess supply or excess demand. According to the authors, this process can be helped and even greatly simplified by using computers. Albert and Hahnel also contend that this allocation process can even lead to a Pareto optimum outcome (Albert and Hahnel, 1991, pp. 73–106). A Pareto optimum outcome is an economic state where it is not possible to improve the situation of one individual without degrading the situation of at least one other.

The third model developed by Cockshott and Cottrell starts from the principle of maintaining a central plan of investment and production at its core. Planners use two essential tools to prepare these plans: first, a network of computers with at least one station in every workplace where 'a local spreadsheet of its production capabilities and raw materials requirements' (Cockshott and Cottrell, 2008, p. 171) is continuously and automatically updated; second, supercomputers that integrate this information into an algorithm designed to allocate raw materials and the labour force according to a set of desired outputs for the whole economy. Equipped with these tools, planners can design a diversity of macroeconomic, strategic and detailed plans with different total output results and workload inputs. These plans are then submitted to a political process for approval or rejection.

As for democracy, Cockshott and Cottrell propose a direct democracy based on sortition, inspired by the Athenian classic democracy (Cockshott and Cottrell, 1993, pp. 157–70). Hence, '[t]he various organs of public authority would be controlled by citizens' committees chosen by lot. The media, the health service, the planning and marketing agencies, the various industries would have their juries.' Local democracy only intervenes *ex post* in Cockshott and Cottrell's model, as it democratically organises the decision taken by the plan, which is written by the Central Planning Bureau and adopted by referendum.

Cockshott and Cottrell accept von Mises' conclusion that 'rational socialist calculation' requires 'an objectively recognizable unit of value, which would permit of economic calculation in an economy where neither money nor exchange were present. And only labour can conceivably be considered as such.' According to this approach, the Marxian model of a communist economy, in its first phase, is characterised by 'planning based on labour-time calculation'.[34] An important ingredient of this model is its reliance on labour values (or time) as the basis of planning calculations, not physical inputs and outputs. The workers are paid in labour tokens directly by the planners. These labour tokens are equal to the amount of labour time a worker has accomplished in a given period. Workers then exchange them for consumer goods. As soon as they do so, the tokens lose their value, like a theatre ticket. The trends in token spending will give the Central Planning Bureau the necessary information to establish market clearing prices in labour value terms.

These as well as other proposals have interesting sides. But the plurality of proposals submitted indicates that in the end it is those who will go through the transition period and further to socialism who will decide which of the three models, if any of them, will be chosen, modified and applied.

This aside, these blueprints share a common drawback, a technicist, mechanical view of a planned economy, which hides the class content of these schemes. Even if it might be difficult to implement it in the first stage of the transition, the technical division of labour inherited from capitalism will have to be revolutionised. Instead of applying the capitalist fragmentation of the labour process in increasingly smaller positions, a process which reduces humans to appendices of machines and destroys their creativity and individuality, the new structure of position, to be consonant with socialism, would have to ensure the maximum development of each individual's personality. The creation of positions encompassing a wide variety of tasks and the rotation of individuals among different positions would ensure that each can realise his/her potentialities to the maximum during his/her working time. This implies necessarily redesigning the means of production (see Carchedi, 2011a).

The computation of the output in terms of labour contents runs against an objection: how to compute the labour time a machine has cost. To know it, we must compute the labour cost of its components in the previous year, and of the components of those components etc. This is the backward ad infinitum argument which has been used to criticise Marx's transformation procedure. In a capitalist economy, it can be solved. Basically, one needs to go back only one year and compute the rate of the new value produced (hours of labour or labour units) to wages and profits. Due to the homogeneity of abstract labour, this ratio can then be applied to the value of the means of production produced in the same (the last) year. Within the temporalist approach, this is also the value of the same means of production at the beginning of this year (see Carchedi, 2011a). This method is to be preferred to the replacement cost of the means of production because it starts the computation from the previous year without falling into the backward ad infinitum trap whereas the replacement cost severs the tie between past and present.

But in a planned economy where the unit of account is the labour contained, how do we compute the hours of labour contained in the assets without falling in the backward ad infinitum trap? One suggestion is that the planners could impute arbitrarily the labour content of the means of production. The argument is that this starting point would become less arbitrary as the years go on. Nevertheless, the calculation would be deprived of a scientific and rational basis. Different initial values would lead to different evaluations of labour contents. No means would be available to decide rationally which initially imputed labour content is to be preferred. Also, by imputing arbitrarily different labour contents to the means of production in the different sectors of the economy, one would direct arbitrarily the social division of labour. The alternative is the replacement cost principle, the computation of how many hours of labour it would cost at the beginning of the planning period to produce those means of production. This would not be arbitrary, but based on technical production relations. Within the temporalist approach, the replacement cost at the beginning of the planning year is also the cost at the end of the pre-planning previous year. This operation would be possible only once. From the first planning year, the labour costs of the inputs could be rationally computed.

Marx assumed that in communism, the market would be abolished and replaced by production using labour certificates or tokens. 'On the basis of communal production, the determination of time remains, of course, essential. ... Economy of time, to this all economy ultimately reduces itself. ... Thus, economy of time, along with the planned distribution of labor time among the various branches of production, remains the first economic law on the basis of the communal production. However, this is essentially different from a measurement of exchange values (labour or products) by labour time' (Marx, 1973, pp. 172–3). The principle of economic coordination in the first stage of communism (socialism) is participatory planning, or planning from below, based on labour time calculation. Accordingly, the individual producer receives back from society – after the deductions have been made – exactly what he gives to it. What he has given to it is his individual quantum of labour. For example, the social working day consists of the sum of the individual hours of work; the individual labour time of the individual producer is the part of the social working day contributed by each worker. The worker receives a certificate from society that is equivalent to that amount of labour (after deducting labour time for the common funds), and with this certificate the worker draws from the social stock of means of consumption as much as the same amount of labour costs. The same amount of labour given to society in one form is received back in another.

It is crucial to stick to planning using labour time, at least in the first phase of communism. Planning without this single accounting unit is simply a contradiction in terms, tantamount to the rejection of planning altogether. Producers are compensated by the labour certificates, which show how much time they worked, after deducting the tax for the common use of labour time, such as investment, collective consumption, support for the disabled etc.

Hence, there is a dual role for a labour time calculus in the classical Marxian approach to the planning of production. First, the basic economic task of the socialist 'association' is conceived in terms of an allocation of social labour in accordance with the proportional production of the use values obtained from the various branches of the division of labour. This proportionality is to be achieved directly, as opposed to the indirect mechanism of the 'law of value' under capitalism. This requires, among other things, the measurement of the labour required to produce specific goods and services. Second, one general objective of socialist planning must be the economisation of labour time – the progressive reduction of the labour necessary for the production of specific use values, or in other words, the progressive augmentation of the quantum of use value which can be produced with any given expenditure of social labour. This all presupposes a system of socialist decision-making.

What Marx and Engels are rejecting is the notion of fixing prices according to actual labour content in the context of a commodity producing economy where production is private. In an economy where the means of production are under communal control, on the other hand, labour does become 'directly social', in the sense that it is subordinated to a pre-established central plan. Here the calculation of the labour content of goods is an important element in the planning process. And here the reshuffling of resources in line with changing social needs and priorities does not proceed via the response of profit-seeking, so the critique of labour money is simply irrelevant. This is the context for Marx's suggestion for the distribution of consumer goods through 'labour certificates'. The labour

certificates Marx talks of here are quite different from money. They do not circulate; rather they are cancelled against the acquisition of consumer goods of
equivalent labour content. And they may be used for consumer goods alone;
they cannot purchase means of production or labour power, and hence cannot
function as capital.[35]

However, the exchange of equal quantities of labour using labour certificates
is not an absolute principle of communism that should be permanently observed
and reproduced, but rather it is part of the remains or 'defects' of capitalism that
need to be overcome 'from the outset' of the first phase of communism. Marx
assumed that even in the first phase of communism, the substantial part of the
total social product will not be distributed to people according to the labour
time they perform, but deducted for the common use 'from the outset': 'Second,
that which is intended for the common satisfaction of needs, such as schools,
health services, etc. [is deducted]. From the outset, this part grows considerably in comparison with present-day society and it grows in proportion as the
new society develops' (Marx, 1989a, p. 85). With the radical shortening of the
working day thanks to the rapid development of artificial intelligence, machine
learning, the Internet of Things, 3D printing etc., the scope of labour certificates would be substantially narrowed in the 21st century. Considering that the
essence of communism is not the domination of labour but its abolition, labour
certificates should be considered a tool for facilitating the tendency of the abolition of labour.

Marx refers to the Robinson Crusoe story, pointing out that 'Nature itself
compels [Robinson] to divide his time with precision between his different
functions. Whether one function occupies a greater space in his total activity
than another depends on the magnitude of the difficulties to be overcome in
attaining the useful effect aimed at.' After discussing the counterpart to the Rob-
insonian calculations in feudal and primitive societies, Marx comes to the case
of socialism.

> Let us finally imagine, for a change, an association of free men, working with
> the means of production held in common, and expending their many differ-
> ent forms of labour-power in full self-awareness as one single labour force.
> All the characteristics of Robinson's labour are repeated here, but with the dif-
> ference that they are social instead of individual ... The total product of our
> imagined association is a social product. One part of this product serves as
> fresh means of production and remains social. But another part is consumed
> by the members of the association as means of subsistence. In such a social-
> ised economy, the (direct) apportionment of labour time 'maintains the
> correct proportion between the different functions of labour and the various
> needs of the associations,' and here 'the social relations of the individual pro-

235

ducers, both towards their labour and the products of their labour, are ... transparent in their simplicity.'

Whatever the exact model of democratic planning is adopted, what the evidence shows is planning in transitional economies is not only necessary, but is rational in concept and practical in application. It must be a key part of the transition out of capitalism and the law of value and towards socialism.

Appendix 1

The Value Theory of Inflation: The Method

To measure the value rate of inflation in the productive sector of the US economy, we use source time series from US Federal Reserve of St Louis (FRED). https://fred.stlouisfed.org/

US CPI: FPCPITOTLZGUSA; US wage growth: B461RC1Q027SBEA

Combined Purchasing Power (CPP) = Net Operating Surplus + Wages; where NOS. W326RC1Q027SBEA; Wages: B461RC1Q027SBEA

M2% has been adjusted by the NFC ratio in total value from BEA NIPA Table S.5.a Nonfinancial Corporate Business lines 102/(lines 102 + 107)

The Value Rate of Inflation = CPP: where NOS (adjusted for corporate tax: NFCPATAX) plus Wages (adjusted for tax and benefits by 0.78 average) PLUS M2% adjusted

For the whole economy, the Value Rate of Inflation = V^* where VRI* = CPP (Wages A4102C1Q027SBEA as adjusted 0.78) + Profits GDINOS adjusted for tax (A053RC1Q027SBEA) plus M2 (MYAGM2USM052N) adjusted for capital consumption ratio (BEA NIPA Table 1.10. Gross Domestic Income by Type of Income lines 8 and 22).

Excel sheet workings are available on request.

Appendix 2

Measuring Unequal Exchange in International Trade

Database series used: Penn World Tables 10.0; www.rug.nl/ggdc/productivity/pwt/

We use the following series in constant prices:

GDP = rgdpna
Capital Stock K = rnna
Depreciation ratio = delta
Internal rate of return = irr

The annual national market price (MP) = So MP = c + V + S

where c = capital used up = K*delta + S = Capital stock rnna * internal rate of return on stock irr + V = GDP rgdpna − S

To compute the annual UE transfer value in trade between two countries or blocs, we use the annual export to GDP ratios (x) for each country's trade with another. Exports between countries are sourced from the IMF Direction of Trade Statistics. https://data.imf.org/?sk=9d6028d4-f14a-464c-a2f2-59b2cd424b85p

Export ratio x = exports/GDP, to produce the annual national market output value (MPx) for exports between each country or bloc: MPx = cx + Vx + Sx

The Penn Tables 10.0 do not separate productive from unproductive sectors. However, this is not an issue here because we can assume that the export sectors are basically productive sectors.

Within a country the national surplus value is *value realised* because it is the sum of the value realised by domestic sectors through the formation of a national rate of profit. So the surplus value before international realisation is the surplus value after national realisation. But *within the international context* the same several national surplus values are *unrealised value* and they must be further redistributed internationally through the formation of a world rate of profit.

In the text we have argued that the formula for the rate of exploitation is RSV = (S + UE)/V. This adds to Marx's formula RSV = S/V because we include the transfer of international surplus value.

238

We calculate UE in two ways: UE based on narrow bilateral trade (*narrow UE*) and UE based on broad trade (*broad UE*). In the narrow UE, the assumption is that two countries trade only with each other. The two countries' average rate of profit $(nRx) = nRx = (S_1x + S_2x)/(c_1x + V_1x + c_2x + V_2x)$.

Given nRx, the two nPPx are $(cx + Vx) + (cx + Vx)^*nRx$ for each country; then the *narrow UEx* = nPPx − MPx for each country. The result will show + or − for each annual UEx which will cancel each other out.

In the broad UE, the assumption is that the two countries trade with *all* other countries as well. So we take the G20 (actually 19) countries as the proxy for the world and calculate a world rate of profit based on these countries. The *world* average rate of profit (WRx) is thus: $WRx = \Sigma Sx/(\Sigma cx + \Sigma Vx)$ for the 19 countries.

We compute the PPx:

Country 1. $PPx = (cx + Vx) + (cx + Vx)^*WRx$
Country 2. $PPx = (cx + Vx) + (cx + Vx)^*WRx$
Countries 17. $PPx = \Sigma(cx + Vx) + \Sigma(cx + Vx)^*WRx$

So the *broad UEx* = PPx − MPx for each country. The result will show + or − for each UEx which will cancel out overall.

The difference between the narrow and the broad UE is found in the computation of the nRx and WRx.

UE is determined by the difference between the organic composition of capital (OCC) and by the rate of surplus value (RSV) for each country. OCC = K/V and RSV = S/V + UE. If the OCC differentials are greater than the RSV differentials, the former contribute more to the flow of value and vice versa.

Notes

INTRODUCTION

1. See Carchedi, 1999, pp. 121–2.
2. Labour is productive of value embodied not only if employed by capital, but also if, as *concrete* labour, it transforms use values into new use values. If it does not transform use values, it is unproductive labour. It allows capital to participate in the redistribution of (surplus) value even if its labourers are unproductive of value.

CHAPTER 1

1. John Bellamy Foster and Brett Clark, 'Marx and Alienated Speciesism', *Monthly Review*, 2018.
2. www.haymarketbooks.org/search?q=Marx-and-Nature, www.amazon.co.uk/Marx-S-Ecology-Materialism-Nature/dp/1583670122
3. Frederich Engels, *Outlines of a Critique of Political Economy*, 1844, www.marxists.org/archive/marx/works/1844/df-jahrbucher/outlines.htm
4. Frederich Engels, *The Dialectics of Nature*, 1883, www.marxists.org/archive/marx/works/1883/don/index.htm
5. David Maybury-Lewis, 'Genocide against Indigenous Peoples', in *Annihilating Difference: The Anthropology of Genocide*, Berkeley, CA: University of California Press, 2002, pp. 43–54.
6. Karl Marx, *Critique of the Gotha Programme*, 1875, www.marxists.org/archive/marx/works/1875/gotha/ch01.htm
7. Karl Marx, *Capital*, Vol. I, New York: Vintage Books, 1977, p. 283.
8. The concept of punctuated equilibrium was, to some, a radical new idea when it was first proposed by Stephen Jay Gould and Niles Eldredge in 1972. Now it is widely recognised as a useful model for one kind of evolutionary change. The relative importance of punctuated and gradual patterns of evolution is a subject of debate and research.
9. Karl Marx, *18th Brumaire of Louis Bonaparte*, 1852, www.marxists.org/archive/marx/works/1852/18th-brumaire/ch01.htm
10. G.M. Lange, Q. Wodon and K. Carey (eds), *The Changing Wealth of Nations 2018: Building a Sustainable Future*, Washington, DC: The World Bank.
11. World Bank, www.worldbank.org/en/topic/natural-capital#1
12. Depankar Basu, 'Marx's Analysis of Ground-Rent: Theory, Examples and Applications', Working Paper 2018-04, University of Massachusetts, Amherst.www.umass.edu/economics/publications/2018-04.pdf
13. Notes on Marx and ground-rent, SPGB, https://socialiststudies.org.uk/marx%20groundrent.shtml
14. Jason W. Moore, *Capitalism in the Web of Life: Ecology and the Accumulation of Capital*, New York: Verso, 2015. ISBN: 9781781689011 (cloth); ISBN: 9781781689028 (paper); ISBN: 9781781689042 (ebook).

15. José A. Tapia, 'From the Oil Crisis to the Great Recession: Five Crises of the World Economy', https://drexel.edu/~/media/Files/coas2/politics/Tapia_From TheOilCrisisToTheGreatRecession%20-%20FiveCrisesOfTheWorldEconomy%20 2014.ashx?la=en

16. James Hamilton, 'Historical Oil Shocks', NBER Working Paper No. w16790, last revised: 19 May 2021.

17. The internal rate of return on capital (IRR) is value added minus labour compensation divided by fixed assets, from the Penn World Tables 10.0, and as such is close (proxy) to the Marxian average rate of profit (ARP).

18. https://amp.theguardian.com/environment/climate-consensus-97-per-cent/2018/ jan/01/on-its-hundredth-birthday-in-1959-edward-teller-warned-the-oil-industry-about-global-warming

19. www.encognitive.com/node/1677

20. Oxfam, 21 September 2020, www.oxfam.org/en/press-releases/carbon-emissions-richest-1-percent-more-double-emissions-poorest-half-humanity

21. The Carbon Majors Database CDP Carbon Majors Report 2017.

22. Daniel Quiggin, Kris De Meyer, Lucy Hubble-Rose and Antony Froggat, 'Climate Change Risk Assessment', September 2021, Chatham House.

23. 'The Human Cost of Disasters', UNDRR, 2020, www.preventionweb.net/files/74124_humancostofdisasters20002019reportu.pdf

24. 'IMF Climate Change and Financial Risk', *Finance & Development*, December 2019, 56(4), www.imf.org/external/pubs/ft/fandd/2019/12/pdf/climate-change-central-banks-and-financial-risk-grippa.pdf

25. R.D. Bressler, 'The Mortality Cost of Carbon', *Nature Communications* 12(4467), 2021, www.nature.com/articles/s41467-021-24487-w?fbclid=IwAR1tCQkJax_QonR4 U2cuUeFWdRaswAMENb-ap9SoCn1IEfJZa4gpX52Io2E

26. Robert Solow, 'A Contribution to the Theory of Economic Growth', *Quarterly Journal of Economics*, 70(1), February 1956, pp. 65–94.

27. Avi J. Cohen and G.C. Harcourt, 'Whatever Happened to the Cambridge Capital Theory Controversies?' *Journal of Economic Perspectives*, 17(1), Winter 2003, pp. 199–214.

28. José A. Tapia Granados and Óscar Carpintero, 'Dynamics and Economic Aspects of Climate Change'. http://deepblue.lib.umich.edu/bitstream/handle/2027.42/93589/ Tapia&Carpintero_Dynamics_of_climate_change.pdf?sequence=1

29. Joe Spearing, 'We Need to Look beyond the Market to Beat Climate Change', *Financial Times*, 14 July 2021, www.ft.com/content/bb92c7aa-aa1d-4797-9739-81ce1054ceaa

30. https://systemchangenotclimatechange.org/article/%E2%80%9Csocial-cost-carbon%E2%80%9D-what-price-existence

31. Michael R. Bloomberg, 'Climate Policy Factbook', 20 July 2021, https://about.bnef. com/blog/new-report-finds-g-20-member-countries-support-fossil-fuels-at-levels-untenable-to-achieve-paris-agreement-goals/

32. www.iisd.org/articles/fossil-fuel-subsidy-reform-could-reduce-co2-emissions-equivalent-those-1000-coal-fired

33. World Energy Outlook 2021, International Energy Agency, https://iea.blob. core.windows.net/assets/888004cf-1a38-4716-9e0c-3b0e3fdbf609/World EnergyOutlook2021.pdf

34. William Nordhaus, https://carbon-price.com/william-nordhaus/

35. Simon Dietz, James Rising, Thomas Stoerk and Gernot Wagner, 'Tipping Points in the Climate System and the Economics of Climate Change', https://thenextrecession. files.wordpress.com/2020/01/tippingpointsintheclimatesystemand_preview.pdf

36. Mark Carney, 'Regulate Business to Tackle Climate Crisis', *Guardian*, 17 July 2021, www.theguardian.com/environment/2021/jul/17/regulate-business-to-tackle-climate-crisis-urges-mark-carney

37. Chevron has been the company behind what is reportedly the biggest CCS project in the world. It is a project in Western Australia. It is expected that it has only captured 30 per cent of the carbon it was supposed to capture, according to Ian Porter, a former oil and gas industry executive who is chair of the advocacy group Sustainable Energy Now WA.

38. IEA, *World Energy Report 2021*, www.iea.org/reports/world-energy-outlook-2020

39. L. Martin Weitzman, 'Fat-Tailed Uncertainty in the Economics of Catastrophic Climate Change', *Review of Environmental Economics and Policy*, 5(2), Summer 2011, pp. 275–92, https://scholar.harvard.edu/files/weitzman/files/fattaileduncertaintyeconomics.pdf

40. Y. Zhang, I. Held and S. Fueglistaler, 'Projections of Tropical Heat Stress Constrained by Atmospheric Dynamics', *Nature Geoscience*, 14, 2021, pp. 133–7, https://doi.org/10.1038/s41561-021-00695-3

41. Jason Hickel, 'Degrowth: A Theory of Radical Abundance', *Real-World Economics Review*, 87(19), 2019, pp. 54–68.

42. Giorgos Kallis, *In Defense of Degrowth: Opinions and Manifestos*, 2018. UK: Uneven Earth Press, pp. 22, 21.

43. Marx, *Capital Vol 3*, New York: Penguin, 1991, p. 180.

44. Matt Huber, 'Fossilized Liberation: Energy, Freedom, and the "Development of the Productive forces"', in B.R. Bellamy and J. Diamanti (eds), *Materialism and the Critique of Energy*, Chicago, IL: MCM Press, 2018, p. 517.

45. Ernest Mandel, 'We Must Dream. Anticipation and Hope as Categories of Historical Materialism', 2020. Originally published at https://iire.org/es/node/940?fbclid=IwAR1GPtMzjOqv-SaTYdAsfGq615haNZn5de-Sp5UVddll_AnAub3-PVomqVs, International Institute for Research and Education (IIRE), 9 September 2020. See also https://mronline.org/guest-author/iire-international-institute-for-research-and-education/, 16 September 2020. Also https://mronline.org/2020/09/16/1978-ernest-mandel-we-must-dream-anticipation-and-hope-as-categories-of-historical-materialism/. Ernest Mandel on Marxism and ecology: 'The Dialectic of Growth', International Institute for Research and Education (IIRE), 17 June 2020, https://iire.org/es/node/940?fbclid=IwAR1GPtMzjOqv-SaTYdAsfGq615haNZn5de-Sp5UVddll_AnAub3-PVomqVs

46. Jason Hickel, *Less Is More: How Degrowth Will Save the World*, February 2021. Windmill Press.

47. https://edition.cnn.com/2018/03/12/health/disease-x-blueprint-who/index.html

48. Ibid.

49. Ibid.

50. Ibid.

51. W. Xia, J. Hughes, D. Robertson and X. Jiang, 'How One Pandemic Led to Another: Asfv, the Disruption Contributing to SARS-Cov-2 Emergence in Wuhan', January 2022, https://europepmc.org/article/PPR/PPR446246, Version 2.

52. Stavros Mavroudeas, 'The Economic and Political Consequences of the COVID-19 Pandemic', *International Critical Thought*, 10(4), 2020, pp. 559–65, doi: 10.1080/21598282.2020.1866235

53. Pierre-Olivier Gourinchas, Professor of Economics, UC Berkeley, visiting Princeton University, 'Flattening the Pandemic and Recession Curves, 13 March 2020, https://clausen.berkeley.edu/wp-content/uploads/2020/03/COVID_2b.pdf

54. www3.weforum.org/docs/WEF_The_Future_Of_Nature_And_Business_2020.pdf

CHAPTER 2

1. Quotations are taken from this work, unless otherwise indicated.

2. Section 1 – The Measure of Value; Section 2 – The Medium of Circulation; 2A. The Metamorphosis of Commodities; 2B. The Currency of Money; 2C. Coin and Symbols of Value; Section 3 – Money; 3A. Hoarding; 3B. Means of Payment; 3C. Universal Money.

3. For the alternative interpretations of abstract labour, see Carchedi, 2010.

4. This is a preview of the theory of price formation through the equalisation of the profit rates to be found in Volume III of *Capital*. It is around this point and thus around the transformation procedure (improperly called problem) that the discussion among Marxists has raged and continues to rage.

5. For a recent example of a value-form approach, see John Milios, *Marx's Value Theory Revisited. A 'Value-Form' Approach*, http://users.ntua.gr/jmilios/F2_3.pdf

6. The example of the ellipse is an analogy and should not be used to argue that for Marx the laws of movement of society are modelled on those of nature.

7. There is another cause of the failure of what Marx calls '*the salto mortale of the commodity*': the buyers' lack of purchasing power. But this aspect belongs to the analysis of crises. Here the assumption is that all commodities are sold. Thus, crises must be explained, not due to, but in the absence of, difficulties of realisation.

8. Karl Marx, *Critique of Political Economy*, 1859, p. 4. The precious metals. This is quite aside from money as a vehicle of imperialist relation and as instrument of money wars. See later.

9. Joseph Schumpeter, *History of Economic Analysis*, New York: Oxford University Press, 1954, p. 1090.

10. Another Chartalist, Pavlina Tcherneva writes: 'Chartalists argue that, since money is a public monopoly, the government has at its disposal a direct way to determine its value. Remember that for Knapp the payments with currency measure a certain number of units of value. For example, if the state required that in order to obtain a high-powered money unit a person must provide one hour of work, then the money would be worth exactly one hour of work. As a monopoly issuer of the currency, the state can determine what the currency will be worth by establishing the terms in which the high-powered money is obtained.' *The Nature, Origins, and Role of Money: Broad and Specific Propositions and Their Implications for Policy*, January 2005, p. 18, http://tankona.free.fr/tcherneva05.pdf. Tcherneva's policy of State 'exogenous pricing' is similar to the views of 19th century utopian socialist John Gray who reckoned that by issuing bonds that were exogenously priced to represent working time, so economies could deliver growth and full employment – a view that Marx rejected.

11. As Cullen Roche, an orthodox Keynesian, put it: 'MMT gets the causality backwards here by starting with the state and working out.' Roche goes on: 'The proper causality

is that private resources necessarily precede taxes. Without a highly productive revenue generating private sector there is nothing special about the assets created by a government and it is literally impossible for these assets to remain valuable. We create equity when we produce real goods and services or increase the market value of our assets relative to their liabilities via productive output.' MMT, 'The Good, the Bad and the Ugly', 31 January 2019, www.pragcap.com/mmt-good-bad-ugly/

12. Roche: 'It is completely illogical and beyond silly to argue that one can just "print" equity from thin air. Government debt is, logically, a liability of the society that creates it. In the aggregate government debt is a liability that must be financed by the productive output of that society.'

13. L. Randall Wray is one of most active writers in this tradition, http://xenophon-mil. org/politicaleconomy/wrraymoney.htm

14. As Rolando Astarita puts it: 'the fundamental difference between the Marxist approach to money and the Chartalist approach revolves around this single point. In Marx's conception, money can only be understood as a social relation. In the Chartalist approach, it is an artifice in which essential social determinations are missing ... it "sweeps under the carpet" the centrality of productive work and the exploitation of work; the true basis on which capitalist society is based.' https://rolandoastarita.blog/2018/11/10/origen-del-dinero-cuestiones-historicas/

15. Scott Fulwiler, 'The Sector Financial Balances Model of Aggregate Demand and Austerity', *New Economic Perspectves*, 9 June 2011, http://neweconomicperspectives. org/2011/06/sector-financial-balances-model-of.html

16. Scott Fulwiler presents a time series graph comparing US Private Net Saving (remember this includes household net saving) with Government deficits and concludes that 'It shows how closely the private sector surplus and the government sector deficit have moved historically, which isn't surprising given they are nearly the opposing sides of an accounting identity.' Scott says: 'What we notice (from these graphs) is that the current rise in the government's deficit is creating net saving for the private sector.'

17. 'The accounting identities equating aggregate expenditures to production and of both to incomes at market prices are inescapable, no matter which variety of Keynesian or classical economics you espouse. I tell students that respect for identities is the first piece of wisdom that distinguishes economists from others who expiate on economics. The second? Identities say nothing about causation.' James Tobin, 'Comment', in B.D. Bernheim and J.B. Shoven (eds), *National Saving and Economic Performance*, Chicago, IL: University of Chicago Press, 1997, p. 300.

18. 'Money is ultimately a creation of government – but that doesn't mean only government deficits determine the level of demand at any one time. The actions and beliefs of the private sector matter as well. And that in turn means you can have budget surpluses and excess demand at the same time, just as you can have budget deficits and deficient demand.' Jonathan Portes, 'Nonsense Economics, the Rise of Modern Monetary Theory', *Prospect*, 30 January 2019, www.prospectmagazine. co.uk/economics-and-finance/nonsense-economics-the-rise-of-modern-monetary-theory

19. Michael Roberts, 'Macro Modelling MMT', 3 March 2019, https://thenextrecession. wordpress.com/2019/03/03/macro-modelling-mmt/

20. 'Bank money does not exist as a result of economic activity. Instead, bank money creates economic activity.' Or this: 'The money for a bank loan does not exist until we, the customers, apply for credit.' Ann Pettifor, 'There Is No Money', UNCTAD,

11 September 2017, https://unctad.org/system/files/non-official-document/Ann_Petifor_PRIME_11_Sept_2017.pdf

21. Bill Mitchell is a leading MMT economist from Australia and has campaigned tirelessly for the government job guarantee. He describes it as 'an open-ended public employment program that offers a job at a living (minimum) wage to anyone who wants to work but cannot find employment ...', 'What Is a Job Guarantee', 4 May 2013, http://bilbo.economicoutlook.net/blog/?p=23719

22. 'The Job Guarantee jobs would "hire off the bottom", in the sense that minimum wages are not in competition with the market-sector wage structure. By not competing with the private market, the Job Guarantee would supposedly avoid the inflationary tendencies of old-fashioned Keynesianism, which attempted to maintain full capacity utilisation by "hiring off the top".

23. The Job Guarantee program is to provide jobs only at the minimum wage. It is similar to the notorious Hartz labour 'reforms' in Germany in the early 2000s that created programmes for the unemployed at the barest minimum wage. The unemployment rate fell but real wages stagnated. While unemployment is at its lowest since German reunification in 1990, some 9.7 per cent of Germans in work still live below the poverty line – defined as income of around €940 per month or less. Indeed, that working poor figure has grown from 7.5 per cent in 2006 and even surpasses the EU average of 9.5 per cent, according to Eurostat data.

24. Under Roosevelt's Works Progress Administration (WPA) many unemployed were put to work on a wide range of government financed public works projects, building bridges, airports, dams, post offices, hospitals and hundreds of thousands of miles of road. This was all on very basic incomes. Did it solve the problem of sky-high unemployment in the Great Depression? Well, in 1933 the unemployment rate reached 25 per cent; in 1938 it was 19 per cent; so not a great success. MMTers will say that this was because it was not done properly as Roosevelt kept trying to balance the government budget, not run deficits permanently.

25. Even leading MMT man Bill Mitchell is aware of this risk: 'Think about an economy that is returning from a recession and growing strongly. Budget deficits could still be expanding in this situation, which would make them obviously pro-cyclical, but we would still conclude the fiscal strategy was sound because the growth in net public spending was driving growth and the economy towards full employment. Even when non-government spending growth is positive, budget deficits are appropriate if they are supporting the move towards full employment. However, once the economy reached full employment, it would be inappropriate for the government to push nominal aggregate demand more by expanding discretionary spending, as it would risk inflation.'

26. R. Auer and D. Tercero-Lucas, 'Distrust or Speculation? The Socioeconomic Drivers of US Cryptocurrency Investments', BIS Working Paper 951, July 2021, www.bis.org/publ/work951.pdf

27. Group of Thirty, 'Digital Currencies and Stablecoins Risks, Opportunities, and Challenges Ahead', July 2020, https://group30.org/images/uploads/publications/G30_Digital_Currencies.pdf

28. We refer to the US CPI as our measure of inflation. There have been many critiques of this index. An assessment lies outside the scope of this work.

29. A debate between these two theories started in the late 1950s in the US (see Johnson, 1963).

30. We use gross value added in the non-financial corporate sector for output.

31. See Friedman, 1970. For a good discussion of monetarism, see Green, 1982.

32. Actually, one should refer to oligopolies rather than monopolies.

33. Jared Bernstein and Ernie Tedeschi, 'Pandemic Prices: Assessing Inflation in the Months and Years Ahead', The White House, 12 April 2021, www. whitehouse.gov/cea/blog/2021/04/12/pandemic-prices-assessing-inflation-in-the-months-and-years-ahead/

34. IMF, World Economic Outlook, October 2016.

35. J. Hazell and colleagues point out that explanations of long-run inflation on the basis of long-run expectations are particularly problematic since the latter are sometimes fairly stable but at other times change sharply. Jonathon Hazell, Juan Herreño, Emi Nakamura and Jón Steinsson, The Slope of the Phillips Curve: Evidence from U.S. States, Working Paper 28005, 2020, p. 41, www.nber.org/papers/w28005 NATIONAL BUREAU OF ECONOMIC RESEARCH www.nber.org/system/files/working_papers/w28005/w28005.pdf

36. Jeremy B. Rudd, Federal Reserve Board, 'Why Do We Think That Inflation Expectations Matter for Inflation?' 23 September 2021.

37. Rudd: 'Most standard tests of the new-Keynesian Phillips curve suffer from such severe potential misspecification issues or such profound weak identification problems as to provide no evidence one way or the other regarding the importance of expectations (much the same statement applies to empirical tests that use survey measures of expected inflation).'

38. Duncan Weldon, 'We Have No Theory of Inflation', Substack, 4 October 2021, https://duncanweldon.substack.com/p/we-have-no-theory-of-inflation

39. Marx, *Critique of Political Economy*.

40. For an account of how the banking controversy influenced Marx view of money, see Lapavitsas, 1994: 'Marx's work was indeed in the anti-Quantity Theory tradition of Steuart (1767), Tooke (1959) and Fullarton (1845), but it was also a significant development of that tradition' (p. 449).

41. As a first approximation, wages and profits (new value) can be considered to be the purchasing power of labour and capital. But wages and profits are not quantitatively equal to the combined purchasing power (CPP). Among the reasons for this discrepancy, the following can be mentioned: first, purchasing power must be net of taxes; second, there are savings and reserves, where income is not spent in one year but set aside and spent subsequently; and third, money is used for the settlement of international payments. We have estimated that quantitatively new value and CPP differ by a ratio of 22 per cent. This ratio has been arrived at in the following way: we looked at total personal income and total personal outlays after removing any income like dividends, which mostly go to employers. The ratio between outlays and income hardly varies at 0.78 per cent over 50 years. So it is a reasonably robust assumption to use the 22 per cent ratio for deductions to get labour's purchasing power spent on consumer goods. Profits have been adjusted for taxes.

42. As Lapavitsas, 1994, p. 451 correctly point out, changes in the money quantity represent value changes rather than changes in (effective) demand.

43. The assumption is that the decrease in wages is not more than compensated by the increase in profits. This is indeed the case, given that the increase in constant capital and thus the decrease in wages, that is, the increase in the OCC, is the tendency and the increase in the rate of surplus value is the counter-tendency. This, in its turn, is confirmed by the tendential fall in the average rate of profit.

44. The ratio of financial assets to total assets rises for the NFC sector since 1959. So the deduction of the total M2 stock each year to get the NFC share rises. Financial assets in the NFC total assets are about 23 per cent in the 1960s to 1980s – our first period. Then from the 1980s that ratio rises sharply to 45 per cent by early 2000 (the second period) and then stabilises. So we adjust the M2 by this ratio.

45. Frederic Boissay, Fiorella De Fiore, Deniz Igan, Albert Pierres-Tejada and Daniel Rees, 'Are Major Advanced Economies on the Verge of a Wage-Price Spiral?' BIS Bulletin No. 53, 4 May 2022.

46. The State of UK Competition Report, April 2022, www.gov.uk/government/publications/state-of-uk-competition-report-2022/the-state-of-uk-competition-report-april-2022

CHAPTER 3

1. 'Marx and the Theory of Economic Crisis', Stavros Mavroudeas, Department of Economics, University of Macedonia.

2. This holds per unit of capital invested. Total employment and the creation of value and surplus value depends also on capital accumulation.

3. *Capital*, Vols I to III.

4. 'In light of the fact that "the principal laws governing crises" are, as all social laws, tendential and contradictory, "to determine mathematically the laws is an impossible task. Mathematics is a branch of formal logic. Premises in formal logic cannot be contradictory. However, to account for the laws of movement in society one has to start from contradictory premises and this is why the laws of movement are tendential. But if it is impossible to determine the laws of crises purely in terms of mathematics, it is certainly possible to analyse the cyclical movement of economic indicators (the ups and downs) by using "higher mathematics". This was Marx's intuition."' G. Carchedi, *Behind the Crisis*, Leiden: Brill, 2011, appendix 3, p. 280.

5. C. Harman, 'The Rate of Profit and the World Today', *International Socialism*, 115, 2007, http://isj.org.uk/the-rate-of-profit-and-the-world-today/

6. G. Carchedi and M. Roberts, 'Turnover and the Rate of Surplus Value', unpublished paper.

7. Karl Marx, *Capital*, Vol. III, Part 3, Chapter 13, p. 218.

8. We would rather stress the actual, rather than the projected increase in investments.

9. Jose Tapia, 'Investment, Profit and Crises: Theories and Evidence', in G. Carchedi and M. Roberts (eds), *World in Crisis*, Chicago, IL: Haymarket, 2018, chapter 3.

10. Ibid.

11. For a fuller analysis of Marx's law and a defence of the critical arguments against it, see G. Carchedi and M. Roberts, 'Old and New Misconceptions of Marx's Law', *Critique: Journal of Socialist Theory*, 41, 2014, pp. 571–94.

12. 'The tendency of the rate of profit to fall and its empirical confirmation highlights the historically limited nature of capitalist production. If the rate of profit measures the vitality of the capitalist system, the logical conclusion is that it is getting closer to its endpoint.' Esteban Maito, 'The Tendency of the Rate of profit to Fall since the 19th Century and a World Rate of Profit', in G. Carchedi and M. Roberts (eds), *World in Crisis*, Chicago, IL: Haymarket, 2018, chapter 4, p. 129.

13. Although Luxemburg's statement in the Anti-Critique that 'There is still some time to pass before capitalism collapses because of the falling rate of profit, roughly until the sun burns out' is well known, less so is the person she is responding to. He was

an anonymous reviewer of 'The Accumulation of Capital' in *Dresdener Volkszeitung* of 21 and 23 January 1913. The author was Miran Isaakovich Nakhimson. Born in 1880, he joined the Bundists in 1898 and became known as one of its most prominent political economists (he remained a Bundist until 1922). He lived for many years in Germany (until returning to Russia after the Revolution) so was in the thick of many of the debates within the SPD – in fact, he authored over a hundred articles in *Die Neue Zeit*. Although virtually forgotten today, he was a considerable presence at the time, authoring such works as 'Die Agrarfrage in Rußland' and 'Die Lage der arbeitenden Klasse in Russland' (both in 1907) and 'Die theory der Volkswirtschaft' (1912). He was one of the first to review Luxemburg's 'Accumulation', beating Pannekoek by a few weeks. Nakhimson headed the Department of Statistics of the International Agrarian Institute in Moscow – which had direct links with the Frankfurt School. One figure from the latter who was influenced by Nakhimson was Henryk Grossman (he discusses Nakhikmson in his 'Law of Accumulation' and the two carried on a correspondence). So it turns out the person Rosa attacked in the harshest of terms turns out to be an inspirer of the man who is widely considered the first to reframe the debates in Marxism around Marx's theory of the rate of profit. Nakhimson was murdered by Stalin's NKVD in 1938. None of his work has been published in English. Source: Email from Peter Hudis, Hudis Oakton Community Collent.ge, Chicago.

14. Anti-Critique, p. 76, www.marxists.org/archive/bukharin/works/1924/impacck/cho5.htm

15. Karl Marx and Friedrich Engels, *The Communist Manifesto*, 1848.

16. Karl Marx, *Capital*, Vol. 1, Moscow: Progress Publishers, 1961, Chapter 25, p. 633.

17. Marx sought the ultimately determining factor. This however does not exclude other factors, which are determined by this one. The critique that Marx's theory is 'mono-causal' reveals methodological ignorance.

18. We shall see that this is the central point in Maksakovsky's theory – see below.

19. Systemic fragility in the global economy. What follows is based on Rasmus' summary of his book in *The European Financial Review*, February–March 2016, pp. 13–20 (EFR from now on)..

20. Karl Marx, *Collected Works*, Vol. 32, London: Lawrence and Wishart, 1973.

21. Karl Marx, *Grundrisse*, 1968, p. 512.

22. M. Brooks, 'Capitalist Crisis – Theory and Practice', *Expedia*, 2012.

23. But it should be stressed that speculation was not due to the workers' greed. Rather, it was fuelled by finance capital, which pushed workers to buy mortgages even if it was clear that workers would never be able to pay for them. A second factor was rising unemployment. See Section 3.5 below.

24. 'The theory of crises most fully (though far from completely) developed in the 1864–65 Manuscript, and already sketched out in earlier drafts, posits an interaction between the tendency of the rate of profit to fall and the cycle of bubble and panic on financial markets, which feeds the accumulation of capital in good times and accomplishes in bad times the destruction of capital required to restore profitability.' A. Callinicos, *Deciphering Capital*, London: Bookmarks, 2014, chapter 6.

25. *Capital*, Vol. III, p. 621.

26. M. Kraetke, Capitalism and Its Crises, www.academia.edu/5545493/Capitalism_and_its_crises

27. Paul Mattick, 'Economic Crisis and Crisis Theory', 1974, www.marxists.org/archive/mattick-paul/1974/crisis/ch02.htm

28. G. Carchedi, 'The Return from the Grave', 12 March 2009, http://gesd.free.fr/carchedi9.pdf

29. Karl Marx, *Theories of Surplus Value*, Vol II, p. 514.

30. A. Pannekoek, 'The Theory of Collapse of Capitalism', 1934, p. 683. First published: unsigned article in *Ratekorrespondenz*, June 1934; translated by Adam Buick in *Capital and Class*, Spring 1977, www.marxists.org/archive/pannekoe/1934/collapse.htm

31. B. Ollman, *Dialectical Investigations*, New York: Routledge, 1993, p. 16.

32. *Capital*, Vol. III, pp. 475ff.

33. Marx, *Capital*, Vol. 2, Moscow: Progress Publishers, 1961, Chapter 20, p. 410.

34. G. Carchedi, 'The Old Is Dying', in G. Carchedi and M. Roberts (eds), *World in Crisis*, Chicago, IL: Haymarket, 2018, chapter 3, p. 48.

35. Marxists supporting this cause include Richard Wolff and Costas Lapavitsas as well as some mainstream Nobel Prize winners like Joseph Stiglitz (in his book *The Price of Inequality*) or the current head of the Indian central bank, Raghuram Rajan (as in his book, *Faultlines*). And there have been a host of books arguing that inequality is the cause of all our problems – *The Spirit Level* by Kate Pickett and Richard Wilkinson. The varied views on this issue were summed up in a compendium, *Income Inequality as a Cause of the Great Recession* (http://gesd.free.fr/treeck12.pdf).

36. A. Mina and A. Sufi, *House of Debt*, Chicago, IL: Chicago Press, 2014.

37. C. Lapavitsas, *Profiting without producing*, London: Verso, 2013.

38. E. Stockhammer, 'Rising Inequality as the Cause of Crisis', *Cambridge Journal of Economics*, 39(3), May 2015, pp. 935–58.

39. Michael D. Bordo and Christopher M. Meissner, 'Does Inequality Lead to a Financial Crisis?' NBER Working Papers 17896, National Bureau of Economic Research, 2012.

40. A.B. Atkinson and Morelli, Salvatore, 'Economic Crises and Inequality', UNDP-HDRO Occasional Papers No. 2011/6, 7 November 2011. Available at SSRN: https://ssrn.com/abstract=2351471

41. J. Weeks, 'A Note on Underconsumption Theory and the Labour Theory of Value', *Science & Society* 192, http://marx2mao.com/PDFs/JW82.pdf

42. The reason for the assumption of the equality between one unit of use values and one unit of the value it contains is that it simplifies the numerical examples. Any other assumption would do.

43. Pavel Maksakovsky, *The Capitalist Cycle: An Essay on the Marxist Theory of the Cycle*, Chicago, IL: Haymarket, 2009.

44. See discussion between Pete Green and Micheal Roberts, https://thenextrecession.wordpress.com/2016/12/02/the-long-depression-and-marxs-law-a-reply-to-pete-green/; also Chris Harman, www.marxists.org/archive/harman/2005/xx/boom-slump.html; Hadas Thier, *A People's Guide to Capitalism: An Introduction to Marxist Economics* (Paperback), chapter 4, www.haymarketbooks.org/books/1481-a-people-s-guide-to-capitalism; Stavros Mavroudeas, www.academia.edu/17849817/The_Capitalist_Cycle_by_Pavel_Maksakovskyhttps://isreview.org/issue/90/systematic-theory-economic-crisis/index.html

45. Maksakovsky summarises his theory of the cycle at p. 138.

CHAPTER 4

1. Stavros Mavroudeas, 'The Marxist Theory of Imperialism: Which Way Forward', 13th Forum, World Association for Political Economy, July 2018, www.academia.edu/37061654/The_Marxist_Theory_of_Imperialism_Which_way_forward and Sam King Imperialism and the Development Myth, MUP, 2020

2. Imperialism is much more than domination. T. Norfield, 2018 uses 'the term "imperialism" in the classical sense to describe the system of domination in the capitalist world economy'. But domination is the consequence of technological and thus economic superiority.

3. For a discussion of the notion of the dialectical relation, see Carchedi, 2011b, chapter 1.

4. See Svee Freeman, 2019 for an approach complementary to the present one.

5. We define the dominated countries as those in the G20 group that are not imperialist (eleven countries). The imperialist countries are defined as the G7 plus Australia in the G20 bloc. There are other smaller imperialist countries in Europe (Sweden, Netherlands, Belgium) and New Zealand, but these are excluded in our calculations.

6. So we agree that 'an injection of surplus value by means of foreign trade would raise the rate of profit and reduce the severity of the breakdown tendency... Marx's conception (is that) the original surplus value expands by means of transfers from abroad ... thus we have a means of partially offsetting a crisis of valorisation in the domestic economy.' And 'at advanced stages of accumulation, when it becomes more and more difficult to valorise the enormously accumulate capital, such transfers become a matter of life and death for capitalism. This explains the virulence of imperialist expansion in the late stage of capitalism.' H. Grossman, 1992, p. 172, quoted in R. Kuhn, 2007, pp. 133–4.

7. For Marx's law of profitability, see Carchedi and M. Roberts, 2018.

8. Marx, *Capital*, Vol. I, Chapter 22, p. 560.

9. See Sam King, 2020b for a detailed sympathetic treatment of Lenin's theory of imperialism.

10. The IMF defines primary income as 'the net flow of profits, interest and dividends from investments in other countries and net remittance flows from migrant workers'. Since remittances from migrant workers are not transfers of surplus value, these data are an overestimation. Nevertheless, in spite of this overestimation, this is a clear measure of cross-border net surplus value flows.

11. Seignorage is not the only advantage of the dollar as the international currency. For example, by closing off this venue of international money, the US can drastically limit the imports and exports of a nation, thus strangling its economy, as in contemporary Venezuela. More generally, the dollar is the instrument through which the US can control the international financial system. For a fuller analysis of US seignorage, see Carchedi, 2001.

12. We do not review here the various theories of trade. For our purposes, the point is not why countries trade (in a different context we would argue for absolute advantage), but given that they do trade, our point is about the appropriation of surplus value inherent in trade.

13. Dialectically, the passage from the unrealised to the realised is the passage from the potential to the realised. That is, what has become realised was potentially present before realisation. Other approaches similar to the present one lack the dialectical dimension.

14. The assumption here is that the two sectors invest the same quantity of value, that is, 100. Then, if the commodities are exchanged at the production prices on the basis of the equalisation of the profit rates, each sector has sufficient purchasing power to buy the other sector's output.

15. The *Monthly Review* school replaces the notion of surplus value with 'surplus'. The replacement is accepted also by other writers. See also Duménil and Lèvy, 2011, p. 9: 'economically, the purpose of this domination is the extraction of a "surplus" through the imposition of low prices of natural resources and investment abroad, be it portfolio or foreign direct investment'. The substitution of surplus value by 'surplus' shifts the level of analysis back to a pre-Marx stage.

16. This thesis is held by authors such as Baran and Sweezy and the *Monthly Review* school. As Amin, 2015 puts it, 'the abolition of competition ... detaches the price system from its basis, the system of values'.

17. We agree with King, 2020b, p. 135 that monopolies can charge prices (market prices) above production prices. But production prices should be accounted for to begin with.

18. For example, Cockshott sees a dispersion of rates of profits and concludes that 'The basic problem with Vol. III of *Capital* is that Marx introduces an imagined hypothesis profit rate equalisation which was not backed up by accurate observations', www.researchgate.net/publication/302897588_Laws_of_chaos--a_probabilistic_approach_to_political_economy?fbclid=IwAR02uk4SoKnYb-t8FW1gFCYfMc6Ee7kHiY2CVz4efMUzpNydNCotE96bhCU. The confusion here is between imagined and tendential.

19. Jason Hickel, Dylan Sullivan and Huzaifa Zoomkawala, 'Plunder in the Post-colonial Era: Quantifying Drain from the Global South Through Unequal Exchange, 1960–2018', *New Political Economy*, 30 March 2021, www.tandfonline.com/doi/abs/10.1080/13563467.2021.1899153?journalCode=cnpe20&journalCode=cnpe20

20. Turan Subasat, 'Can Differences in International Prices Measure Unequal Exchange in International Trade?' October 2013, Sage Journals, www.semanticscholar.org/paper/Can-Differences-in-International-Prices-Measure-in-Suba%C5%9Fat/5e8b90e9c5723136ced3e0714b2301b49a3d4286

21. Below we too speak of broad and narrow UE, but from quite a different perspective.

22. Ruy Marini, 'Plusvalía extraordinaria y acumulación de capital', *Cuadernos Políticos*, núm. 20, México, abril–junio, 1979, pp. 19–39.

23. Super-exploitation 'consiste en reducer el consume del obrero más allá de su límite normal'. R.M. Marini, *Dialéctica de la dependencia*, Ediciones Era, México, 1991, p. 22. Elsewhere, Marini seems to think of super-exploitation as 'labour being remunerated below its value' (1991, p. 25).

24. Higginbottom, 2013; Mayer, 2018; Smith, 2011, 2015, 2016, 2018.

25. Karl Marx, *Capital*, Vol. III, International Publishers, New York, 1967, p. 238.

26. Similar conclusions are reached by Akkermans, 2017, p.13. 'One of the most striking facts is the development of core countries ... most FDI of developed countries has flown to other developed countries.'

27. Smith, 2016, p. 35.

28. Higginbottom, 2013; Utsa Patnaik and Prabhat Patnaik, 2015; ibid.

29. King, 2020b, p. 73.

30. We explain in detail our sources and the methods we adopt in order to do this in Appendix 1 and 2.

31. The missing economy in the G20 is the EU as a whole.

32. This is our measure of 'narrow' UE of trade between two blocs without reference to trade outside the blocs. Given that the G20 constitutes over 70 per cent of global GDP, there is no necessity to consider the broad UE measure in this case.

33. We disregard within this context the ecological crisis, the most threatening consequence of the destructive nature capitalism. See Chapter 1 of this work.

CHAPTER 5

1. This chapter is a shortened version of G. Carchedi and M. Roberts, 'The Ontology of Knowledge, Machine Thinking and Marxism', unpublished paper.

2. Economies in a graph originally constructed by John Smith in his excellent paper 'Imperialism in the Twenty-First Century: Globalization Super-Exploitation and Capitalism's Final Crisis' published by Monthly Review Press, 2016.

3. We shall see later that the term 'intelligence' as applied to both humans and machines hides a fundamental difference. Quantitatively as well as qualitatively, machines will never be intelligent as humans are.

4. Paul Krugman, 'Human versus Physical Capital', New York Times blog, 11 November 2012, http://krugman.blogs.nytimes.com/2012/12/11/human-versus-physical-capital/

5. International Labour Organization, 'Global Labour Income Share and Distribution, Key Findings', July 2019, www.ilo.org/wcmsp5/groups/public/---dgreports/---stat/documents/publication/wcms_712232.pdf

6. Marco Annunziata, 'The Next Productivity Revolution', 7 December 2012, www.voxeu.org/article/next-productivity-revolution-industrial-internet

7. Kenneth Rogoff, 'Technology Stagnation and Advanced Countries Slow Growth', Project Syndicate, 4 December 2013, www.project-syndicate.org/commentary/kenneth-rogoff-asks-whether-we-need-to-know-what-s-ailing-the-advanced-economies-in-order-to-boost-growth

8. Paul Krugman, 'Robots and Robber Barons', New York Times blog, 10 December 2020, www.nytimes.com/2012/12/10/opinion/krugman-robots-and-robber-barons.html

9. Paul Mason, Post Capitalism, a Guide to Our Future, London: Allen Lane, 2015.

10. McKinsey Institute, 'Disruptive Technologies', May 2013, www.mckinsey.com/~/media/McKinsey/Business%20Functions/McKinsey%20Digital/Our%20Insights/Disruptive%20technologies/MGI_Disruptive_technologies_Full_report_May2013.ashx

11. John Lanchester, 'The Robots Are Coming', London Review of Books, Vol. 37, No. 5, March 2015, www.lrb.co.uk/the-paper/v37/n05/john-lanchester/the-robots-are-coming

12. George Graetz and Guy Michaels, 'Robots at Work', Centre for Economic Policy Research, March 2015, https://cepr.org/active/publications/discussion_papers/dp.php?dpno=10477

13. Carl Benedikt Frey and Michael Osborne, 'The Future of Employment', 17 September 2013, Oxford Martin School, University of Oxford, www.oxfordmartin.ox.ac.uk/downloads/academic/The_Future_of_Employment.pdf

14. Paul Krugman, 'The Accidental Theorist', Slate, 24 January 1997, http://web.mit.edu/krugman/www/hotdog.html. See Richard Serlin's critique of this example, 'AI and Krugman's Hot Dogs', 18 September 2016, https://richardhserlin.blogspot.com/2016/09/ai-and-krugmans-hot-dogs.html

15. Karl Marx, *Capital*, Vol. 1, Chapter 15.
16. For a critique of underconsumption, see Chapter 3 on crises in this work.
17. Jeffrey Sachs, 'How to Live Happily with Robots', The American Prospect, 3 August 2015, https://prospect.org/labor/live-happily-robots/
18. Martin Ford, *The Rise of the Robots: Technology and the Threat of a Jobless Future*, New York: Basic Books, 2015.
19. Martin Wolf, 'If Robots Divide Us, They Will Conquer', *Financial Times*, 4 February 2014, www.ft.com/content/e1046e2e-8aae-11e3-9465-00144feab7de#axzz3k72z2kiJ
20. Lanchester, 'The Robots Are Coming'.
21. David Graeber, *Bullshit Jobs*, London: Penguin Random House, 2018.
22. William Nordhaus, 'Are We Approaching Economic Singularity?', Cowles Foundation Discussion Paper, September 2015, SSRN-id2658259.
23. Thomas Rotta and Rodrigo Teixeira, 'The Commodification of Knowledge', in *The Oxford Handbook of Karl Marx*, June 2019, doi:10.1093/oxfordhb/9780190695545.013.23
24. Quoted in the Encyclopedia2.thefreedisctionary.com
25. A complete critique of workerism is beyond the scope of this work. See Carchedi, 2012; Henninger, 2007; Starosta, 2012. For some authors, especially of a workerist persuasion, the notion of 'immaterial' seems to resemble that of 'mental' in this work. Even so the gulf is unbridgeable because workerism rejects Marx's labour theory of value while the present work builds a Marxist epistemology upon it.
26. Rey, 2012, p.406 is one of many holding this view.
27. See Carchedi, 2011b, pp. 39–44 for a more detailed treatment.
28. Here dialectics is a method of social research and it applies to social life. We leave aside whether it applies to nature. See ibid., pp. 37–8. Kangal, 2017 dissents. A fuller discussion of dialectical logic and related aspects can be found in Carchedi, 2011, chapter 1.
29. Marx, *Capital*, Vol. II, Chapter 6.
30. The only exception are the production relations which are determinant in the last instance.
31. Just three operations (AND, OR and NOT) can perform all logic functions.
32. Here we consider the mainstream Copenhagen interpretation. Alternative interpretations have been formulated, both in the West and in the former Soviet Union (see Cross, 1991; Kojevnikov, 2013). For example, in 1944 Blokhintsev accepted the Copenhagen view, but in 1949 he rejected it, arguing instead that the wave function provided an objective description of the wave function (Cross, 1991, p. 740). Fock 'argued that the wave-function described observer-independent "potential possibilities", one of which was "actualized" as an objective state when a measurement was made. Thus he took the controversial step of extending materialism to potential situations' (Cross, 1991, p. 741). In 1955 Lurcat stressed that 'it was important to distinguish the physics of the theory from the idealistic philosophy of some physicists' (Cross, 1991, p. 749). Following these and other authors, we sympathised with a formulation of quantum mechanics and more specifically with a notion of potentiality consistent with a dialectical, materialist causality.
33. Quoted in Daniel, 1989, p. 252.
34. Humans generate a new knowledge also when they replicate an existing knowledge (see Section 5.7 below). But when a computer replicates existing knowledge by repeating a computation, no new knowledge is generated because human synapses

are not involved. The outcome of computation becomes a means for the generation of new knowledge when used by humans in the mental labour process. Quantum computers, just as traditional computers, can compute, but cannot think, that is, cannot think like humans.

35. There is a branch of formal logic, fuzzy logic, that claims to reproduce human thinking better than classical binary logic because the human brain can reason with vague assertions or claims that involve uncertainties or value judgement (Kosko and Isaka, 2021). In this fuzzy area, statements can be both true and false. The point here is quantification: statements are to some extent true and to some extent false. For example, a statement can be 60 per cent true and 60 per cent false. But then one returns to the binary system: if a statement is (60 per cent) true, it is not (60 per cent) false. Gerla, 2017 p. 442 gives a more formal demonstration that 'a fuzzy logic cannot be alternative to classical logic since it is a construct of this logic and, at the same time fuzzy logic is an attempt to extend classical logic'. If fuzzy logic is not an alternative to binary logic but an extension of it, the claim that fuzzy logic approaches human thinking more than classical binary logic is unfounded.

36. See: Bohr–Einstein debates, *Wikipedia*.

37. Karl Marx, *Economic and Philosophic Manuscript of 1844*, p. 137.

38. For Bauchspies, Croissant and Restivo, 2006, p. 46, knowledge is explained in terms of 'networks and connections'. This is similar to the approach in this work inasmuch as it stresses the social determination of knowledge.

39. This section relies on Carchedi, 2011b, chapter 4.

40. Tanner Mirrlees, 'Power, Privilege and Resistance in the Digital Age', 1 May 2019, www.policyalternatives.ca/authors/tanner-mirrlees

41. For a much more detailed exposition, see Carchedi, 2010b, chapter 4.

42. For similar arguments see '2 + 2 Doesn't Always Equal 4', YouTube, www.youtube.com/watch?v=0WPY5cfOOIM&ab_channel=SabineHossenfelder

43. Noble, 1978.

44. Some positions entail both the coordination of labour and contemporaneously its control. In some cases, it might be impossible to separate the two functions, but analytically this separation can and should be made.

CHAPTER 6

1. Robert C. Allen, 'The Rise and Decline of the Soviet Economy', *Canadian Journal of Economics*, 34(4), November 2001, www.jstor.org/stable/3131928; 'A Reassessment of the Soviet Industrial Revolution', https://warwick.ac.uk/fac/soc/economics/staff/mharrison/archive/noticeboard/bergson/allen.pdf; *Farm to Factory: A Reinterpretation of the Soviet Industrial Revolution*, Princeton: Princeton University Press, 2003, p. xviii.

2. Source: Mike Edwards, *National Geographic*, March 1993.

3. J. Sachs, *New York Times magazine*, 27 June 1993, Section 6, p. 21.

4. Janos Kornai's study, *The Socialist System, The Political Economy of Communism*, Oxford: Oxford University Press, 2007.

5. The term 'trapped transition' was first used by Minxin Pei in his book, *Trapped Transition, the Limits of Developmental Autocracy*, Cambridge, MA: Harvard University Press, 2009. Ironically, Pei used to describe the failure of China to move towards a 'full market economy' which had been blocked by regional CP authorities. Our use is the opposite: China's move towards socialism has been blocked by a

bureaucratic CP elite which stops the formation of workers' democratic institutions and by the pressure of the large capitalist sector.

6. A large body of analysis that argues that conceptual and statistical frailties in China's statistical work has led to an exaggeration of China's real GDP growth since the 1949 revolution and especially since the 'market reform' period initiated by Deng started after 1978. The main source of this view comes from the US Conference Board, a mine of statistical information on the GDP, GDP per head, productivity and employment for most countries of the world. The Conference Board has adjusted China's real GDP growth rate going back to the 1950s to produce a much lower rate of growth than the official data. The CB finds that while the official data reckon that real GDP growth in China from 1949 to 2019 was 8.5 per cent a year, it was really only 5.9 per cent a year, some 30 per cent slower. The gap is even greater in the post-Mao period up to 2000, with China's official real GDP growing at 9.7 per cent a year while the CB finds it grew at 6.3 per cent a year or 35 per cent slower. After that, the gap between the two measures narrows somewhat. With real GDP per capita growth (taking into account population growth), the gap between the official data and the CB data is even greater.

7. Anton Cheremukhin, Mikhail Golosov, Sergei Guriev and Aleh Tsyvinski, 'The Economy of People's Republic of China from 1953', Working Paper 21397, National Bureau Of Economic Research, July 2015, www.nber.org/papers/w21397.

8. https://thenextrecession.files.wordpress.com/2021/01/howchinaescapedshock therapy_themar_preview-2.pdf

9. In 1921 Lenin had been forced to introduce the New Economic Policy (NEP), which imposed a capitalist superstructure on the USSR. Lenin called this stage 'state capitalism'. Che Guevara argued that Lenin would have reversed the NEP had he lived longer. However, Lenin's followers 'did not see the danger and it remained as the great Trojan horse of socialism, according to Guevara. A capitalist superstructure became entrenched, influencing the relations of production and creating a 'hybrid system of socialism with capitalist elements' that inevitably provoked conflicts and contradictions that were increasingly resolved in favour of the superstructure. In short, capitalism was returning to the Soviet bloc. See H. Yaffe, *Science & Society*, 26(1), January 2012, pp. 11–40.

10. Elias Jabbour, Alexis Toribio Dantas and Carlos Espíndola, 'China and Market Socialism: A New Socioeconomic Formation', www.tandfonline.com/doi/abs/10.1080/21598282.2021.1886147?journalCode=rict20

11. In our measure, we use the internal rate of return (IRR) on net capital as provided by the Penn World Tables. The IRR is GDP less employee compensation divided by the net stock of fixed assets. So it is a proxy for the Marxian rate of profit measure.

12. Adalmir Marquetti, Catari Vilela Chaves, Leonardo Costa Ribeiro and Eduardo da Motta e Albuquerque, 'Rate of Profit in the United States and in China (2007–2014): Introductory Comparison of Two Trajectories', Textos para Discussão Cedeplar-UFMG 577, Cedeplar, Universidade Federal de Minas Gerais, 2018.

13. Minqi Li, 'China: Imperialism or Semi-periphery?', *Monthly Review*, July 2021, https://monthlyreview.org/2021/07/01/china-imperialism-or-semi-periphery/

14. Zhiming Long and Remy Herrera in 'The Enigma of China's Growth', *Monthly Review*, 1 December 2018, using the Penn World Tables database, find ten periods of negative profit rate growth but there were not ten periods of negative real GDP growth, which suggests that the profitability of the capitalist sector was not decisive. However, the authors adopt a 'broader concept of crisis' to include 'structural

difficulties even though the appearance of a strong GDP growth suggests that all is going well' to justify their conclusion that movements in the rate of profit in the economy drive movements in China's real GDP. This broadening of the Marxist concept of crisis beyond slumps in investment and production as used for capitalist economies seems dubious. See https://monthlyreview.org/2018/10/01/on-the-nature-of-the-chinese-economic-system/

15. Y. Yongding, 'Don't Bet on a Chinese Financial Meltdown, at Least for Now', *China-US Focus*, 9 April 2014.

16. Andrew Szamosszegi and Cole Kyle, A'n Analysis of State-Owned Enterprises and State Capitalism in China', 26 October 2011, US-China Economic and Security Review Commission.

17. Tony Cliff, 'Russia a Marxist Analysis', www.marxists.org/archive/cliff/works/1964/russia/ch18.htm

18. Leon Trotsky, *The Class Nature of the Soviet State*, www.marxists.org/archive/trotsky/1933/10/sovstate.htm

19. Tony Cliff, *Stalinist Russia: A Marxist Analysis*, 1964, www.marxists.org/archive/cliff/works/1964/russia/index.htm

20. Sometimes it is argued that Engels did consider that a capitalist state could exist with just one capital where competition among capitals has disappeared. In *Socialism Utopian and Scientific*, Engels says: 'The modern state, no matter what its form, is essentially a capitalist machine – the state of the capitalists, the ideal personification of the total national capital. The more it proceeds to the taking over of productive forces, the more does it actually become the national capitalist, the more citizens does it exploit. The workers remain wage-workers – proletarians. The capitalist relation is not done away with.' This seems to suggest that you could have a state form of capitalism – state capitalism. But read on: 'The capitalist relation is not done away with. It is, rather, brought to a head. But, brought to a head, *it topples over*. State-ownership of the productive forces is not the solution of the conflict, but concealed within it are the technical conditions that form the elements of that solution.' So state ownership does not get rid of capitalist property relations, for example, wage labour, but there is a qualitative change (a 'toppling over') from the capitalist mode of production with many capitals competing on a market. Engels continues: 'The proletariat seizes political power and turns the means of production into State property.' The first act by virtue of which the state really constitutes itself as the representative of the whole of society – the taking possession of the means of production in the name of society – this is, at the same time, its last independent act as a state. State interference in social relations becomes, in one domain after another, superfluous, and then dies out of itself; the government of persons is replaced by the administration of things, and by the conduct of processes of production. The state is not 'abolished'. It dies out. Workers seize political power, expropriate the capitalists and then there is a period of transition that eventually removes the remaining capitalist property relations, that is, wage labour, money and the (capitalist) state machine itself. So there is a transition period where the state exists (but is supposedly withering away); and where wage labour continues but is supposedly being gradually eliminated as 'the technical conditions' deliver the 'solution'. This is not 'state capitalism' but the state in a transitional economy.

21. Trotsky: 'The Soviet economy was supposed to obey the normal laws of capitalism, and so forth. However, such an argument immediately found itself entangled in a host of contradictions. To look no further, we must point out that, if the Soviet

Union was capitalist (or state capitalist, it makes no real difference to the substance of the argument), then it had to have the same law of motion as capitalism – i.e., booms and slumps. However much you twist and turn, you will not find any such phenomenon. Thus, the adoption of a false theory necessarily leads to the abandonment of the basic standpoint of Marxism. Here we have a kind of capitalism which has succeeded in eliminating the fundamental contradiction of a market economy – a capitalism without unemployment, capable of developing the means of production at unheard-of rates of growth, uninterrupted by crises of overproduction.' L. Trotksy, *The Revolution Betrayed, Appendix: Socialism in One Country?* 1936, www.marxists.org/archive/trotsky/1936/revbet/index.htm

22. Credit Suisse, *Global Wealth Report*, 2021. www.credit-suisse.com/about-us/en/reports-research/global-wealth-report.html
23. Ammar A. Malik, Bradlet Parks, Brooke Russell et al., 'Banking on the Belt and Road', AidData, September 2021.
24. Ching Kwan Lee, 'Against the Law: Labor Protests in China's Rustbelt and Sunbelt'.
25. As Xi put it in a long speech in July 2021 to party members: 'Realizing common prosperity is more than an economic goal. It is a major political issue that bears on our Party's governance foundation. We cannot allow the gap between the rich and the poor to continue growing – for the poor to keep getting poorer while the rich continue growing richer. We cannot permit the wealth gap to become an unbridgeable gulf. Of course, common prosperity should be realized in a gradual way that gives full consideration to what is necessary and what is possible and adheres to the laws governing social and economic development. At the same time, however, we cannot afford to just sit around and wait. We must be proactive about narrowing the gaps between regions, between urban and rural areas, and between rich and poor people. We should promote all-around social progress and well-rounded personal development, and advocate social fairness and justice, so that our people enjoy the fruits of development in a fairer way. We should see that people have a stronger sense of fulfilment, happiness, and security and make them feel that common prosperity is not an empty slogan but a concrete fact that they can see and feel for themselves.' And Xi perceptively admitted in this speech about the demise of the Soviet Union: 'The Soviet Union was the world's first socialist country and once enjoyed spectacular success. Ultimately however, it collapsed, mainly because the Communist Party of the Soviet Union became detached from the people and turned into a group of privileged bureaucrats concerned only *with protecting their own interests* (our emphasis). Even in a modernized country, if a governing party turns its back on the people, it will imperil the fruits of modernisation.'
26. Ernest Mandel, 'In Defence of Socialist Planning', September 1986, www.marxists.org/archive/mandel/1986/09/planning.html
27. http://library.freecapitalists.org/books/Ludwig von Mises/Economic Calculation in the Socialist Commonwealth.pdf
28. This latter position was taken by Hayek in the 1935 book in which he reprinted Mises' article along with two essays of his own: the Austrians thereby retreated from an untenable strong impossibility claim, to the weaker claim that socialist calculation would face practical difficulties – in effect, it was being claimed that the socialists could not solve all the necessary equations, while the market mechanism could.
29. Alec Nove, *The Economics of Feasible Socialism*, London: Harpers Collins, 1989.

30. Haerdin, 'Planning Complexity for Model Economies', www.haerdin.se/blog/2021/02/24/planning-complexity-for-model-economies/
31. Robin Hahnel, Mitchell Szczepanczyk and Michael Weisdorf, 'Computer Simulations Experiments of Participatory Annual Planning', Computer SimulationExperimentsOfParti_powerpoint.pdf, Portland State University.
32. Frederic Legault and Simon Tremblay-Pepin, 'A Brief Sketch of Three Models of Democratic Economic Planning', https://innovationsocialeusp.ca/wp-content/uploads/2021/04/Note-2-Legault-and-Tremblay-Pepin-Democratic-Planning.pdf
33. Robin Hahnel, 'Democratic Economic Planning', 2021 www.taylorfrancis.com/chapters/mono/10.4324/9781003173700-1/introduction-robin-hahnel
34. Paul Cockshott and Allin Cottrell, 'Value, Markets and Socialism', *Science & Society*, 61(3), 1997 pp. 330–57, www.jstor.org/stable/40403641
35. https://thenextrecession.files.wordpress.com/2018/10/sovietplanningltc_seongjin_urpe20180928.pdf, but see www.communistvoice.org/DSWV-181014.html

Bibliography

Adaman, F. and Devine, P. (1996), The Economics Calculation Debate: Lessons for Socialists, *Cambridge Journal of Economics*, 20(5), 523–37.

Akkermans, H.M. (2017), Net Profit Flow Per Country from 1980 to 2009: The Long-Term Effects of Foreign Direct Investment, *PLoS One*, 12(6): e0179244. https://doi.org/10.1371/journal. pone.01792440

Albert, M. and Hahnel, R. (1991), *The Political Economy of Participatory Economics*, Princeton, NJ: Princeton University Press.

Altvater, E., Blanke, B. and Neusiiss, C. (1971), Kapitalistischer Weltmarkt und Welt-wahrungskrise, *Probleme des Klassenkampfs*, 1(5), 117.

Arvidsson, A. and Colleoni, E. (2012), Value in Informational Capitalism and on the Internet, *The Information Society*, 28(3), 135–50.

Auer, R. (2019), Beyond the Doomsday Economics of 'Proof-of-Work' in Cryptocurren-cies, BIS Working Papers, No. 765, January.

Auer, R. and Claessens, S. (2004), Cryptocurrency Market Reactions to Regulatory News, Federal Reserve Bank of Dallas, Working Paper, April.

Banks, J.A. and Deuze, M. (2009), Co-creative Labour, *International Journal of Cultural Studies*, 12(5), 4194–431.

Bauchspies, W.K., Croissant, C. and Restivo, R. (2006), *Science, Technology and Society*, Oxford: Blackwell.

Beggs, M. (2018), The Dumb Money, *The Jacobin*, 4 October.

Bohr, N. (1958), *Atomic Physics and Human Knowledge*, New York: John Wiley & Sons.

Bond, P. (2018), East-East/North-South – or Imperial – Subimperial? The BRICS, Global Governance and Capital Accumulation, *Human Geography*, 1–18.

Brown, F. (2015), Thoughts on Inflation and the 'Real Wage', from a Marxist Perspective, *Anti-Imperialism.org*.

Brown, R. (1978), The Theory of Unequal Exchange: The End of the Debate? *ISS Occa-sional Papers*, No. 65, The Institute of Social Studies, The Hague.

Busch, K., Scholler, W. and Seelow, W. (1971), Weltmarkt und Weltwahrungskrise (Bremen: 1971). … Of Capital and the Nation State, *New Left Review*, 67.

Canning, P. and Tsigas, M. (2000), Regionalism, Federalism and Taxation, a Food and Farm Perspective, USDA Technical Bulletin 1882, March.

Carchedi, G. (1977), *On the Economic Identification of Social Classes*, London: Routledge and Kegan Paul.

Carchedi, G. (1983), *Problems in Class Analysis*, London: Routledge and Kegan Paul.

——(1984), *The Logic of Prices as Values, Economy and Society*, 13(4), 431–55.

—— (1989), Classes and Class Analysis, in E.O.Wright (ed.), *The Debate on Classes*, London: Verso.

——(1991), *Frontiers of Political Economy*, London: Verso.

——(1999), A Missed Opportunity: Orthodox Versus Marxist Crises Theories, *Historical Materialism*, 4(1), January, 33–55.

—— (2001), *For Another Europe. A Class Analysis of European Economic Integration*, London: Verso.

——(2005), On the Production of Knowledge, *Research in Political Economy*, 22, 267–304.

——(2011a), Behind and beyond the Crisis, *International Socialism*, No. 132.

——(2011b), *Behind the Crisis: Marx's Dialectics of Value and Knowledge*, Chicago, IL: Haymarket.

——(2012), *Behind the Crisis*, Chicago, IL: Haymarket.

Carchedi, G. and Roberts, M. (2018), *The World in Crisis*, London: Pluto Press.

——(2019), *World in Crisis*, Chicago, IL: Haymarket.

Cockshott, P. (2019), Comments on Michael Roberts blog post, 8 July.

Cockshott, P. and Cottrell, A. (1993), *Towards a New Socialism*. Spokesman. Nottingham: Russell Press.

——(2008), Computers and Economic Democracy, *Revista de Economía Institucional*, 1, 161–205.

Cole, M., Radice H. and Umney, C. (2021), The Political Economy of Datafication and Work: A New Digital Taylorism? *Socialist Register*.

Congressional Research Service (2020), *Monetary Policy and the Federal Reserve: Current Policy and Conditions*, Updated 6 February 2020, https://crsreports.congress.gov

Corcoran, J. (2001), Second Order Logic, in A. Anderson and M. Zeleny (eds), *Logic, Meaning and Computation*, Dordrecht: Kluwer Academic.

Cross, A. (1991), The Crisis in Physics: Dialectical Materialism and Quantum Theory, *Social Studies of Science*, 21(4), November, 735–59.

Daniel, W. (1989), Bohr, Einstein and Realism, *Dialectica*, 43(3), 249–61.

Day, R. (1975), Preobrazhensky and the Theory of the Transition Period, *Soviet Studies*, Vol. 27, April.

de Ronde, C. and Massri, C. (2019), The Logos Categorical Approach to Quantum Mechanics, *International Journal of Theoretical Physics*, 60(2), 429–56.

Dean, J. (2010), *Blog Theory*, Cambridge: Polity Press.

Den Haan, W., Ellison, M., Ilzetzki E., McMahon, M. and Reis, R. (2017), Economists Relaxed about Bitcoin: New CFM-CEPR Expert Survey on Cryptocurrencies, the Financial System, and Economic Policy, https://voxeu.org/article/economists-relaxed-about-bitcoin-new-cfm-cepr-survey (accessed July 2022).

Denton, P.H. and Restivo, S. (2008), *Battleground Science and Technology*, Westport, CT: Greenwood Press.

Deubner, C., Rehfeldt, U., Schlupp, F. and Ziebura, G. (1979), *Die Internationali- sierung des Kapitals. Neue Theorien in der Internationalen Diskussion*, Frankfurt: Campus Verlag.

Devine, I. (2000), The Rise and Fall of Stagflation, Preliminary Results, *Review of Radical Political Economics*, 32(3), 398–407.

Devine, P. (1988), *Democracy and Economic Planning. The Political Economy of a Self-Governing Society*, Boulder, CO: Westview Press.

Duménil, G. and Lèvy, D. (2011), *The Crisis of Neo-liberalism*, Cambridge, MA: Harvard University Press.

Dyer-Witheford, N. and de Peute, G. (2009), *Games of Empire*, Minneapolis, MN and London: University of Minnesota Press.

Emmanuel, A. (1972), Unequal Exchange: A Study of Imperialism in Trade, Monthly Review Press, www.worldcat.org/title/unequal-exchange-a-study-of-the-imperialism-of-trade/oclc/1151844117 (accessed July 2022)

Engels, F. (1939), *Herr Eugen Dühring's Revolution in Science (Anti-Dühring)*, New York: International Publishers.

——(1979), *The Housing Question*, Moscow: Progress Publishers.

Foley, S., Karlsen, J. and Putriins, T. (2019), Sex, Drugs and Bitcoin, *Review of Financial Studies*, May.

Foster, J.B. (2015), The New Imperialism of Globalized Monopoly-Finance Capital, An Introduction. *Monthly Review*, 1 July.

—— (2019), Late Imperialism. Fifty Years after Harry Magdoff's *The Age of Imperialism*, *Monthly Review*, 1 July, https://monthlyreview.org/2019/07/01/late-imperialism/ (accessed July 2022).

Freeman, A. (2019), The Sixty-Year Downward Trend of Economic Growth in the Industrialised Countries of the World, University of Manitoba GERG Data Group Working Paper, No. 1.

Freeman, A. and Carchedi, G. (eds) (2019), *Marx and Non-Equilibrium Economics*, Cheltemham, UK: Edward Elgar.

Friedman, M. (1970), *The Counter-Revolution in Monetary Theory*, IEA Occasional Paper, No. 33, Institute of Economic Affairs.

Froewis, M. and Boehme, R. (2017), In Code We Trust? Measuring the Control Flow Immutability of All Smart Contracts Deployed in Ethereum, in J. Garcia-Alfaro, G. Navarro Arribas, H. Hartenstein and J.Herrera-Joancomarti (eds), *Data Privacy Management, Cryptocurrency and Blockchain Technology*, Luxembourg: Springer, pp. 357–72.

Fuchs, C. (2010), Class, Knowledge and New Media, in *Media, Culture and Society*, Vol. 32, Los Angeles, CA and London: Sage, pp. 141–50.

Fullwiler, S. (2011), The Sector Financial Balances Model of Aggregate Demand and Austerity, *New Economic Perspectives*, 9 June.

Gerla, G. (2017), Vagueness and Formal Fuzzy Logic: Some Criticisms, *Logic and Logical Philosophy*, 26, 431–60.

Ghosh, J. (2019), A Brave New World, or the Same Old Story with New Characters? *Development and Change*, 50(2), 379–93.

Gibson, R. (1980), Unequal Exchange: Theoretical Issues and Empirical Findings, *Review of Radical Political Economics*, 12(3), 15–35.

Gobierno Bolivariano de Venezuela (n.d.), *Petro Hacia la Revolución Digital Económica*, www.minci.gob.ve/petro-hacia-la-revolucion-digital-economica/ (accessed 2 October 2018).

Goodhart, C. (2020), Inflation after the Pandemic: Theory and Practice, 13 June, *voxeu. org*.

Goodman, J. (2018), Russia Bank Helps Venezuela Defy US Cryptocurrency Sanctions, copyhttps://apnews.com/b745c5132a544735a71e9480582240f4 (accessed 14 May 2018).

Gorton, G.B. and Zhang, J.Y. (2021), *Taming Wildcat Stablecoins*, htps://ssrn.com/abstract=3888752

Green, R. (1982), Money, Output and Inflation in Classical Economics, *Contributions to Political Economy*, 1, 59–85 (p. 59).

Grossmann, H. (1971), ëDie Fortentwicklung des Marxismus bis zur Gegenwartí, in Henryk Grossmann and Carl Grünberg, *Anarchismus, Bolschewismus, Sozialismus*, Frankfurt am Main: Europäische Verlagsanstalt, pp. 281–336.

——(1992), *The Law of Accumulation and Breakdown of the Capitalist System: Being Also a Theory of Crises*, London: Pluto Press.

——(2015), *Marx, Classical Political Economy and the Problem of Dynamics*, Introduced, edited and newly translated by Rick Kuhn, Kindle.

Harman, C. (1979), Do Wages Cause Inflation? *Socialist Review*, No. 10, March, 34–9.

Hazell, J., Herreño, J., Nakamura. E. and Steinsson, J. (2020), The Slope of the Phillips Curve: Evidence from U.S. States, https://eml.berkeley.edu/~jsteinsson/papers/StateLevelCPIs.pdf, Revised May 2021: www.nber.org/system/files/working_papers/w28005/w28005.pdf

Heisenberg, W. (1958), *Physics and Philosophy*, he Internet Encyclopedia of Philosophy, London: Ruskin House, p. 42.

Henninger, M. (2007), Doing the Math: Reflections on the Alleged Obsolescence of the Law of Value under Post-Fordism, *Ephemera*, 7(1), 158–77.

Higginbottom, A. (2013), Structure and Essence in Capital I: Extra Surplus-Value and the Stages of Capitalism, *Journal of Australian Political Economy*, 70(70), 251–70.

Herrera, R., Long, Z., Feng, Z. and Li, B. (2020), Guerra commerciale USA-Cina: il vero ladro finalmente smascherato Materialismo Storico, No. 1/2020 (Vol. VIII).

Howard, M.C and King, J.E. (1992), *A History of Marxian Economics*, Vol. II, London: Macmillan.

Huang, Y. and Mayer, M. (2022), Digital Currencies, Monetary Sovereignty, and U.S.–China Power Competition, *Policy and Internet*, 6 June.

Huberman, G., Leshno, J. and Moallemi, C.M. (2017), The Economics of the Bitcoin Payment System, 16 December, *voxeu.org*.

Huws, U. (2014), *Labor in the Global Digital Economy*, New York: Monthly Review Press.

International Trade Administration (2016), *Jobs Attributable to Foreign Direct Investment in the United States*, www.trade.gov/mas/ian/build/groups/public/@tg_ian/documents/webcontent/tg_ian_005496.pdf

Ivanova, M.N. (2020), Marx's Theory of Money: A Reappraisal in the Light of Unconventional Monetary Policy, *Review of Radical Political Economics*, 52(1), 1–15.

Jefferies, W. (2019), Piero Sraffa's Physical Price System and Reproduction without Production, *Capital and Class*, 44(2), 1–21.

Johnson, H.G. (1963), A Survey of Theories of Inflation, *Indian Economic Review*, 6(3), 29–69 (p. 33).

Kangal, K. (2017), Carchedi's Dialectics: A Critique, *Science & Society*, 81(3), 427–36.

Katz, C. (2018), 'Successes and Problems of Super-exploitation in Mauro Marini's Theory', *O Olho da Historia*, March (Federal University of Bahia), https://ri.conicet.gov.ar/handle/11336/136029 (accessed July 2022).

Keen, S. (2014), The Cost of Climate Change, *Economics*, 14 July, https://evonomics.com/steve-keen-nordhaus-climate-change-economics/ (accessed July 2022).

Kharif, O. (2020), Bitcoin Whales' Ownership Concentration Is Rising, Bloomberg, 18 November.

King, S. (2020a), China and the Third World Are Not 'Catching up' to the Rich Countries, *Labor and Society*, 21, 447–70.

——(2020b), Twenty-First Century Imperialism: How the Rich Countries Rule, Draft.

Köhler, G. (1998), The Structure of Global Money and World Tables of Unequal Exchange, *Journal of World-Systems Research*, 4, 145–68.

Kojevnikov, A. (2013), Probability, Marxism, and Quantum Ensembles, www.semanticscholar.org/paper/PROBABILITY%2C-MARXISM%2C-AND-QUANTUM-ENSEMBLES- (accessed July 2022).

Kornai, J. (2016), The System Paradigm Revisited. Clarification and Additions in the Light of Experiences in the Post-Socialist Region, *Acta Oeconomica* (Akadémiai Kiadó, Hungary), 66(4), December, 547–96.

Kosko, B. and Isaka, S. (2021), *Fuzzy logic*, Doster.

Kostakis, V. (2010), Identifying and Understanding the Problems of Wikipedia's Peer Governance. The Case of Inclusionists versus Deletionists, *First Monday*, 15(3).

—— (2012), The Political Economy of Information Production in the Social Web: Chances for Reflection on Our Institutional Design, *Contemporary Social Science*, 29 June, 1–15, www.tandfonline.com/doi/abs/10.1080/21582041.2012.691988 (accessed July 2022).

Kotz, D.M. (1982), Monopoly, Inflation, and Economic Crisis. *Review of Radical Political Economics*, 14(4), 1–17.

Krogstrup, S. and Oman, W. (2019), Macroeconomic and Financial Policies for Climate Change Mitigation: A Review of the Literature, IMF Working Paper, September.

Kuhn, R. (2006), *Henryk Grossman and the Recovery of Marxism*, Leiden: Brill.

Küklich, J. (2005). Precarious Playbour: Modders and the Digital Games Industry, *The Fibreculture Journal*, No. 5.

Lakhani, K.R. and Wolf, R.G. (2005), Why Hackers Do What They Do: Understanding Motivation and Effort in Free/Open Source Software Projects, in J. Feller, B. FitzGerald, S. Hissam and K. Lakhani (eds), *Perspectives on Free and Open Source Software*, Cambridge, MA: The MIT Press.

Lange, O. (1967), The Computer and the Market, in C. Feinstein (ed.), *Socialism, Capitalism and Economic Growth: Essays Presented to Maurice Dobb*, Cambridge: Cambridge University Press.

Lapavitsas, C. (1994), The Banking School and the Monetary Thought of Karl Marx, *Cambridge Journal of Economics*, 18, 447–61.

Legault, M-J. (2013), IT Firms Working Time (de)Regulation Model: A By-product of Risk Management Strategy and Project-Based Work Management, *Work Organization, Labour and Gobalization*, 7(1), Summer, 76–94.

Lenin, V.I. (1917 [1963]), *Imperialism, the Highest Stage of Capitalism, Selected Works*, Moscow: Progress Publishers.

—— (1972), *Materialism and Empirio-criticism, Collected Works*, Vol. 14, Moscow: Progress Publishers.

Lobkowicz, Nikolaus (1961), The principle of contradiction in recent Soviet Philosophy, *Studies in Soviet Thought*, SOVA, Vol. 7.

Lohmann, L. (2021), Interpretation Machines: Contradictions of 'Artificial Intelligence' in 21st-Century Capitalism, *Socialist Register*, 50–78.

Louwerse, J. (2017), *International Seigniorage, the US Dollar and the American Trade Deficit*, Rotterdam: Erasmus University Rotterdam.

Lovink, G. (2011), *Ossessioni collettive*, Milano: Università Bocconi Editore.

Maddison, A. (1995a), Explaining the Economic Performance of Nations 1982–1989, Australian National University.

——(1995b), *Monitoring the World Economy, 1820–1992*, Paris: OECD.

——(2001), *The World Economy – a Millennial Perspective*, Paris: OECD Development Centre Studies.

Maito, E. (2019) The Tendency of the Rate of Profit to Fall since the 19th Century and a World Rate of Profit, in G. Carchedi and M. Roberts, *The World in Crisis*, London: Pluto Press, chapter 4.

Mandel, E. (1990), Karl Marx, in J. Eatwell, M. Milgate and, P. Newmam (eds), *Marxian Economics*, London: Macmillan, pp. 1–38.

Marvit, M.Z. (2014), How Crowdworkers Became the Ghosts in the Digital Machine, *The Nation*, 4 February.

Marx, K. 1973, *Grundrisse*.

——(1859), Critique of Political Economy.

—— (1867), On the Lausanne Congress, www.marxists.org/archive/marx/iwma/documents/1867/lausanne-call.htm

——(1961), *Capital*, Vols 1 and 2, Moscow: Progress Publishers.

——(1966), *Critique of the Gotha Programme*, New York: International Publishers.

——(1967), *Capital*, Vol. I, New York: International Publishers.

——(1967), *Capital*, Vol. II, New York: International Publishers.

——(1967), *Capital*, Vol. III, New York: Intemrnational Publishers.

——(1971), *Critique of Political Economy*, London: Lawrence and Wishart, p. 105.

——(1971), *The Economic and Philosophic Manuscript of 1844*, New York: International Publishers.

——(1971), *Theories of Surplus Value*, Pt. III, Moscow: Progress Publishers.

——(1973), *Grundrisse*, London: Vintage Books.

—— (1974), Inaugural Address of the International Working Men's Association, in David Fernbach (ed.), *The First International and After*, New York: Random House, pp. 73–81.

——(1975), *Karl Marx and Frederick Engels, Collected Works*, New York: International Publishers, p. 422.

——(1976), *Capital*, Vol. I, London: Penguin Books.

——(1981), *Capital*, Vol. 3 Chapter 15, London: Penguin Books.

——(1985), The Civil War in France', in Karl Marx and Frederick Engels, *On the Paris Commune*, Moscow: Progress Publishers, pp. 48–181.

——(1989a), Epilogue to *Revelations Concerning the Communist Trial in Cologne*, in *Collected Works,* Vol. 24, New York: International Publishers, pp. 51–4.

——(1989b), Drafts of the Letter to Vera Zasulich, and Letter to Vera Zasulich (March 8, 1881), in Karl Marx and Frederick Engels, *Collected Works*, Vol. 24, New York: International Publishers, pp. 346–71.

——(1995), Capital, Vol. One, English edition, 1887, Moscow: Progress Publishers.

Marx, K. and Engels, F. (1968), Manifesto of the Communist Party, in Karl Marx and Frederick Engels, *Selected Works* (one volume), London: Lawrence and Wishart, pp. 35–63.

——(1976), *The German Ideology*, Moscow: Progress Publishers.

——(2010), *Manifesto of the Communist Party, Marx and Engels Collected Works*, Vol. 6, London: Lawrence and Wishart.

Mattick, P. (1977), Economics, Politics and The Age of Inflation, *Marxists.org*.

Mavroudeas, S.D. (2018), The Marxist Theory of Imperialism: Which Way Forward, Paper presented at the13th Forum of the World Association for Political Economy, Berlin School of Economics and Law, 16–18 July.

Mavroudeas, S. and Seretis, S. (2018), Imperialist Exploitation and the Greek Crisis, *East-West Journal of Economics and Business*, XXI(1–2), 43–64.

Mayer, A. (2018), Dissolving Empire: David Harvey, John Smith, and the Migrant, 10 April, http://roape.net/2018/04/10/dissolving-empire-david-harvey-john-smith-and-the-migrant/

Milios, J. (2003), *Marx's Value Theory Revisited. A 'Value-Form' Approach*, http://users.ntua.gr/jmilios/F2_3.pdf

Mirrlees, T. (2021), Socialists and Social Media Platforms: Communicating within and against Digital Capitalism, *Socialist Register*, 112–37.

Mitchell, B. (2021), (Modern) Marx and MMT – Part 2, blog, Thursday, 30 September, http://bilbo.economicoutlook.net/blog/?p=48426

Münchau, W. (2020), A Flexible Inflation Target Is Not a Panacea, *Financial Times*, 20 July.

Nakamoto, S. (2008), Bitcoin: A Peer-to-Peer Electronic Cash System, 31 October. https://nakamotoinstitute.org/bitcoin/

Nakjima, A. and Izumi, H. (1995), Economic Development and Unequal Exchange among Nations – Analysis of the USA, Japanese and South Korean Economies for the Years 1960–1985 Using Total Labor Inputs, *Kyoto University Economic Review*, 64(2), 33–48.

Noble, D. (1978), Social Choice in Machine Design: The Case of Automatically Controlled Machine Tools and a Challenge for Labour, *Politics and Society*, 8, 3–43, 313–47.

Norfield, T. (2014a), British Imperialism and Finance: A Contribution to the Theory of Contemporary Imperialism, PhD Thesism SOAS, University of London. https://doi.org/10.25501/SOAS.00020315

——(2014b), *The City: London and the Global Power of Finance*, London:Verso.

—— (2018), Finance, Imperialism and Profits, *Economics of Imperialism*, https://economicsofimperialism.blogspot.com/2018/11/finance-imperialism-and-profits.html (accessed July 2022).

——(2019), Imperialism, a Marxist Understanding, *Socialist Economist*.

Nove, A. (1977), *The Soviet Economic System*, London: George Allen & Unwin.

Patnaik, U. and Patnaik, P. (2015), Imperialism in the Era of Globalization, *Monthly Review*, 67(3).

Pettifor, A. (2013), The Power to 'Create Money out of Thin Air', *Open Democracy*.

Pfeiffer, S. (2013), Web, Value and Labour, *Work Organisation, Labour & Globalization*, 7(1), 12–30.

Phillips, A.W. (1958), The Relationship between Unemployment and the Rate of Change of Money Wages in the United Kingdom 1861–1957, *Economica*, 25(100), 283–99. doi:10.1111/j.1468-0335.1958.tb00003.x

Ossinger, J. and Hunter, G. (2021), Dogecoin Surges 77%, Bloomberg, 28 January, www.bloomberg.com/news/articles/2021-01-28/dogecoin-surges-77-as-retail-fever-pitch-stretches-into-crypto#xj4y7vzkg

Philosophical Issues in Quantum Theory (2016), *The Stanford Encyclopedia of Philosophy*, Stanford University.

Pitts, F. (2013), 'A Science to It': Flexible Time and Flexible Subjectivity in the Digital Workplace, *Work Organisation, Labour & Globalization*, 7(1), 95–105. https://doi.org/10.13169/workorgalaboglob.7.1.0095

Portes, J. (2019), Nonsense Economics, the Rise of Modern Monetary Theory, *Prospect*, 30, January, www.prospectmagazine.co.uk/economics-and-finance/nonsense-economics-the-rise-of-modern-monetary-theory (accessed August 2022).

Prahalad, C.K. and Ramaswamy, V. (2000), Co-opting Customer Competence, *Harvard Business Review*, January.

Preobrazhensky,Y. (1965), *The New Economics*, trans. Brian Pearce, London: Oxford University Press.

Rasmus, J. (2019), Financial Imperialism: The Case of Venezuela, *Counterpunch*, 5 March.

Restivo, S. (1992), *Mathematics in Society and History*, New York: Springer.

Reveley, J. (2013), The Exploitative Web: Misuses of Marx in Critical Social Media Studies, *Science & Society*, 77(4), 512–35.

Rey, P.J. (2012), Alienation, Exploitation, and Social Media, *American Behavioral Scientist*, 56(4), 399–420.

Ricci, A. (2018), Unequal Exchange in the Age of Globalization, *Review of Radical Political Economy*, September.

Riehle, D. (2007), The Economic Motivation of Open Source Software: Stakeholder Perspectives, *IEEE Computer Society*, 25–32.

Roberts, M. (2016), Monocausality and Crisis Theory – a Reply to David Harvey, in T. Subasat (ed.), *The Great Financial Meltdown*, Cheltenham: Edward Elgar, chapter 4.

——(2020a), Deficits, Debt and Deflation after the Pandemic, *Michael Roberts* blog, 29 June.

——(2020b), The FED in a Hole, *Michael Roberts* blog, 28 August.

Roche, C. (2019), MMT – The Good, the Bad and the Ugly, *Pragcap*.

Rodolsky, R. (1977), *The Making of Marx's Capital*, London: Pluto Press.

Rosenthal, M. and Yudin, P. (1949), *Handbook of Philosophy*, edited and adapted by H. Selsam, translated from the Russian, New York: International Publishers.

Ross, D. (2013), The Place of Free and Open Source Software in the Social Apparatus of Accumulation, *Science & Society*, 77(2), 202–26.

Saad-Filho, A. (2000), Inflation Theory: A Review and a Research Agenda, Value, Capitalist Dynamics and Money, in P. Zarembka (ed.), *Research in Political Economy*, Vol. 18. pp. 335–62.

Sangster, J. (2021), The Surveillance of Service Labour: Conditions and Possibilities of Resistance, *Socialist Register*, 175–200.

Santomero, A.M. (2002), What Monetary Policy Can and Cannot Do, *Business Review*, Federal Reserve Bank of Philadelphia.

Sawyer, M.C. (1988), Theories of Monopoly Capitalism, *Journal of Economic Surveys*, March.

Sayers, S. (1983), Materialism, Realism and the Reflection Theory, *Radical Philosophy*, Spring.

Schumpeter, J. (1954), *History of Economic Analysis*, New York: Oxford University Press.

Senf, B. (1978), Politischeĉkonomiedes Kapitalismus, *Mehrwert*, No. 18.

Shaikh, A. (2012), Competition Matters: China's Exchange Rate and Balance of Trade, *The Forum*, Summer.

—— (2016), Explaining Inflation and Unemployment: An Alternative to Neo-liberal Economic Theory, in *Capitalism, Competition, Conflict, Crises*, New York: Oxford University Press, chapter 15.

Shaikh, A. and Antonopoulos, R. (2013), Explaining Long Term Exchange Rate Behavior in the United States and Japan, in J.K. Moudud, C. Bina and P.L. Mason (eds), *Alternative Theories of Competition*, London: Routledge, chapter 9.

Shuster, S. (2018), Exclusive: Russia Secretly Helped Venezuela Launch a Cryptocurrency to Evade U.S. Sanctions, *Time.com*.

Siegel, T. (1984), Politics and Economics in the Capitalist World Market: Methodological Problems of Marxist Analysis, *International Journal of Sociology*, 14(1), i–v.

Smith, A. (1970), *The Wealth of Nations*, 1776, London: Penguin edition.

Smith, J. (2011) Imperialism and the Law of Value, *Global Discourse* [Online], 2(I), http://global-discourse.com/contents.

——(2015), Imperialist Realities vs. the Myths of David Harvey, *roape.net*.

——(2016) *Imperialism in the Twenty-First Century*, New York: Monthly Review Press.

——(2018), Imperialist Realities vs. the Myths of David Harvey, 19 March, http://roape. net/2018/03/19/imperialist-realities-vs-the-myths-of-david-harvey/ (accessed July 2022).

Stalder, F. (2013), *Digital Solidarity, PML and Mute Books*, Leuphana University, www. metamute.org/sites/www.metamute.org/files/u1/Digital-Solidarity-Felix-Stalder-9781906496920-web-fullbook.pdf (accessed July 2022).

Starosta, G. (2012), Cognitive Commodities and the Value Form, *Science & Society*, 76, 365–92.

Struik, D. (1948), Marx and Mathematics, *Science & Society*, 12(1), 181–96.

Sweezy, P. (1942), *Theory of Capitalist Development*, London: Dobson Books.

Tcherneva, P.R. (2005), *The Nature , Origins , and Role of Money: Broad and Specific Propositions and Their Implications for Policy*, http://tankona.free.fr/tcherneva05.pdf (accessed July 2022).

Terranova, T. (2000), Free Labor: Producing Culture for the Digital Economy, *Social Text*, 63, 18(2), Summer, 33–57.

Tobin, J. (1997), *Money, Credit and Capital*, New York: McGraw-Hill.

Trigg, A. (2013), Towards a Marxian Critique of Inflation Targeting, *International Journal pf Pluralism and Economics Education*, 4(3), 278.

Tsaliki, P., Paraskevopoulou, C. and Tsoulfidis, L. (2018), Unequal Exchange and Absolute Cost Advantage: Evidence from the Trade between Greece and Germany, *Cambridge Journal of Economics*, 42(4), July, 1043–86.

Twomey, D. and Mann, A. (2020), Fraud and Manipulation within Cryptocurrency Markets, in C. Alexander and D. Cumming (eds), *Corruption and Fraud in Financial Markets: Malpractice, Misconduct and Manipulation*, Hoboken, NJ: John Wiley & Sons, p. 214.

Von Mises, L. (1935), *Economic Calculation in the Socialist Commonwealth, Collectivist Economic Planning: Critical Studies on the Possibilities of Socialism*, London: George Routledge, pp. 87–130.

——(1949), *Human Action: A Treatise on Economics*, New Haven, CT: Yale University Press.

Walch, A. (2019), Deconstructing 'Decentralization': Exploring the Core Claim of Crypto Systems, in *Crypto Assets: Legal & Monetary Perspectives*, Oxford: Oxford University Press.

West, J. and Gallagher, S. (2006), Challenges of Open Innovation: The Paradox of Firm Investment in Open-source Software, *R&D Management*, 36, 3.

Wichita State University, Department of Mathematics and Statistics, https://scholar-works.sjsu.edu/cgi/viewcontent.cgi?article=1002&context=org_mgmt_pub (accessed July 2022).

Wray, R. (1998), Modern Money, Levy Economics Institute Working Paper No. 2.

Wroughton, L. and Ellsworth, B. (2018), U.S. Sanctions Venezuela Officials, Trump Slams Maduro, *Reuters.com*.

Yaffe, H. (2012), Che Guevara and the Great Debate, Past and Present, *Science & Society*, 76(1), January, 11–40.

Index

Thanks to our Patreon subscribers:

Andrew Perry
Ciaran Kane

Who have shown generosity and
comradeship in support of our publishing.

Check out the other perks you get by subscribing
to our Patreon – visit patreon.com/plutopress.

Subscriptions start from £3 a month.